Teach Yourself VISUALLY™

Android Phones and Tablets

Guy Hart-Davis

Visual™
A Wiley Brand

Teach Yourself VISUALLY™
Android Phones and Tablets

Published by
John Wiley & Sons, Inc.
10475 Crosspoint Boulevard
Indianapolis, IN 46256

www.wiley.com

Published simultaneously in Canada

Wiley publishes in a variety of print and electronic formats and by print-on-demand. Some material included with standard print versions of this book may not be included in e-books or in print-on-demand. If this book refers to media such as a CD or DVD that is not included in the version you purchased, you may download this material at http://booksupport.wiley.com. For more information about Wiley products, visit www.wiley.com.

Library of Congress Control Number: 2013935670

ISBN: 978-1-118-64661-8 (pbk); 978-1-118-67530-4 (ebk); 978-1-118-67531-1 (ebk); 978-1-118-73710-1 (ebk)

Manufactured in the United States of America

10 9 8 7 6 5 4 3

Trademark Acknowledgments

Contact Us

For general information on our other products and services please contact our Customer Care Department within the U.S. at 877-762-2974, outside the U.S. at 317-572-3993 or fax 317-572-4002.

For technical support please visit www.wiley.com/techsupport.

Credits

Acquisitions Editor
Aaron Black

Project Editor
Jade L. Williams

Technical Editor
Dennis Cohen

Copy Editor
Kim Heusel

Editorial Director
Robyn Siesky

Business Manager
Amy Knies

Senior Marketing Manager
Sandy Smith

Vice President and Executive Group Publisher
Richard Swadley

Vice President and Executive Publisher
Barry Pruett

Project Coordinator
Patrick Redmond

Graphics and Production Specialists
Ronda David-Burroughs
Andrea Hornberger
Jennifer Mayberry
Melissa Smith

Proofreading
Cynthia Fields

Indexing
BIM Indexing & Proofreading Services

About the Author

Guy Hart-Davis is the author of *Teach Yourself VISUALLY iPad & iPad mini,*
Teach Yourself VISUALLY iPhone 5, Teach Yourself VISUALLY Mac mini, Teach
Yourself VISUALLY iMac, 2nd Edition, iMac Portable Genius, 4th Edition, iLife
'11 Portable Genius, and *iWork Portable Genius.*

Author's Acknowledgments

My thanks go to the many people who turned my manuscript into the highly
graphical book you are holding. In particular, I thank Aaron Black for asking
me to write the book; Jade Williams for keeping me on track and guiding
the editorial process; Kim Heusel for skillfully editing the text; Dennis
Cohen for reviewing the book for technical accuracy and contributing
helpful suggestions; Ronda David-Burroughs and Melissa Smith for creating
the art; Cynthia Fields for providing a final proofreading; and BIM Indexing
& Proofreading Services for creating the index.

How to Use This Book

Who This Book Is For

This book is for the reader who has never used this particular technology or software application. It is also for readers who want to expand their knowledge.

The Conventions in This Book

① Steps

This book uses a step-by-step format to guide you easily through each task. **Numbered steps** are actions you must do; **bulleted steps** clarify a point, step, or optional feature; and **indented steps** give you the result.

② Notes

Notes give additional information — special conditions that may occur during an operation, a situation that you want to avoid, or a cross-reference to a related area of the book.

③ Icons and Buttons

Icons and buttons show you exactly what you need to click to perform a step.

④ Tips

Tips offer additional information, including warnings and shortcuts.

⑤ Bold

Bold type shows command names or options that you must click or text or numbers you must type.

⑥ Italics

Italic type introduces and defines a new term.

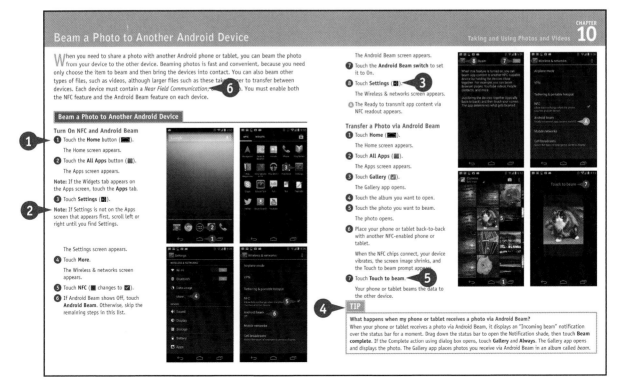

Table of Contents

Chapter 3   Working with Text and Voice

Table of Contents

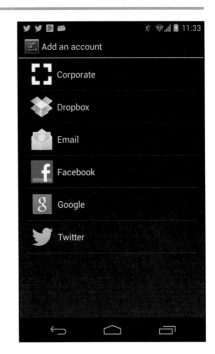

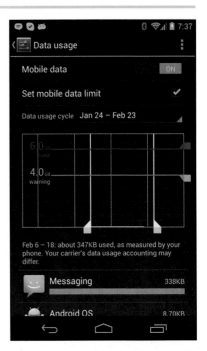

Chapter 6   Making Calls and Instant Messaging

Chapter 7   Enjoying Social Networking

Table of Contents

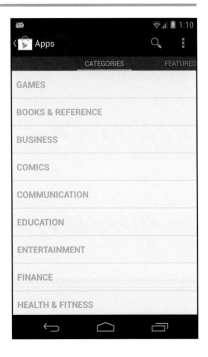

Chapter 10   Taking and Using Photos and Videos

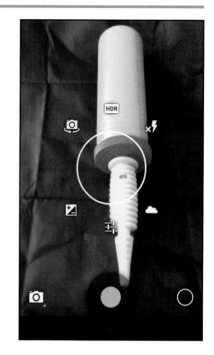

Chapter 11   Using Maps, Google Earth, and Clock

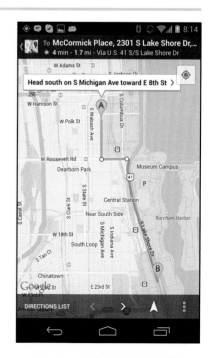

Table of Contents

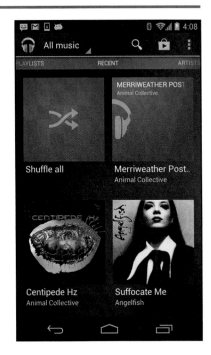

CHAPTER 1

Getting Started with Android

In this chapter, you set up your Android phone and tablet, meet its hardware controls, and learn to navigate it. You also learn to transfer files from your PC or Mac to your device.

Discover the Types of Android Devices

Android is an operating system created by Google for use on mobile computing devices. Android runs on both smartphones and tablet computers and is widely used on both types of device. Various hardware manufacturers install Android as the operating system for their devices, and as a result, you can buy many different Android devices with widely varying capabilities and prices. Android has a standard user interface that is referred to as *stock Android*. But some manufacturers add an overlay called a *skin* to Android, giving it a different look, changing its built-in functionality, and adding features.

Android Smartphones

Android smartphones are cellular phones that run on the Android operating system. Android provides a wide range of features, from sending e-mail and browsing the Internet to making phone calls and taking photos. Most Android phones include a rear camera with which you can take high-quality photos, using the screen as a viewfinder, and a front camera for taking self-portraits and for enjoying video chat sessions. Android phones also include one or more microphones you can use to record audio and voice memos. Android smartphones come in many sizes, designs, and price levels. This book uses the Google Nexus 4 phone as a reference Android smartphone that runs unmodified Android version 4.2, which is known as Jelly Bean.

Android Tablets

Google designed Android to run tablet computers as well as smartphones. Tablets come in a wide range of sizes, ranging from pocket size to table-top size. Smaller tablets have screen sizes such as 7 inches or 8.9 inches. Full-size tablets have screen sizes such as 10 inches. Oversize tablets have screens sizes such as 13 inches. Monster tablets have screens as big as 22 inches. This book uses the Google Nexus 7 tablet as a reference Android tablet. In general, tablets are larger than

smartphones, although bigger smartphones now approach the size of smaller tablets. Smartphones have cellular phone capability whereas tablets do not. Some tablets have cellular data connectivity but cannot make cellular phone calls.

Manufacturers of Android Devices

Many hardware manufacturers make Android devices, including Archos, Asus, Dell, HP, HTC, LG, Motorola, Samsung, Sony, Toshiba, and ViewSonic. Some manufacturers make both Android smartphones and Android tablets, whereas other manufacturers produce only smartphones or only tablets. When looking for an Android smartphone or tablet, you can choose from a wide range of devices, so it is a good idea to spend time deciding exactly what you need and carefully researching the devices that appear to meet your needs. Apart from studying the specifications for the devices, you can benefit from reading both professional reviews and user reviews of them to learn their strengths and weaknesses. The Amazon website, http://www.amazon.com, is a good place to find user reviews of many devices.

Versions of the Android Operating System

As of this writing, Google has released seven main versions of the Android operating system. Each version has a code name from a sweet food. For example, the code name for Android versions 4.1 and 4.2 is Jelly Bean, whereas Android 4.0's code name is Ice Cream Sandwich. When Google releases a new version of Android, each hardware manufacturer must customize a version for its phones and tablets. Each new version may take weeks or months to arrive — or a manufacturer may decide not to create a new version for its older phones and tablets. For this reason, when considering buying an Android device, you should check carefully the Android version it is running and updates that are available.

Android Skins

Android Jelly Bean is a full-featured operating system with an easy-to-use user interface. But hardware manufacturers can alter or extend the Android user interface by applying extra software called a *skin*. For example, Samsung adds a skin called TouchWiz to many of its Android devices, and HTC adds a skin called HTC Sense. A skin can modify many aspects of the standard *stock* or *pure* Android Jelly Bean interface. For example, the TouchWiz skin gives the Home screen and the lock screen a different look, adds extra features and graphics to the Settings app, and replaces key apps such as the Camera app with custom versions.

Unbox and Charge Your Phone or Tablet

Once you have your Android phone or tablet, your first move is to take it out of the box, identify the components, and set the device to charge. To get the best battery life out of your phone or tablet, you should first fully charge the battery even if it came partly charged. So no matter how eager you are to set up your phone or tablet, load your data and media onto it, and start using it, take a few hours to charge it fully first.

Unbox and Charge Your Phone or Tablet

1 Open the box for the phone or tablet, and remove its contents.

2 Check to make sure you have the phone or tablet itself, and identify its components. The components vary depending on the phone or tablet, but these components are typical for a phone:

Ⓐ The phone or tablet itself.

Ⓑ A headset.

Ⓒ A USB cable.

Ⓓ A power adapter.

3 If the phone or tablet has protective stickers on its front or back, peel them off.

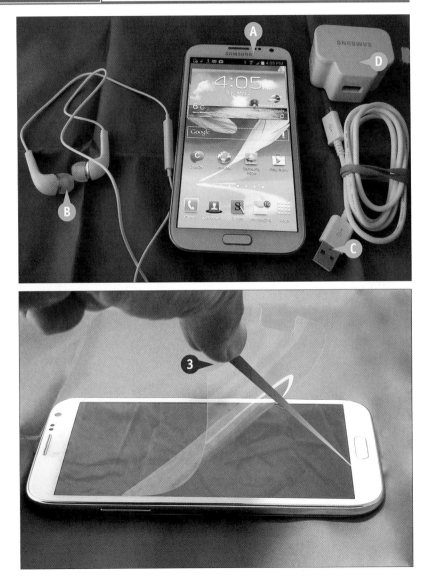

4 Connect the USB end of the USB cable to the power adapter.

5 Plug the power adapter into a power socket.

6 Connect the opposite end of the USB cable to the phone or tablet.

Note: Many Android phones and tablets use a standard USB cable with a micro-B USB connector at the device's end. Check the orientation of the port on the phone or tablet is before you try to connect the cable.

When you have connected a power source, some form of charging readout appears on-screen.

7 Leave the phone or tablet to charge until the battery readout shows that the battery is fully charged.

TIP

My phone or tablet does not include a power adapter. Where can I get one?
You can get a suitable adapter either from the manufacturer of the phone or tablet or from an online or real-world electronics store. Although many phones and tablets charge satisfactorily from generic chargers, look first for a charger designed to work with your phone or tablet. Such a charger delivers exactly the current and voltage the phone or tablet requires, which will charge it as quickly as possible and keep the battery in good condition. If you need to charge your phone or tablet when you are on the road, consider buying a car adapter or a battery pack as well.

Meet Your Device's Controls

After charging your phone or tablet, turn it on and meet its controls. Although different Android phone and tablet models have different controls and layouts, many devices have standard hardware buttons such as a Power button and a volume rocker or two volume buttons. Android devices also have three buttons — Back, Home, and Recent Apps —at the bottom of the screen, normally implemented as soft buttons built into the screen. Many stores and carriers insert a SIM card in your phone or cellular-capable tablet if it does not come with a SIM. In some cases, you may need to insert a suitable SIM card yourself.

Meet Your Device's Controls

1 Press and hold the Power button on the phone or tablet for a couple of seconds.

As the phone or tablet starts, the Google logo appears on the screen.

A This is the micro-USB port. Google refers to this as the Charger/USB/SlimPort port.

B This is a microphone on the base of the device.

C This is the front-facing camera.

D This is the headphone socket.

E This is a microphone at the top of an Android phone.

F This is the rear-facing camera.

G This is the camera flash.

2 Turn the phone or tablet so that you can see the side that contains the volume button or volume buttons.

3 Press the upper part of the volume rocker to increase the ringer volume.

4 Press the lower part of the volume rocker to decrease the ringer volume.

5 When the lock screen appears, touch the **lock circle** (🔘) and then drag the lock to any point on the circle that appears.

The phone or tablet unlocks, and the Home screen appears.

H You can touch the **Home** button (▬) to display the Home screen.

I You can touch the **Back** button (◀) to display the previous screen.

J You can touch the **Recent Apps** button (▭) to display a list of recent apps.

TIP

How do I insert a SIM card in my phone or tablet?

If the store or carrier has not inserted a SIM card, you will need to insert one yourself. Consult the device's documentation to learn which kind of SIM card it needs — for example, a micro-SIM or a nano-SIM — and get a SIM card of that type. You must also consult the documentation about inserting the SIM card in the phone or tablet. Some devices have an external SIM slot that you open using a SIM ejection tool or the end of a straightened paper clip. Other devices require you to take the back off the device in order to access the SIM compartment and insert the SIM card.

Perform the Initial Setup Routine

To get your phone or tablet working, you must perform the initial setup routine. This is a one-time procedure in which you select essential settings and connect the device to a wireless network. The first time you turn on your phone or tablet, Android displays the Welcome screen. You can then choose which language to use, connect to a Wi-Fi network, set up your Google Account, and choose other settings including backup and restore settings and Google & location settings.

Perform the Initial Setup Routine

1 Turn on the phone or tablet by pressing and holding the **Power** button.

2 On the Welcome screen, touch the language.

3 Touch **Start**.

4 On the Select Wi-Fi screen, touch the Wi-Fi network you want to use.

A If the Wi-Fi network does not appear in the list, touch **Other network**. The network may be one that does not broadcast its name.

B If you do not want to connect to a network now, touch **Skip**. Go to step **8**.

5 Type the password for the Wi-Fi network.

C You can touch **Done** to reveal more options.

D You can touch **Show password** (■ changes to ✓) if you need to see the characters.

E You can touch **Show advanced options** (■ changes to ✓) if you need to choose proxy settings or Internet Protocol settings.

6 Touch **Connect**.

Your phone or tablet connects to the Wi-Fi network.

7 On the Got Google? screen, touch **Yes** if you already have a Google Account, such as Gmail or YouTube. Otherwise, touch **No** and follow the instructions to set up an account.

8 Type the e-mail address for your Google Account.

9 Type your password.

10 Touch **Next** (◧) or **Next** on the keyboard.

11 In the dialog box that opens, touch **OK**.

12 On the Entertainment screen, touch **Set up credit card** or **Not now**.

13 On the backup and restore screen, touch **Restore from my Google Account to this phone** (■ changes to ☑) if you have saved data to your Google Account.

14 Touch **Keep this phone backed up with my Google Account** (■ changes to ☑).

15 Touch **Next** (◧).

16 On the Google & location screen, select whether you want to share your location.

17 Touch **Next** (◧).

18 On the Setup complete screen, touch **Finish**.

TIP

Should I back up my phone or tablet to my Google Account?

Normally, it is a good idea to back up your Android phone or tablet to your Google Account, because doing so enables you to recover your data and your device's configuration after hardware or software problems. But if you prefer not to entrust your data to Google, do not back up your phone or tablet to your Google Account. Be aware that if you store a lot of content on your device, you may exceed the free storage allocation of your Google account and have to pay for extra space.

Connect to a Wireless Network

If you use your phone or tablet in multiple locations, you may need to connect to several wireless networks. You can quickly connect your device to wireless networks when you want to connect to the Internet. Many networks broadcast the network name, and often you need only provide the password to make a connection. If the network does not broadcast its name, you will need to type the name to connect. For some networks, you may need to specify an IP address or proxy server details.

Connect to a Wireless Network

Connect to a Wireless Network That Broadcasts Its Name

1 On a phone, touch the status bar and drag down.

The Notification shade open.

2 Touch **Quick Settings** (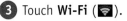).

The Quick Settings pane appears.

Note: On a tablet, touch the right side of the status bar and drag down to open the Quick Settings pane.

3 Touch **Wi-Fi** (🛜).

The Wi-Fi screen appears.

4 If the Wi-Fi switch is set to Off, touch **On**.

5 Touch the network to which you want to connect the phone or tablet.

A dialog box for connecting to the network appears.

Note: If the network does not use security, Android connects to the network without displaying the connection dialog box.

6 Type the password.

7 Touch **Connect**.

Android connects to the network.

Connect to a Network That Does Not Broadcast Its Name

1 Repeat steps **1** to **3** in the previous section to display the Wi-Fi screen.

2 Touch **Add** ().

3 On the Add network screen, touch Network SSID and type the network name.

4 Touch Security and then touch the security type — for example, WPA/WPA2 PSK.

5 Touch **Password** and type the password.

6 Touch **Save**.

Connect to a Network and Specify Settings

1 Repeat steps **1** to **3** in the previous section to display the Wi-Fi screen.

2 Touch the network.

3 Touch **Password** and type the password.

4 Touch **Show advanced options** (■ changes to ☑).

5 To set proxy server information, touch **Proxy Settings**, touch **Manual**, and then choose the settings.

6 To set IP address information, touch **IP Settings**, touch **Static**, and then choose the settings.

7 Touch **Connect**.

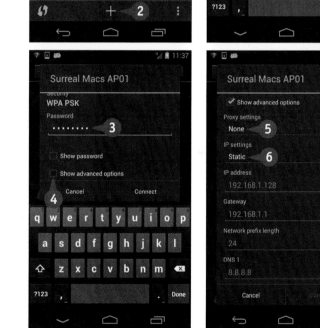

How do I stop using a particular wireless network?
Touch the upper-right corner of the screen and drag down to open the Notification shade, then touch **Wi-Fi** (📶). On the Wi-Fi screen, touch the network's name. In the dialog box that opens, touch **Forget**.

How else do I set up a wireless network?
If the wireless network has *Wi-Fi Protected Setup*, or WPS, touch **WPS** (🔘) on your phone or tablet, and then press the WPS button on the wireless network router. Wi-Fi Protected Setup sets up the network connection automatically.

Download and Install Companion Software

While you can use your Android phone or tablet as a stand-alone device, you may find it helpful to sync data such as contacts, photos, and songs between the phone or tablet and your PC or Mac. You can sync data between your Android device and your computer in two main ways. You can use companion software that syncs the data for you, such as the Samsung Kies app or the HTC Sync app, or you can sync your data via your Google Account or another online service.

Determine Whether Companion Software Is Available

Some manufacturers of Android phones and tablets provide companion software for syncing data to their devices. For example, Samsung provides the Kies app for Windows and for Mac OS X, whereas HTC provides the HTC Sync app for Windows. The easiest way to find out if the manufacturer provides companion software for your device is to open your web browser and go to the manufacturer's website. If the manufacturer does not provide companion software, you may be able to find third-party sync software by searching on the web. Alternatively, you can copy files to your device manually.

Download the Companion Software

If you find suitable companion software or third-party sync software to use between your computer and your Android phone or tablet, download the software to your computer using your web browser. When downloading the installer file, your browser may offer you the choice between saving it and running it. Normally, saving the installer file is the better choice, because you can then run the installation again if necessary. If you locate the software by searching rather than by browsing the manufacturer's website, make sure you download it from the manufacturer's website rather than from a third-party site that may provide a version containing spyware or malware.

Install the Companion Software

After downloading the companion software, run its installer to install the software on your computer. On Windows, User Account Control prompts you to confirm that you want to allow the software to make changes to your computer; if you are not an administrator, you will need to provide an administrator password to proceed. On the Mac, you will need to authenticate as an administrator user in order to install the software for all users. Follow through the installer, evaluating all options and choosing settings suitable to your needs. When installing third-party software, be careful to read all the prompts on-screen so that you can avoid installing any extra features, such as browser toolbars, that you do not want. After the installer finishes, restart your computer if prompted to do so.

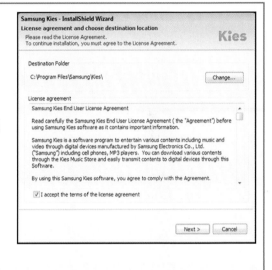

Run the Companion Software and Sync Your Files

Run the companion software from the Start menu or from a desktop shortcut on Windows or from the Launchpad on Mac OS X. The first time you run the software, you may need to choose which language to use and set some other options. Connect your Android phone or tablet and verify that the app detects it. For example, in Samsung Kies, the phone or tablet appears in the Connected devices list in the upper-left corner of the window. You can then select items and transfer them between your computer and the device by dragging them from one to the other. Depending on the app, you may also be able to install new versions of Android on your phone or tablet and back it up to your computer.

Transfer Files from Your PC to Your Device

You can load files on your phone or tablet by connecting the device to your PC via a USB cable and transferring files. If the manufacturer of your Android phone or tablet does not provide companion software for syncing files between your computer and the device, you can transfer files directly between the two. To do so, you can use Windows Explorer, the file-management program that comes built in to Windows. The storage space on your phone or tablet appears as a drive in Windows Explorer.

Transfer Files from Your PC to Your Device

1 Connect your phone or tablet to your PC via the USB cable.

Note: If the device's screen is protected with a PIN or password, unlock the device to allow your computer to access it.

The AutoPlay dialog box opens.

2 Click **Always do this for this device** (☐ changes to ☑) if you want Windows to automatically open Windows Explorer when you connect your device in the future.

3 Click **Open device to view files**.

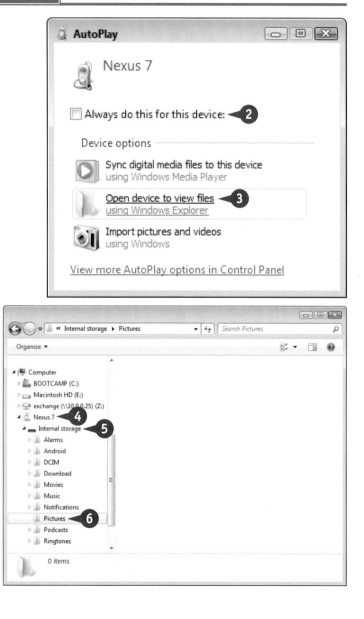

A Windows Explorer window opens showing your device's contents.

4 Double-click your device's name.

5 Double-click **Internal storage**.

6 Click the appropriate folder. For example, if you want to copy pictures to your device, click Pictures.

The Windows Explorer window shows the contents of the folder you clicked on the device.

7 Click **Start**.

The Start menu opens.

8 Click the appropriate folder. For example, to copy pictures, click Pictures.

The library or folder you chose opens. For example, if you click Pictures, the Pictures library in your user account opens.

9 Click the first item you want to copy.

10 Hold down **Shift** and click the last item you want to copy.

Windows selects the range of items.

11 Drag the items to the destination folder on your device.

Windows copies the files.

12 When Windows finishes copying the files, disconnect your phone or tablet from your computer.

How can I see how much space is free on my phone or tablet?

1 Connect your phone or tablet to your PC.

2 If the AutoPlay dialog box opens, click **Open device to view files**.

3 In the Windows Explorer window, click the device's name.

4 Look at the Internal Storage readout in the details pane.

Transfer Files from Your Mac to Your Device

If you have a Mac rather than a Windows PC, you need to add an app for transferring files to or from your Android device. Android phones and tablets do not appear in the Mac OS X Finder, but you can use an app called Android File Transfer to transfer files. Android File Transfer is free, and it works well with standard Android devices. But if your device is designed to work with companion software, such as Samsung Kies, you should use that software instead of Android File Transfer.

Transfer Files from Your Mac to Your Device

Download and Install Android File Transfer

1 Click **Safari** (◉) on the Dock.

A Safari window opens.

2 Click in the Address box.

The contents of the Address box become selected.

3 Type **www.android.com/ filetransfer** and press **Return**.

The Android File Transfer web page appears.

4 Click **Download Now**.

The download begins.

5 When the download completes, click **Downloads**.

The Downloads stack opens.

6 Click **androidfiletransfer.dmg**.

A Finder window opens showing the contents of the Android File Transfer disk image.

7 Drag **Android File Transfer** (◈) to the Applications icon (▨).

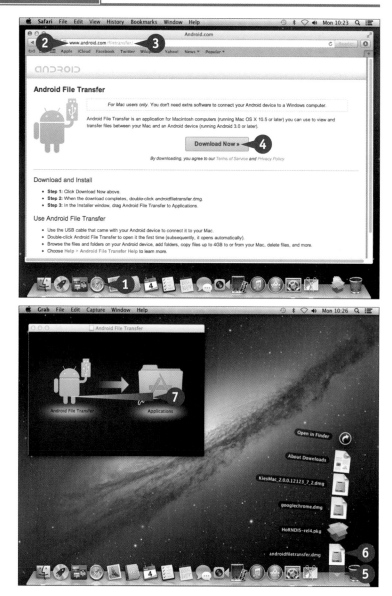

Launch Android File Transfer and Transfer Files

1 Connect your phone or tablet to your Mac via USB.

2 Click **Launchpad** (🚀).

The Launchpad screen appears.

3 Click **Android File Transfer** (🤖).

Android File Transfer opens and displays the contents of your device.

4 Control +click or right-click **Finder** (🗔).

The context menu opens.

5 Click **New Finder Window**.

A new Finder window opens.

6 Navigate to the folder that contains the files you want to copy to your device.

7 Select the files.

8 Drag the files to the appropriate folder on your device. For example, drag song files to the Music folder.

Android File Transfer copies the files.

9 When you finish using Android File Transfer, disconnect your phone or tablet from your Mac.

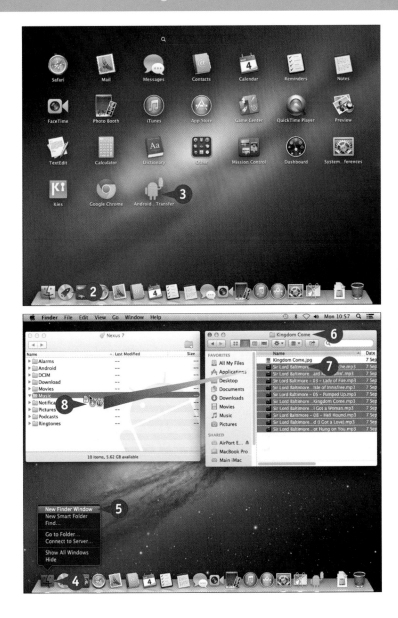

TIPS

How can I see how much free space my device has?

After launching Android File Transfer, look at the status bar. The readout shows the amount of free space — for example, 5.55 GB available.

What other actions can I take with Android File Transfer?

You can delete a file or folder by Control +clicking or right-clicking it and then clicking **Delete** on the context menu. You can create a new subfolder by Control +clicking or right-clicking in the existing folder in which you want to create the subfolder, clicking **New Folder**, typing the name, and then pressing Return .

Explore the User Interface and Launch Apps

When you press the Power button to wake your phone or tablet from sleep, Android displays the lock screen. You then unlock the phone or tablet to reach the Home screen, which contains a Favorites tray of icons for running frequently used apps plus the All Apps icon for accessing the full list of apps installed on the device. You can add other icons to the Home screen as needed. When you launch an app, its screen appears. From the app, you can return to the Home screen by pressing the Home button. You can then launch another app.

Explore the User Interface and Launch Apps

1 Press the Power button.

Note: If your device has a physical Home button rather than a soft button, you can normally press **Home** to wake the device instead of pressing the Power button.

The device's screen lights up and shows the lock screen.

2 Drag the lock symbol (🔒) to the edge of the unlocking circle. You can drag in any direction.

The Home screen appears.

Note: If Android displays an app rather than the Home screen, touch **Home** (⬠) to display the Home screen.

3 Touch **All Apps** (▦).

The Apps screen appears.

Note: If the Widgets tab is displayed on the Apps screen, touch the **Apps** tab.

4 Touch **Calculator** (▦).

The Calculator app opens.

5 Touch the buttons to perform a calculation.

A The result appears.

6 Touch **Home** (⬠).

The Home screen appears.

7 Touch **All Apps** (⊞).

The Apps screen appears.

8 If the screen is full of apps, swipe your finger from right to left across the screen.

Note: If the Apps screen is not full, most likely there is no second screen of apps to display. Swiping left then displays the Widgets screen.

The next screen of apps appears.

9 Touch an app to launch it. For example, touch Settings (⊞) to open the Settings app, which you use to configure Android.

TIPS

Is there just one Home screen, or are there several?

Android provides five Home screens. You can navigate among them by swiping right or left when a Home screen is displayed. When you touch the Home button (⬠), your phone or tablet displays the Home screen you used last.

Where do I get more apps to perform other tasks?

You can find a wide selection of apps — both free and ones you must pay for — in the Apps section of Google's Play Store. See Chapter 8 for instructions on finding and downloading the apps you need.

Understanding Skinned Versions of Android

Google's Android is currently the most widely used operating system for smartphones and tablets. At this writing, the latest version of Android is version 4.2, which is known as Jelly Bean. This book shows Jelly Bean in its regular form. But many manufacturers add overlays called *skins* to Android. The skins typically add extra functionality, modify the interface for existing apps and features, and make Android look different. If your Android phone or tablet uses a skin, you can still use this book, but you may need to consult your device's documentation to learn about differences and extra functionality.

Establish Whether Your Android Device Uses a Skin

You can easily establish whether your Android phone or tablet uses a skin. Touch Home (▬) to display the Home screen, and then see if it looks like the left screen in the illustration or significantly different, as the right screen does. The left screen shows stock Jelly Bean; the right shows Jelly Bean with a skin. If your device's screens look like those in most of the screens in this book, your device uses stock Android Jelly Bean. But if your phone or tablet is from a manufacturer that uses a skin — such as Samsung, HTC, Motorola, or Sony — most likely it uses a skin rather than stock Android.

Major Android Skins

The four major skins are Samsung's TouchWiz, HTC's Sense, and the skins from Motorola and Sony, neither of which has a formal name. These four skins are substantially different from each other, so Samsung's Android devices look significantly different from HTC's devices, which in turn look different from those that Motorola and Sony produce. Amazon's Kindle Fire devices also use a highly customized skin, but it is built on older versions of Android. Some manufacturers put skins on all their Android devices, whereas other manufacturers put skins on some devices but not all.

Advantages of Skins

Skins have several advantages over stock Android. First, skins can provide extra features and greater functionality than stock Android. For example, Samsung's TouchWiz skin includes support for the S Pen stylus in Android devices such as the Note II, enabling you to draw accurately on the screen and making note-taking easier. Second, a skin can provide greater integration with the specific hardware in a particular phone or tablet, so a manufacturer can make it easier for you to take full advantage of the hardware built in to the device. At the same time, the manufacturer can disable some of Android's stock functionality to encourage you to use the features it has added to the skin. Third, a skin can simply make Android look better, but this is, of course, a subjective judgment.

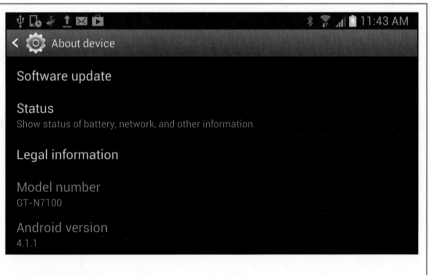

Disadvantages of Skins

If your phone or tablet uses a skin, you may not be able to update to the latest version of Android until a long time after its release. This is because after Google releases each new Android version, a manufacturer must create a new skinned version of Android customized to its phones and tablets. Often, manufacturers decide not to create a new custom version of Android for their older devices that are reaching the end of their product life cycles. This leaves the devices stuck on an older version of Android. If you are considering buying an older Android device, bear in mind that you may not be able to update it to newer versions of Android. Skinned versions of Android may also run more slowly than regular versions. While high-end devices can run skinned Android at full speed, you should test a device for speed before buying it.

continued ▶

Skinned versions of Android typically customize first the areas in which phone and tablet users spend the most time and second the features and apps from which users will derive most benefit. Four of the major areas in which skins often change the Android user interface are the Home screen, including the Favorites tray; the lock screen; the Notification shade; and the Settings app. Depending on the skin, you may also find that the manufacturer has provided an enhanced Camera app to make full use of the hardware features your device offers.

Home Screen

Most skins customize the Home screen, because it is a screen where each user will normally spend a lot of time taking actions. By providing different wallpapers, a manufacturer can give its Android devices a distinct look; and by building additional functionality into the interface, the manufacturer can make its phones and tablets faster and easier to use. Most skins customize the Favorites tray that appears at the bottom of the Home screen. For example, Samsung's TouchWiz skin rearranges the icons, putting the Apps icon on the right rather than in the middle.

Lock Screen

Most skins customize the lock screen, adding functionality to it in various ways. For example, in Samsung's TouchWiz skin, you can swipe an item in the Favorites tray at the bottom of the lock screen to open that item instead of displaying the Home screen or the last app you used. By contrast, in stock Android, you can swipe left from the lock screen to open the Camera app, which is useful for taking photos quickly. If your phone or tablet uses a skin, check the documentation to learn about any extra actions you can take from the lock screen, such as switching straight into apps or adding lock-screen widgets.

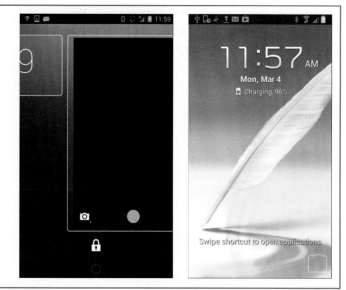

Notification Shade

The Notification shade, which you learn to use at the end of this chapter, brings together all your notifications — such as incoming calls and messages, app updates, and operating-system updates — into a single pane that you can easily access by dragging down the status bar at the top of the screen. Most skins customize the Notification shade to put frequently needed items right at your fingertips. For example, whereas the Notification shade in stock Jelly Bean provides a Quick Settings icon () that you can touch to display the Quick Settings panel, the top of the Notification shade in TouchWiz displays a scrollable list of essential settings to give you instant access to a wider range of settings. TouchWiz also uses a more graphical look for the Notification shade than stock Android does.

Settings App

Most skins also customize the Settings app, the app that you use to manipulate the settings on your Android device. Changes to the Settings app include adding settings for extra features; removing access to features that the skin disables; and changing the overall look of the Settings app itself for cosmetic reasons. For example, the TouchWiz skin changes the icon for not only the Settings app itself but also each of the settings categories. TouchWiz adds extra features, such as Blocking mode and the Power saving mode, to the main Settings screen. TouchWiz also provides access to Samsung's custom Application manager app, which you use to control the apps that are running and to force-quit any app that stops responding to the user interface.

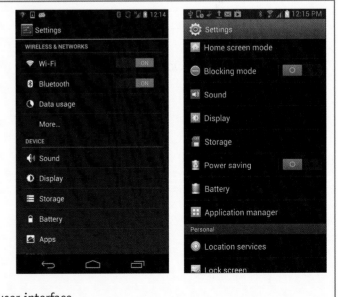

Navigate with Gestures

To navigate the Android user interface smoothly and swiftly, you can use seven main gestures. To trigger the default action for an item, you touch it and raise your finger. To access extra functionality, you touch and hold for a moment. To select text or zoom in to content, you double-tap. To scroll from one screen to another, you swipe right, left, up, or down. To move a shorter distance, you drag a finger. To zoom in or out, you pinch apart or pinch inward with two fingers.

Navigate with Gestures

1 Touch **Home** (▱), pressing your finger briefly to the screen and then lifting it.

The Home screen appears.

2 Touch **All Apps** (▦).

The Apps screen appears.

Note: If the Widgets tab is displayed on the Apps screen, touch the **Apps** tab.

3 Touch **Maps** (▨).

Note: If Maps is not on the Apps screen that appears first, scroll left or right until you find Maps.

The Maps app opens and displays the area around your current location.

4 Swipe left by moving your finger rapidly from the right side of the screen to the left side.

The map scrolls, following the direction you swiped.

5 Double-tap with one finger an item or area of interest on the screen.

Note: The double-tap gesture is also called *double-touch*.

26

The map zooms in on the area you double-tapped.

Note: In the Maps app, double-tapping zooms in by increments. You can zoom out by the same increments by double-tapping with two fingers.

⑥ Place two fingers, or your thumb and finger, close together on the screen and then move them apart. This is the "pinch apart" or "pinch open" gesture.

The map zooms in on the point where you pinched apart.

Note: To zoom back out, place two fingers, or your thumb and finger, apart on the screen and then pinch them inward. This is the "pinch in" or "pinch close" gesture.

⑦ Touch and hold a road on the screen for a moment.

Note: The touch and hold gesture is also called "long press."

A pop-up box appears.

⑧ Touch the pop-up box.

An information screen appears.

⑨ Touch **Street view**.

The Street view of the location appears, showing photos of the road.

⑩ Touch the **Street view figure** () and drag it in the direction you want to move.

The view shifts to follow the figure.

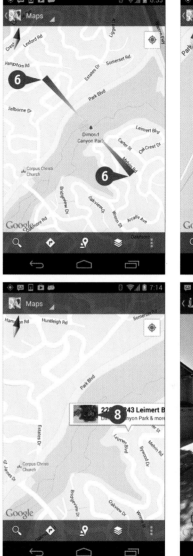

TIPS

What is the difference between swiping and dragging?
The difference between swiping and dragging is that swiping is a more expansive gesture than dragging. You swipe to move from one screen to another, whereas you drag to move within a screen.

Are there other gestures I can use with my phone or tablet?
Yes. Android supports other gestures that you can use within particular apps or features. You will learn about such gestures later in this book.

Use the Notification Shade

As your communications hub, your phone or tablet handles many types of alerts for you: missed phone or video calls, text messages, reminders, meetings, and so on. Android integrates all these alerts into the Notification shade, an area you can pull down from the top of the screen over whichever screen is currently displayed. You can quickly open the Notification shade from the Home screen or almost any other screen. With the Notification shade open, you can go to the app that raised a particular alert, dismiss an alert, dismiss all alerts, or simply close the Notification shade again.

Use the Notification Shade

Open the Notification Shade

1 Touch **Home** (⬛).

The Home screen appears.

Note: You can open the Notification shade from almost any Android app. A few apps, such as the Camera app, are exceptions.

2 On a phone, touch the status bar at the top of the screen and drag downward. On a tablet, touch the left side of the status bar and drag downward.

The Notification shade opens.

Note: On a phone, the Notification shade takes up the whole screen. On a tablet, the Notification shade takes up the upper-left area of the screen.

Go to the App That Raised an Alert

1 Touch the appropriate alert.

The app opens and displays the source of the alert.

You can now work in that app.

2 Drag or swipe open the Notification shade when you want to work with other alerts.

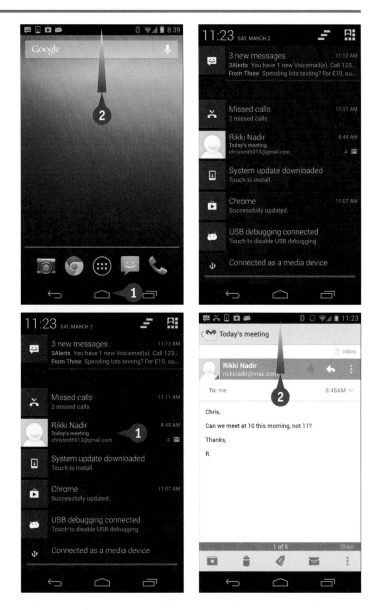

Dismiss One or More Alerts

1 To dismiss an alert, swipe the alert to the left or right.

The alert disappears from the list.

2 To dismiss all alerts, touch **Dismiss all** (⊟).

Android dismisses all the alerts that do not require your attention.

Android closes the Notification shade.

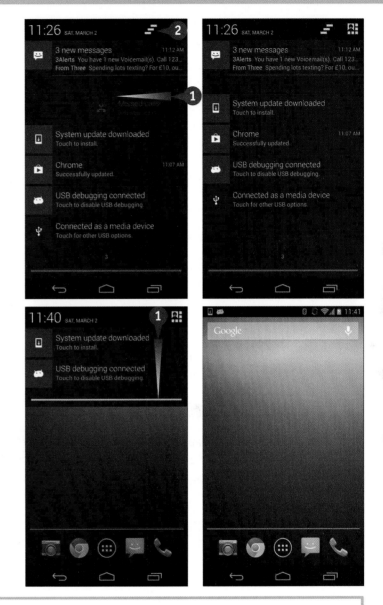

Close the Notification Shade

1 If you do not dismiss all alerts, as explained above, touch the bar at the bottom of the Notification shade and drag up to close the shade.

Note: You can also swipe up the screen from the bottom to close the Notification shade.

The Notification shade closes, and the desktop or app that was underneath the shade appears.

TIPS

Do I drag or swipe down to open the Notification shade?

You can either drag or swipe. Dragging the status bar down enables you to peek at the contents of the Notification shade without opening it fully. Swiping opens the Notification shade fully at once.

What other actions can I take in the Notification shade?

When you miss a phone call, you can touch **Call back** in the notification to return the call, or touch **Message** to send a text message instead. When you receive a notification for new e-mail messages, drag your finger down the notification to expand the list of messages.

CHAPTER 2

Customizing Your Phone or Tablet

To make your phone or tablet work the way you prefer, you can configure its many settings. This chapter shows you how to access the most important settings and use them to personalize the phone or tablet. You learn how to control notifications, audio preferences, screen brightness, and other key aspects of the device's behavior.

Find the Settings You Need

To configure your phone or tablet, you use the Settings app. This app contains settings for the Android operating system and the features your phone or tablet includes. To reach the settings, display the Settings screen and then display the appropriate category of settings. Some apps provide access to settings through the apps themselves. If you cannot find the settings for an app on the Settings screen, look within the app.

Find the Settings You Need

Display the Settings Screen

1 On a phone, touch the bar at the top of the screen and drag your finger down.

Note: On a tablet, touch the right side of the bar at the top of the screen and drag your finger down to open the Quick Settings pane. Touch and drag down the left side of the bar to open the Notification shade.

The Notification shade opens.

2 Touch **Quick Settings** (⊞).

The Quick Settings pane appears.

3 Touch **Settings** (⊞).

The Settings screen appears.

4 Drag your finger up to scroll down to display other settings categories.

Display a Settings Screen

 On the Settings screen, touch the button for the settings you want to display. For example, touch Sound to display the Sound screen.

 Touch **Settings** (▦) when you are ready to return to the Settings screen.

Display the Settings for an App

 With the app running, touch **Menu** (⋮).

The menu appears.

② Touch **Settings** (▦).

The Settings screen appears.

Note: At this point, you may need to choose among different categories of settings by touching the appropriate category. For example, in the Gmail app used in the example here, touch General Settings to display the General Settings screen.

③ Touch the setting you want to change. For example, ☐ changes to ☑ .

④ When you finish changing the settings, touch **Back** ( ) to return to the app.

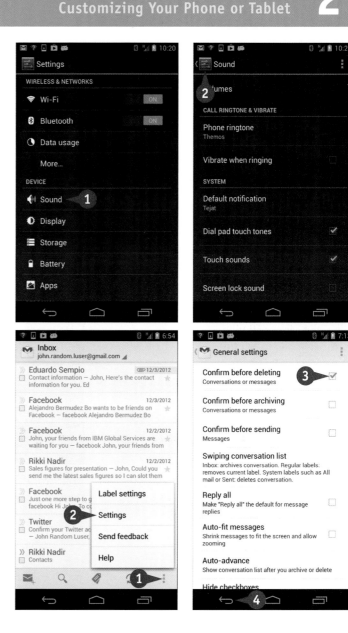

How can I access key settings quickly?
You can access key settings directly from the Quick Settings panel. On a phone, touch the bar at the top of the screen and drag your finger down to open the Notification shade, then touch **Quick Settings** (▦) to display the Quick Settings panel. On a tablet, touch and drag down the right side of the bar at the top of the screen to open the Notification shade. You can then touch the setting you want to change.

Choose Which Notifications to Receive

S ome apps can display notifications to alert you when an event has occurred — for example, to remind you of an upcoming calendar appointment, to announce the arrival of an e-mail message, or to mark the availability of a software update. Notifications are great for keeping track of vital information, but you will probably want to choose which notifications you receive rather than receive all notifications. You can choose which apps give notifications. If your phone or tablet has a notification light, you can choose whether to have the light pulse to alert you to notifications.

Choose Which Notifications to Receive

1 Touch **Home** (⬜).

The Home screen appears.

2 Touch **All Apps** (⊞).

The Apps screen appears.

Note: If the Widgets tab is displayed on the Apps screen, touch the **Apps** tab.

3 Touch **Settings** (⊞).

Note: If the Settings app is not on the Apps screen that appears at first, swipe left to display the next Apps screen. Swipe again if necessary.

Note: You can also open the Settings app by opening the Notification shade and then touching **Settings** on it.

The Settings screen appears.

4 Touch **Apps**.

The Apps screen appears.

5 Touch the app you want to affect.

The App info screen for the app appears.

6 Touch **Show notifications** (■ changes to ✓) if you want to see notifications from this app. Otherwise, deselect **Show notifications** (✓ changes to ■).

7 Touch **Settings** (▦).

The Apps screen appears.

8 Repeat steps **5** to **7** to choose settings for other apps as needed.

9 Touch **Settings** (▦) on the Apps screen.

The Settings screen appears.

10 Touch **Display**.

The Display screen appears.

11 Touch **Pulse notification light** (■ changes to ✓) if you want the phone's or tablet's notification light to pulse when you have a notification. Otherwise, deselect **Pulse notification light** (✓ changes to ■).

12 Touch **Settings** (▦).

The Settings screen appears.

13 Touch **Home** (⌂).

The Home screen appears.

TIP

What other actions can I take on the App info screen for an app?
You can take several other actions on the App info screen for an app:

- Touch **Force stop** to force the app to stop if it has ceased to respond to your touches.
- Touch **Uninstall** to begin the process of uninstalling the app from your phone or tablet.
- Touch **Clear data** to delete the app's data files, including account details you have entered and settings you have chosen.
- Touch **Clear cache** to clear any data the app has stored in its cache for future use.

Choose Volume and Sound Settings

To control the playback volume of sounds and music on your phone or tablet, you can use either the hardware volume controls or the on-screen controls. To control your phone's or tablet's audio feedback, choose settings on the Sound screen. Here, you can control the ringtone and vibration for a phone, set the default notification sound, and choose whether to play sounds to give feedback on touching the screen, locking the screen, or docking the phone or tablet.

Choose Volume and Sound Settings

1 Touch **Home** (▬).

The Home screen appears.

2 Touch **All Apps** (⊞).

The Apps screen appears.

Note: If the Widgets tab is displayed on the Apps screen, touch the **Apps** tab.

3 Touch **Settings** (⊞).

Note: If Settings is not on the Apps screen that appears first, scroll left or right until you find Settings.

The Settings screen appears.

4 Touch **Sound**.

The Sound screen appears.

5 If you want to set the volume, touch **Volumes**.

6 On the Volumes screen, drag the **Music, video, games, & other media** slider.

7 Drag the **Ringtone & notifications** slider or the **Notifications** slider.

8 Drag the **Alarms** slider.

9 Touch **OK**.

10 On the Sound screen, touch **Phone Ringtone** on a phone.

11 On the Phone ringtone screen, touch a ringtone to listen to it.

12 Touch **OK**.

13 On the Sound screen, select (☑) or deselect (■) **Vibrate when ringing**.

14 Touch **Default Notification**.

15 On the Default notification screen, touch a tone to listen to it.

16 Touch **OK**.

17 On the Sound screen, select (☑) or deselect (■) **Dial pad touch tones**.

18 Touch to select (☑) or deselect (■) **Touch sounds**.

19 Touchto select (☑) or deselect (■) **Screen lock sound**.

20 Touch to select (☑) or deselect (■) **Vibrate on touch**.

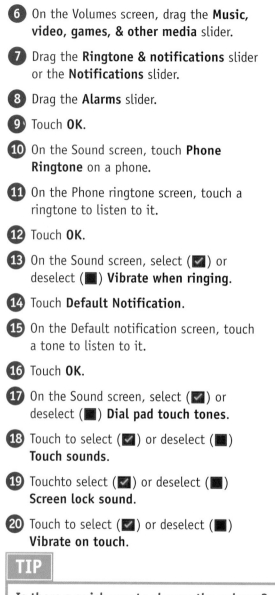

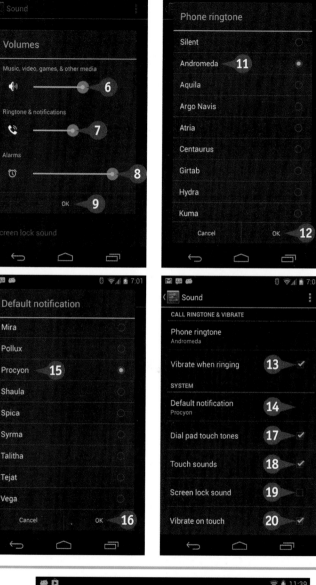

TIP

Is there a quick way to change the volume?

If your phone or tablet has a physical Volume control, press the upper side of the control to increase the volume, or press the lower side to decrease the volume. A volume control appears on the screen, showing the volume setting. If **Options** (▦) (Ⓐ) appears, touch it to display other volumes you can set, then drag 🔘 to set the volume.

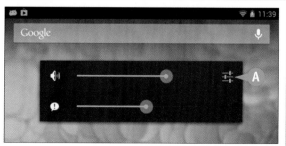

Set Display Brightness and Wallpaper

To make the display easy to see, you can change its brightness. You can also have your device's Auto-Brightness feature automatically set the display brightness to a level suitable for the ambient brightness that the light sensor detects. To make the display attractive to your eye, you can choose which picture to use as the wallpaper that appears in the background. You can choose a picture of your own from the Gallery app, select one of the built-in static wallpapers, or pick a live wallpaper that changes while the lock screen or a Home screen is displayed.

Set Display Brightness and Wallpaper

 Touch **Home** ( ).

The Home screen appears.

 Touch **All Apps** ( ).

The Apps screen appears.

Note: If the Widgets tab is displayed on the Apps screen, touch the **Apps** tab.

 Touch **Settings** ( ).

Note: If Settings is not on the Apps screen that appears first, scroll left or right until you find Settings.

The Settings screen appears.

 Touch **Display**.

The Display screen appears.

 Touch **Brightness**.

Note: You can quickly change the wallpaper from any Home screen. Touch and hold the wallpaper until the Choose wallpaper from dialog box opens, then touch **Gallery**, **Live Wallpapers**, or **Wallpapers**, as appropriate.

The Brightness dialog box appears.

6 Touch **Automatic brightness** (■ changes to ☑) if you want your phone or tablet to set the display brightness automatically. Otherwise, drag the slider to set the brightness.

7 Touch **OK**.

The Brightness dialog box closes.

8 Touch **Wallpaper**.

The Choose wallpaper from screen appears.

9 Touch the wallpaper source: **Gallery**, **Live Wallpapers**, or **Wallpapers**. This example uses Wallpapers.

10 On the screen that appears, touch the picture, live wallpaper, or wallpaper you want.

Note: Live wallpaper can be attractive to look at, but it requires more power than static wallpaper, so it reduces battery runtime.

11 Touch **Set wallpaper**.

12 Touch **Home** (◖▬◗).

The wallpaper appears on the Home screens.

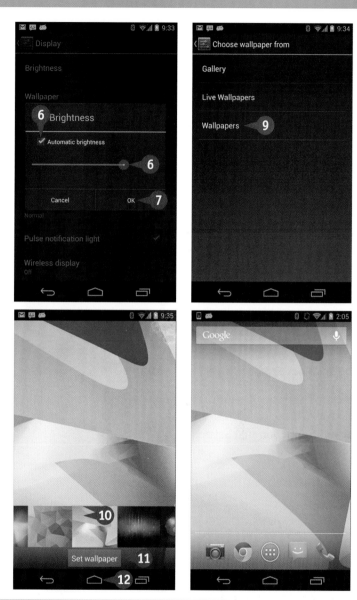

TIP

Is there a quick way to change the display brightness?

You can quickly change the display brightness from the Quick Settings pane. On a phone, touch the top of the screen, drag open the Notification shade, and then touch **Quick Settings** (▦). On a tablet, touch the right side of the top of the screen and drag open the Quick Settings pane. Touch **Brightness** to display the Brightness control, then touch **Auto** or drag the slider as needed.

Choose Location Access Settings

Your Android phone or tablet can determine your location using satellites in the Global Positioning System, or GPS, known wireless networks, and cellphone towers. Android and your apps can use your location information to tag your photos, customize your searches, and provide local information. In Android, you can choose whether to allow location access and — if you allow it — which means of determining location to use. You adjust location access separately for Google apps and for other apps.

Choose Location Access Settings

1 Touch **Home** ().

The Home screen appears.

2 Touch **All Apps** (🔲).

The Apps screen appears.

Note: If the Widgets tab is displayed on the Apps screen, touch the **Apps** tab.

3 Touch **Settings** (🔡).

Note: If Settings is not on the Apps screen that appears first, scroll left or right until you find Settings.

4 Touch **Location access**.

Note: On a phone, you may need to scroll down to display the Location access button.

The Location access screen appears.

5 Touch **Access to my location** to move the switch to On or Off, as needed.

Note: If you move the switch to On, the Location consent dialog box appears. Touch **Agree** to close the dialog box.

6 Touch to select (☑) or deselect (■) **GPS satellites**, as appropriate.

7 Touch to select (☑) or deselect (■) **Wi-Fi & mobile network location**, as appropriate.

8 Touch **Settings** (🔡).

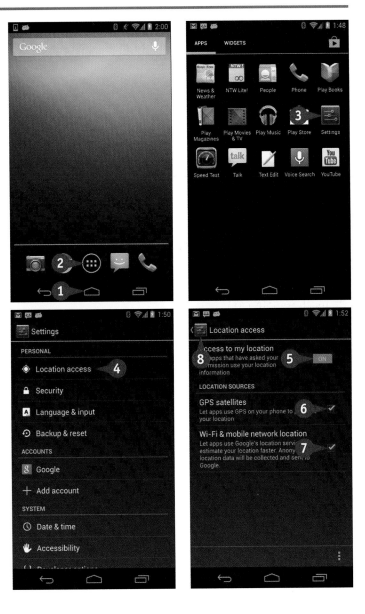

The Settings screen appears again.

9 In the Accounts list, touch **Google**.

The Google screen appears, showing your Google account.

10 Touch **Location settings**.

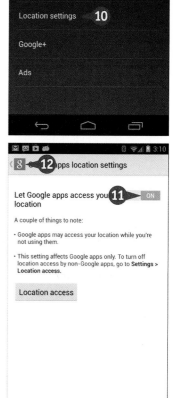

The Google apps location settings screen appears.

11 Touch the **Let Google apps access your location** switch to set it to On or Off, as needed.

Note: On the Google apps location settings screen, you can touch **Location access** to display the Location access screen for other apps.

12 Touch **Google** ().

The Google screen appears.

13 Touch **Settings** ().

The Settings screen appears.

TIP

Should I grant location access when apps request it?

This is entirely up to you. Each time an app requests location access, make sure it has a good reason for using location access and is not just snooping on your movements. Granting location access to apps can help you to get more out of your phone or tablet, but it also raises privacy concerns. For example, allowing social-media apps to access your location lets your friends keep up with your movements, but it can also enable people to stalk you. Similarly, adding location information to your photos enables you to sort them by location, which is helpful. However, if you post photos containing location information online, other people can tell exactly where you took them.

Secure Your Phone or Tablet with a PIN

To prevent anyone who picks up your phone or tablet from accessing your data, you can lock the device with a Personal Identification Number, or PIN. This numeric code takes effect when you lock your phone or tablet or it locks itself. To unlock the device, you must provide the PIN. If you need tighter security than a PIN can provide, you can use a password, which offers greater entropy and so is harder to crack.

Secure Your Phone or Tablet with a PIN

1 Touch **Home** (▬).

The Home screen appears.

2 Touch **All Apps** (▦).

The Apps screen appears.

Note: If the Widgets tab is displayed on the Apps screen, touch the **Apps** tab.

3 Touch **Settings** (▤).

Note: If Settings is not on the Apps screen that appears first, scroll left or right until you find Settings.

The Settings screen appears.

4 Touch **Security**.

Note: On a phone, you may need to scroll down to display the Security button.

The Security screen appears.

5 Touch **Screen lock**.

The Choose screen lock screen appears.

6 Touch **PIN**.

Note: At this point, you can choose a different means of security by touching **Slide**, **Face Unlock**, **Pattern**, or **Password**. See the tip for more information.

The Choose your PIN screen appears.

7 Type a pin of four digits or more.

8 Touch **Continue**.

A second Choose your PIN screen appears, prompting you to confirm your PIN.

9 Type the same PIN.

10 Touch **OK**.

The Security screen appears, now showing other options.

11 Touch **Power button locks instantly** (■ changes to ✓) if you need tight security.

12 Touch **Automatically lock**.

The Automatically lock screen appears.

13 Touch the appropriate time button — for example, 5 seconds.

The Security screen appears.

14 Touch **Settings** (▦).

The Settings screen appears.

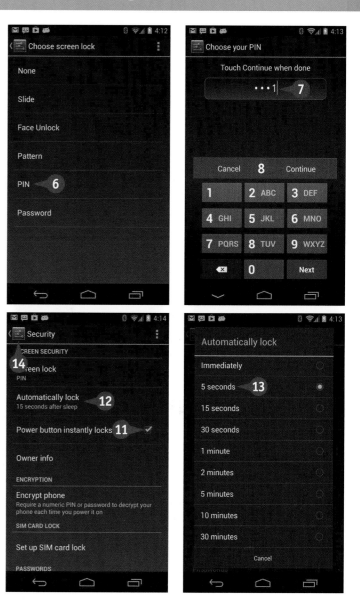

TIP

What alternatives do I have to a PIN for securing my Android device?
On the Choose screen lock screen, you can choose four other means of unlocking the screen. Slide is the default method, requiring you only to slide your finger across the screen. Face Unlock captures photos of your face and uses the camera to authenticate you. Pattern requires you to draw a pattern on a grid of nine dots. Password requires you to type a password. Alternatively, choose None to have no lock.

Encrypt Your Phone or Tablet for Security

After you secure your phone or tablet with a PIN or password, you can protect your valuable data by also encrypting all the data on your phone or tablet. Encryption scrambles the data on the device so that it can be read only by someone who enters the PIN or password. Before encrypting your phone or tablet, you must charge its battery fully. During encryption, the phone or tablet must also be connected to a power source. Android requires both a charged battery and a power source to ensure that encryption can finish even if the power is cut.

Encrypt Your Phone or Tablet for Security

① Plug your phone or tablet into a power source — either a power adapter or the USB port on a computer or powered USB hub — and charge it fully. Leave the phone or tablet connected to the power source.

② Touch **Home** (◼).

The Home screen appears.

③ Touch **All Apps** (◼).

The Apps screen appears.

Note: If the Widgets tab is displayed on the Apps screen, touch the **Apps** tab.

④ Touch **Settings** (◼).

Note: If Settings is not on the Apps screen that appears first, scroll left or right until you find Settings.

The Settings screen appears.

⑤ Touch **Security**.

Note: On a phone, you may need to scroll down to display the Security button.

The Security screen appears.

⑥ Touch **Encrypt phone** or **Encrypt tablet**.

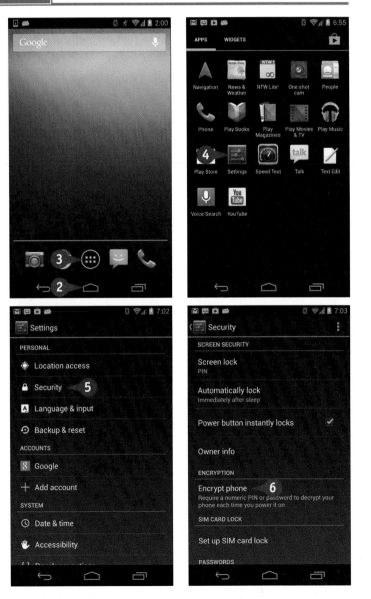

The Encrypt phone screen or the Encrypt tablet screen appears.

Note: If your phone or tablet is not plugged in to a power source, the Encrypt phone button or Encrypt tablet button is dimmed and unavailable.

 Touch **Encrypt phone** or **Encrypt tablet**.

The Confirm your PIN screen appears.

Note: If your device uses a password rather than a PIN, the Confirm your password screen appears.

 Type your PIN.

9 Touch **Next**.

The Encrypt? screen appears, warning you that encryption is irreversible and that you must not interrupt it.

10 Touch **Encrypt phone** or **Encrypt tablet**.

Android begins encrypting the phone or tablet, displaying a progress readout on-screen as it does so.

The Type password to decrypt storage screen appears.

11 Type your PIN.

12 Touch **Done**.

The lock screen appears.

13 Type your PIN.

14 Touch ↵.

The Home screen appears, and you can start using your device normally.

TIP

How do I remove encryption from my phone or tablet?
After encrypting your phone or tablet, you cannot remove the encryption and leave the data in place. Instead, you must perform a factory data reset, which wipes the data from the device and restores factory settings. See Chapter 13 for instructions on performing a factory data reset.

Choose Language and Input Settings

To be able to use your phone or tablet easily, you will want its user interface to use your language. Android supports many languages, and you can quickly switch among them. Android also provides various ways of entering text, ranging from assorted keyboard layouts to speech to typing via the Google voice feature. You can configure your input methods, the spell-checker, and other language options in Language & input settings.

Choose Language and Input Settings

 Touch **Home** (▬).

The Home screen appears.

 Touch **All Apps** (▦).

The Apps screen appears.

Note: If the Widgets tab is displayed on the Apps screen, touch the **Apps** tab.

 Touch **Settings** (▦).

Note: If Settings is not on the Apps screen that appears first, scroll left or right until you find Settings.

The Settings screen appears.

 Touch **Language & input**.

Note: On a phone, you may need to scroll down to display the Language & input button.

The Language & input screen appears.

 To change the language, touch **Language**, touch the appropriate language on the Language screen, and then touch **Settings** (▦).

 To use the spell-checker, select **Spell checker** (▪ changes to ☑).

 To configure the spell-checker, touch **Options** (▦).

Note: To enter set phrases quickly, use Personal dictionary. See the tip for details.

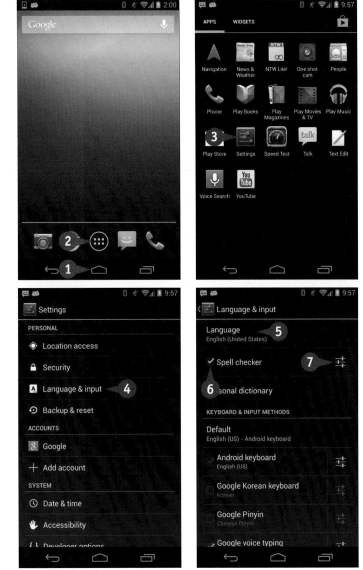

8 On the Spell checker screen, touch **Options** (⊞).

9 On the Spell checking settings screen, touch **Look up contact names** (■ changes to ☑) if you want the spell-checker to look up names in your contact list.

10 Touch **Spell Checker** (▣).

11 In the Language dialog box, touch the language you want to use (○ changes to ◉).

12 In the Keyboard & input methods area, select each keyboard or input method you want to use (■ changes to ☑).

13 To configure Voice Search, touch **Voice Search** and work on the screen that appears.

14 To configure the text-to-speech feature, touch **Text-to-speech output** and work on the screen that appears.

15 To change the pointer speed for an attached mouse, trackball, or trackpad, touch **Pointer speed** and work on the screen that appears.

TIP

What is a personal dictionary and how do I use it?

A personal dictionary is a list containing terms you can enter quickly by typing a shortcut. For example, if you add the term Vice President for Sales & Marketing with the shortcut vpsm, you can quickly enter the term by typing **vpsm** and touching the term on the spelling suggestions bar.

Customize the Home Screens

To make your phone or tablet easy to use, you can customize your Home screens by adding the apps and widgets you find most useful and removing any apps or widgets you do not need. You can reposition the apps and widgets on each Home screen as best suits you, and you can customize the Favorites tray at the bottom of the Home screen with essential apps. You can also resize the widgets to their optimum sizes.

Customize the Home Screens

Put an App on a Home Screen

1. Touch **Home** (▱).

   The Home screen appears.

2. Navigate to the Home screen on which you want to put the app.

3. Touch **All Apps** (▦).

   The Apps screen appears.

Note: If the Widgets tab is displayed on the Apps screen, touch the **Apps** tab.

4. Touch and hold the app you want to add to the Home screen.

   The Home screen appears with the app at the top.

5. Drag the app to where you want it.

6. Release the app.

Customize the Favorites Tray

1 Touch **Home** (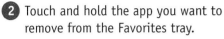).

The Home screen appears.

Note: If the Favorites tray is full of apps, you must remove an app before you can add another app.

2 Touch and hold the app you want to remove from the Favorites tray.

Ⓐ The Remove button appears.

3 Drag the app out of the Favorites tray onto the main part of the Home screen and release it.

4 Touch and hold the app you want to add to the Favorites tray.

The Remove button appears.

5 Drag the app to the Favorites tray and release it.

Put a Widget on the Home Screen

1 Touch **Home** (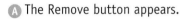).

The Home screen appears.

2 Navigate to the Home screen to which you want to add the widget.

3 Touch **All Apps** ().

The Apps screen appears.

4 Touch **Widgets**.

TIP

What are widgets?

Widgets are miniature apps that display useful information or give you quick access to frequently used apps. For example, the Analog clock widget and Digital clock widget simply display the time on the Home screen at an easy-to-see size. The Gmail widget displays the contents of a folder, and you can touch a message to open it in the Gmail app. Android comes with a wide range of built-in widgets, but you can also download other widgets from the Play Store and other online sources.

continued ▶

To organize the Home screens, you can arrange the apps into folders. You create a folder by dragging one icon onto another icon. Doing this creates a folder containing both items. You can then name the folder. You can create folders both on the main part of the Home screen and in the Favorites tray. After creating a folder, you can populate it with as many apps as needed. You can quickly open an app from within the folder, and you can remove an app from the folder if necessary.

Customize the Home Screens (continued)

The Widgets screen appears.

5 Touch and hold the widget you want to add.

The Home screen appears with the widget at the top.

6 Drag the widget to where you want it.

7 Release the widget.

Note: After you add the widget, you may need to choose options for it — for example, the Photo Gallery widget prompts you to choose which photos to display.

Resize a Widget

1 Touch **Home** (⬛).

The Home screen appears.

2 Touch and hold the widget.

B A blue box and adjustment handles appear around the widget.

3 Drag a handle to resize the widget.

4 Touch outside the widget to deselect it.

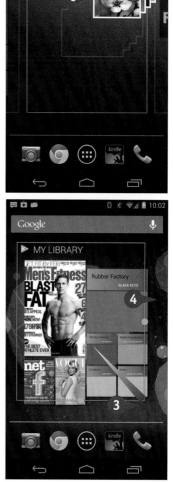

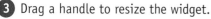

Create a Folder

1 Touch **Home** ().

The Home screen appears.

2 Touch and hold an app you want to put in the new folder.

The Remove button appears.

3 Drag the app to another app destined for the folder.

Android creates an unnamed folder containing the two apps.

4 Touch the folder.

The folder opens.

5 Touch **Unnamed Folder**.

6 Type the folder name.

7 Touch outside the folder.

Note: You can now drag other apps to the folder.

Note: To launch an app from the folder, touch the folder, and then touch the app.

TIP

How do I remove an app or a widget from the Home screen?
Touch and hold the app or widget until the Remove button appears at the top of the screen. Drag the app or widget to the Remove button, and then drop it.

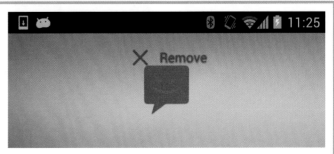

Customize the Lock Screen

The lock screen appears when you turn on your phone or tablet or wake it from sleep. You can customize the lock screen by adding controls that display reference information. For example, if you add the Gmail widget and the Calendar widget to your lock screen, you can monitor your e-mail messages and your upcoming events without having to unlock your phone or tablet and go into the Gmail app or the Calendar app. You can touch an item in the widget to go to that item in the app — for example, to open a message in the Gmail app.

Customize the Lock Screen

1 Press the Power button to put your phone or tablet to sleep.

2 Press the Power button to wake the phone or tablet.

The lock screen appears.

3 Swipe right.

A lock screen with an Add icon () appears.

Note: If your phone or tablet has a camera, swipe left from the lock screen to quickly access the camera.

4 Touch **Add** (+).

A graphical list appears showing widgets such as Calendar, Digital clock, Gmail, and Messaging.

5 Touch the widget you want to use. This example uses Gmail. This widget displays the latest messages in your chosen mailbox on the lock screen.

6 If the widget displays a screen of options, touch the option you want. For example, for the Gmail widget, touch the folder on the Choose folder screen.

The widget appears on the lock screen.

Note: The next time you wake the phone or tablet, you can display the lock screen widget by swiping left from the initial lock screen.

7 If you want to add further widgets, repeat steps **3** to **6**.

8 To navigate from one widget to another, swipe left or right on the lock screen.

9 To unlock your phone or tablet, touch **Unlock** (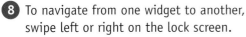).

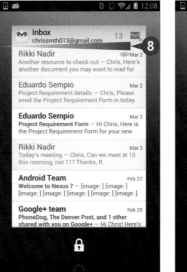

The widget shrinks to the top of the screen.

10 Drag the **lock icon** (🔒) to unlock the phone or tablet as usual.

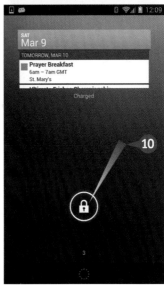

How do I remove a widget from the lock screen?

Touch and hold the widget until the Remove button appears at the top of the screen, then drag the widget to the Remove button. When the widget turns red, release it.

Set Up Sleep and Daydream

Android 4.2 Jelly Bean includes Daydream, a feature similar to screen savers on computers. By turning on Daydream and choosing settings, you can make your phone or tablet display information or graphics on-screen while it sleeps or charges. For example, you can display a clock or a photo frame that shows a selection of photos. Whether you choose to use Daydream or not, you can control how long your phone or tablet stays awake before going to sleep automatically.

Set Up Sleep and Daydream

 Touch **Home** (⬜).

The Home screen appears.

 Touch **All Apps** (⊞).

The Apps screen appears.

Note: If the Widgets tab is displayed on the Apps screen, touch the **Apps** tab.

 Touch **Settings** (⊞).

Note: If Settings is not on the Apps screen that appears first, scroll left or right until you find Settings.

The Settings screen appears.

 Touch **Display**.

The Display screen appears.

 Touch **Sleep**.

The Sleep dialog box opens.

6 Touch the length of time before your device sleeps (■ changes to ◉).

The Sleep dialog box closes.

7 Touch **Daydream**.

The Daydream screen appears.

8 If the Daydream switch is Off, touch to move it to On.

9 In the list, touch the Daydream type to use: **Clock**, **Colors**, **Currents**, **Photo Frame**, or **Photo Table**. This example uses Photo Frame.

10 If you chose Clock, Photo Frame, or Photo Table, touch **Settings** (▦). Choose options on the resulting screen, and then touch **Back** (◄).

11 Touch **When to daydream**.

The When to daydream dialog box opens.

12 Touch **While docked**, **While charging**, or **Either**, as appropriate (■ changes to ◉).

13 Touch **Start now**.

A preview of the Daydream runs.

14 Touch anywhere on the screen.

The preview ends.

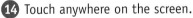

What is the difference between the Photo Frame theme and the Photo Table theme?

Photo Frame shows one photo at a time and is good for enjoying your photos. Photo Table gradually arranges miniature versions of your photos on a table-like surface and is more of a decorative effect.

What is the Currents theme in Daydream?

The Currents theme displays a series of screens containing brief news items. You can touch an item to display it full screen. From there, you can touch the **Open in Google Currents** link to display the full story in the Currents app.

Set Up Accessibility Features

To make your phone or tablet easier and more convenient to use, Android offers a set of accessibility features. You can reach these features through the Settings app. If you have difficulty reading the text on-screen, you can turn on the Large text feature to enlarge the text and you can make the screen easy to magnify. You can also turn on text-to-speech conversion to enable you to listen to the text on-screen. Another option is to have your device speak passwords aloud to you.

Set Up Accessibility Features

1 Touch **Home** (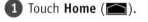).

The Home screen appears.

2 Touch **All Apps** ().

The Apps screen appears.

Note: If the Widgets tab is displayed on the Apps screen, touch the **Apps** tab.

3 Touch **Settings** (⚙).

Note: If Settings is not on the Apps screen that appears first, scroll left or right until you find Settings.

The Settings screen appears.

Note: On a phone, you may need to scroll down to display the Accessibility button.

4 Touch **Accessibility**.

The Accessibility screen appears.

5 To use magnification, touch **Magnification gestures**.

Note: With magnification gestures on, triple-tap to magnify what is on-screen. Drag two or more fingers across the screen to pan. To magnify temporarily, triple-tap and hold; while holding, you can pan by dragging. Pinch in or out with two fingers to adjust the zoom level.

6 On the Magnification gestures screen, touch the **Magnification gestures switch** to set it to On.

7 Touch **Settings** (■).

8 To use large text, touch **Large Text** (■ changes to ✓).

9 Touch **Power button ends call** (■ changes to ✓) if you want to end calls by pressing the Power button.

10 Touch **Auto-rotate screen** (■ changes to ✓) to enable automatic rotation.

11 Touch **Speak passwords** (■ changes to ✓) to have Android speak passwords you type.

12 Touch **Accessibility shortcut**.

13 On the Accessibility shortcut screen, touch the **Accessibility shortcut switch** to set it to On.

14 Touch **Settings** (■).

15 Touch **Touch & hold delay**.

16 In the Touch & hold delay dialog box, touch **Short**, **Medium**, or **Long** (■ changes to ●).

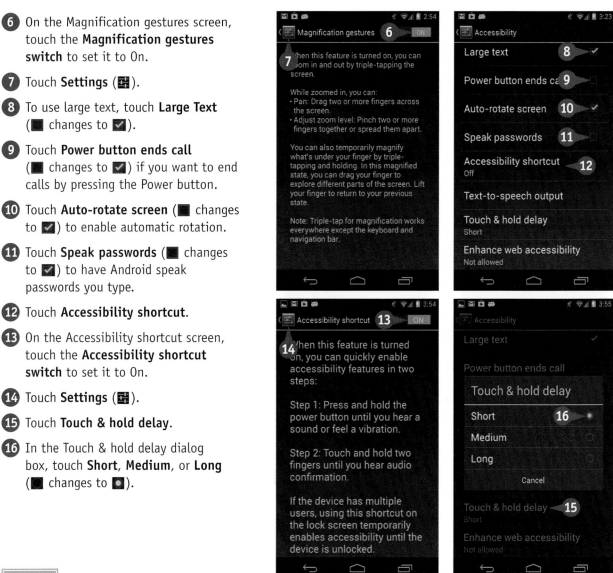

TIPS

How do I use the Accessibility shortcut?

Hold down the Power button until your device beeps or vibrates, then touch and hold with two fingers until your device beeps.

How do I use the Text-to-speech feature?

On the Accessibility screen in Settings, touch **Text-to-speech output** to display the Text-to-speech output screen. In the Preferred Engine list, select the text-to-speech engine to use (■ changes to ✓), then touch ■ and choose settings. In the General area, touch **Speech rate** and then touch **Very Slow**, **Slow**, **Normal**, **Fast**, or **Very Fast** in the Speech rate dialog box.

Use TalkBack and Explore by Touch

If you find it hard to see items on the screen of your phone or tablet, you can use the TalkBack feature to read the screen to you. TalkBack says the name of the current screen or dialog box and announces the items you touch on-screen, enabling you to navigate your device by listening. If you turn on TalkBack, you can also use the Explore by Touch feature, which announces what is under your finger on the screen.

Use TalkBack and Explore by Touch

1 Touch **Home** (⬟).

The Home screen appears.

2 Touch **All Apps** (⊞).

The Apps screen appears.

Note: If the Widgets tab is displayed on the Apps screen, touch the **Apps** tab.

3 Touch **Settings** (⊞).

Note: If Settings is not on the Apps screen that appears first, scroll left or right until you find Settings.

The Settings screen appears.

Note: On a phone, you may need to scroll down to display the Accessibility button.

4 Touch **Accessibility**.

The Accessibility screen appears.

5 Touch **TalkBack**.

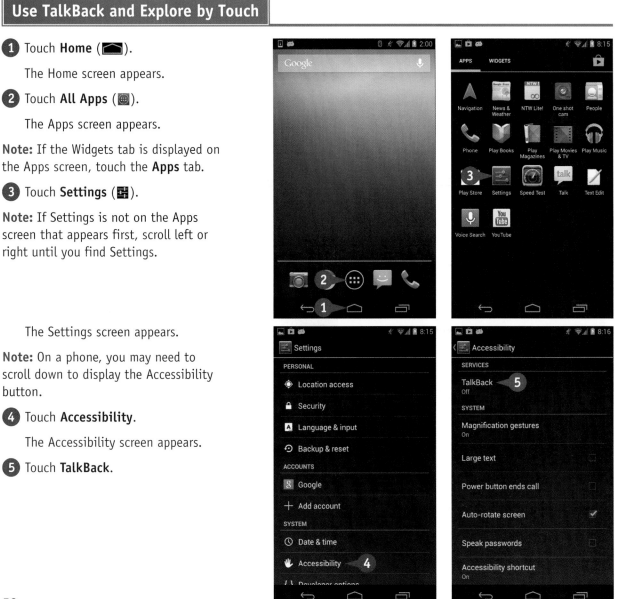

6 On the TalkBack screen, touch the **TalkBack switch** to set it to On.

7 In the Use TalkBack? dialog box, touch **OK**.

The TalkBack tutorial starts.

8 Touch **Next** to select the button, touch again to activate it, and follow through the tutorial.

9 When the tutorial ends, touch **Settings**.

The TalkBack Settings screen appears.

10 Touch **Use pitch changes** (■ changes to ☑) if you want keyboard feedback to use a lower-pitched voice.

11 Touch **Use proximity sensor** (■ changes to ☑) if you want TalkBack to stop when you bring your phone to your face.

12 Touch **Speak caller ID** (■ changes to ☑) if you want TalkBack to announce incoming call numbers.

13 Touch **Explore by touch** (■ changes to ☑) if you want to use Explore by touch.

14 Touch **Launch "Explore by touch" tutorial** to view the tutorial.

15 Touch **Manage shortcut gestures** and choose gestures on the Manage shortcut gestures screen.

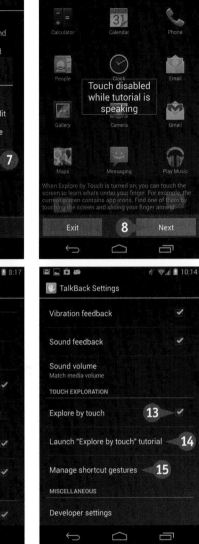

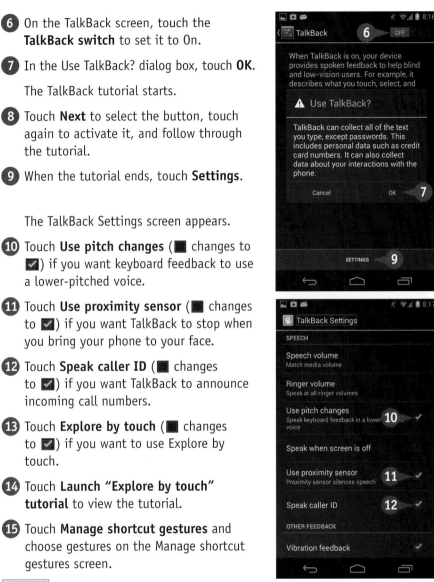

TIP

What settings can I choose for shortcut gestures?
On the Manage shortcut gestures screen, you can choose how Android interprets gestures. For example, you can map swiping down and then right to the Back button or to opening the Notification shade. Touch the gesture you want to change, and then touch the button or action in the dialog box that opens (■ changes to ●).

Install Credentials

To connect your phone or tablet to the network or e-mail servers in a company or organization, you may need to use credentials. These are digital certificates, encrypted chunks of code that uniquely identify a computer and are protected against tampering. Before you can use a digital certificate, you must install it on your phone or tablet. You can install it easily from the device's Download folder. If the certificate is not already in the Download folder, you will need to put it there, as explained in the tip.

Install Credentials

Note: If you have not already protected your phone or tablet with a PIN or password, do so now. The device must have a PIN or password before you can install a certificate.

1 Touch **Home** (▭).

The Home screen appears.

2 Touch **All Apps** (▦).

The Apps screen appears.

Note: If the Widgets tab is displayed on the Apps screen, touch the **Apps** tab.

3 Touch **Settings** (⊞).

Note: If Settings is not on the Apps screen that appears first, scroll left or right until you find Settings.

The Settings screen appears.

Note: On a phone, you may need to scroll down to display the Security button.

4 Touch **Security**.

The Security screen appears.

Note: On a phone, you may need to scroll down to display the Install from storage button.

5 Touch **Install from storage**.

If your device's storage contains multiple certificates, the Choose a certificate screen appears.

 Touch the certificate you want to install.

The Confirm Your PIN screen appears.

Note: If your device uses a password rather than a PIN, the Confirm your Password screen appears. Type your password.

 Type your PIN.

8 Touch **Next**.

The Name the certificate dialog box appears.

9 Edit the name as needed.

10 Touch **OK**.

 Android installs the certificate and displays a message saying it has done so.

11 Touch **Back** ( ).

The Security screen appears.

Note: To remove all the certificates from your phone or tablet, open the Security screen in Settings, and then touch **Clear credentials**.

TIP

How do I put a certificate file in my device's storage?
E-mail is the easiest way to install a digital certificate on your phone or tablet. Send the digital certificate as an attachment to a message and then open the message on the device. In the Attachments area, touch for the attachment, and then touch **Save**. If you cannot use e-mail to install a certificate, use an app such as Windows Explorer or Android File Transfer to copy the certificate file to the Download folder.

Set Up Multiple Users on a Tablet

If you have a tablet running Android 4.2 Jelly Bean, you can set it up for multiple users by creating a separate account for each user. When you do this, each user has his or her Home screens and app settings, enabling each user to keep e-mail, calendars, and other data private. To set up a new user account, you start from your owner account, the account that set up the tablet. You then hand the tablet to the person who will use the new account so that he or she can set it up.

Set Up Multiple Users

1 Touch **Home** (▱).

The Home screen appears.

2 Touch **All Apps** (▦).

The Apps screen appears.

Note: If the Widgets tab is displayed on the Apps screen, touch the **Apps** tab.

3 Touch **Settings** (⊞).

Note: If Settings is not on the Apps screen that appears first, scroll left or right until you find Settings.

The Settings screen appears.

4 Touch **Users**.

The Users screen appears.

5 Touch **Add user**.

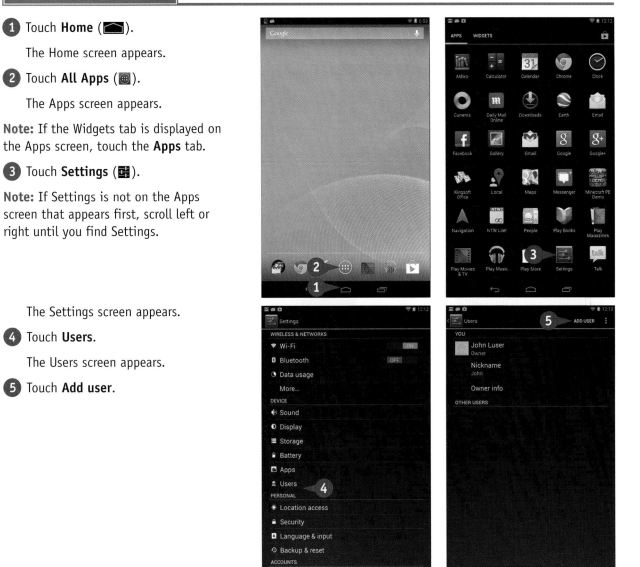

The Add new user dialog box appears.

6 Touch **OK**.

The Set up user now? dialog box appears.

7 Touch **Set up now**.

The lock screen appears showing circles for the accounts.

Ⓐ The circle for the new user is larger, indicating it is selected.

8 Give the tablet to the person who will use the account.

9 Drag the **lock icon** 🔒 in any direction to unlock the tablet.

The Welcome screen appears.

10 Touch **Next** (▶) and follow through the process of setting up the user account.

TIP

How do I remove a user account?

To remove a user account, you must log on to the tablet from your owner account, the account that set up the tablet. A nonowner account cannot remove another account. After logging on to your owner account, touch **All Apps** (⊞) to display the Apps screen, then touch **Settings** (⊞) to open the Settings app. Touch **Users** to display the Users screen. In the Other users list, touch **Delete** (🗑) for the user you want to remove. In the Remove user dialog box, touch **Delete**. Android then removes the user.

Switch Users on a Multiuser Tablet

When you have set up multiple users on a tablet, you and the other users can switch among your accounts quickly from the lock screen. Using separate accounts enables each of you to enjoy customized settings and content and to keep your private data secure from others. When you need to switch accounts, you can display the lock screen either from the Quick Settings panel or by putting the tablet to sleep and then waking it. After displaying the lock screen, you unlock the tablet by using your chosen unlocking method, such as typing a PIN or a password.

Switch Users on a Multiuser Tablet

Display the Lock Screen

1 Touch the right side of the bar at the top of the screen and drag down.

The Quick Settings panel opens.

2 Touch the user button. This button shows the name of the current user.

The current user's lock screen appears.

Note: On a multiuser tablet, each user has his or her own lock screen.

Note: You can also display the lock screen by pressing the Power button to put the tablet to sleep, and then pressing the Power button again to wake the tablet.

Switch Users

1 On the lock screen, touch your user's circle.

Your lock screen appears.

2 To unlock your screen, type your PIN or password, gaze at Face Unlock, or slide the lock icon.

The tablet unlocks, and you can start using your account.

TIP

How do I share my apps with other users?

You cannot share your apps with other users. Each user must install apps on his own user account — for example, buying the apps from the Play Store. The only good news here is that when a user buys an app that is already installed on the tablet, Android uses the copy on the tablet rather than installing it again and taking up twice the space. However, even in this case, Android simulates the download, as if the user was installing a new app.

Accessorize Your Phone or Tablet

To turn your phone or tablet into a go-anywhere, do-anything device, you will most likely want to add accessories. For example, you might decide to protect your device with a case, buy a stand to hold the device in a position for viewing or reading, or mount your device in your car, so you can play music through the car's stereo. You can shop both online and offline for a wide range of accessories for Android phones and tablets. Online sites such as Amazon and eBay are good for getting an idea of the many types of accessories available.

Protect Your Phone or Tablet with a Case

To protect your phone or tablet against damage, put a case on it. Many cases are available, made of various materials and offering different features such as the ability to prop your phone or tablet up in different positions for work or play. Some cases are mostly decorative, but others offer heavy-duty protection against falls and the elements. Some cases are even waterproof.

Charge Your Phone or Tablet Wherever You Go

If you regularly use your phone or tablet both at home and at work, get an extra charging unit so you can have one at home and one at work and keep your device well charged. If you need to charge your phone or tablet in your car, investigate your options. If your car includes an AC outlet, you can plug in a regular charger; if your car offers powered USB outlets, you can simply plug in the USB cable. If your car has only a 12-volt socket, look for a charging unit with a 12-volt adapter. If you travel abroad with your phone or tablet, look for a travel adapter that will work in all the countries you visit.

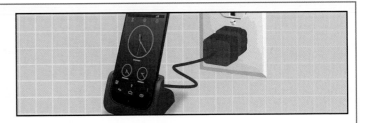

Park Your Phone or Tablet with a Dock or Stand

If your phone or tablet lives on your desk, consider getting a dock or stand so you can park the device neatly and charge it if necessary. Some docks also provide an audio line-out port for connecting the phone or tablet to powered speakers or your stereo so you can play music. You may also be able to use other accessories with the dock, such as a keyboard or mouse.

CHAPTER
2

Customizing Your Phone or Tablet

Play Music from Your Phone or Tablet Through Your Stereo

Your phone or tablet cannot only carry your music library for you to enjoy through headphones, but it can play music through external speakers so that others can enjoy it as well. To connect your device to your stereo, you can either connect a standard headphone cable with a 3.5mm jack to the headphone port or connect an audio or audio-and-video cable to the SlimPort.

Play Movies from Your Phone or Tablet on Your TV

When you want to share a video with others, you can connect your phone or tablet to a TV and play the video on the TV's screen. To connect the device to the TV, you can make a cable connection using a SlimPort-to-HDMI connector or a wireless connection using a Wireless Display–enabled receiver attached to the TV.

Mount Your Phone or Tablet in Your Car

If you take your phone or tablet everywhere, you will certainly want to use it in your car. You can buy a wide variety of car mounts to fix your phone or tablet firmly to the windshield, dashboard, or a cup holder. You can then connect your phone or tablet to your vehicle stereo for entertainment, or use its GPS functionality for navigation.

Type Fast with a Wireless Keyboard

If you need to enter a lot of text on your phone or tablet, buy a Bluetooth keyboard. A wide variety of Bluetooth keyboards is available, ranging from stand-alone keyboards to keyboards with docks for specific Android devices. Some other Bluetooth keyboards come built in to cases that enable you to prop up the phone or tablet at a helpful angle as you type on the keyboard.

CHAPTER 3

Working with Text and Voice

In this chapter, you learn to input text using the on-screen keyboard, the Gesture Typing feature, and dictation. You also learn to use Cut, Copy, and Paste, Voice Actions, and Voice Search.

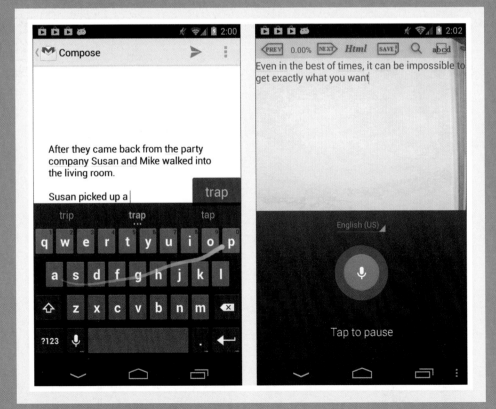

Use the On-Screen Keyboard and Gesture Typing

The most straightforward way to enter text in an app is by touching the keys on the on-screen keyboard. Android automatically displays this keyboard when you touch an input field. As well as straightforward typing, the keyboard in Android Jelly Bean 4.2 provides a feature called Gesture Typing. In Gesture Typing, you touch the first letter of a word, and then slide your finger to each of the other letters in turn. When you stop, Android automatically inserts the most likely matching word.

Use the On-Screen Keyboard and Gesture Typing

Open an App That Allows Text Input

Note: This example uses the Gmail app, but you can use another app that allows text input.

1 Touch **Home** (⬠).

2 On the Home screen, touch **All Apps** (▦).

3 On the Apps screen, touch **Gmail** (✉).

4 In Gmail, touch **New Message** (✉).

A new message opens.

Type on the On-Screen Keyboard

1 Touch in the **Compose email** field in the new message.

A The keyboard switches to uppercase at the beginning of a paragraph or sentence.

2 Type the words you want.

Note: After the first letter of a sentence or paragraph, Android turns off Shift, so the keyboard types lowercase letters unless you apply Shift. You can turn on Caps Lock by double-tapping Shift.

B As you type, the Suggestions bar shows words you may be typing.

3 If a suggestion is correct, touch it. Otherwise, keep typing.

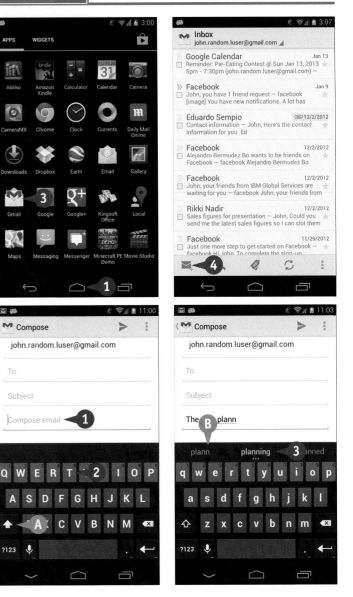

C The word appears in the document.

D The Suggestions bar shows likely next words. If one is suitable, touch to insert it.

4 Touch **?123**.

The numeric keyboard appears, and you can type numbers and symbols.

E To type other symbols, touch **=\<**. The symbols keyboard appears.

5 Touch **ABC** to display the letter keyboard again.

Note: To enter an alternative or related character, touch and hold the base character, then touch the character or symbol on the pop-up panel.

Use Gesture Typing

1 Touch the first letter of the word.

2 Without raising your finger, slide to each successive letter in turn.

3 If the pop-up suggestion is correct, lift your finger to accept it. Otherwise, continue to the end of the word.

TIPS

Why does Gesture Typing not work on my device?
You may need to turn it on. Touch **Home**, touch **All Apps**, and then touch **Settings**. Touch **Language & input**, then touch **Options** (▦) to the right of Android keyboard. Select **Enable Gesture Typing** (■ changes to ☑). You can also select (☑) or deselect (■) **Dynamic floating preview** and **Show gesture trail**.

How can I speed up my typing on my phone or tablet?
Gesture Typing is usually faster than touching individual keys. Use the Personal Dictionary feature to enter standard terms faster by using abbreviations. However, if you need to enter serious amounts of text, connect a hardware keyboard to your phone or tablet.

Edit Text and Use Cut, Copy, and Paste

When you work with text, you often need to edit what you have written. Android makes it easy to edit existing text and select part or all of your text. After selecting text, you can cut it or copy it to the clipboard and then paste it elsewhere. Cutting text removes it from the document, whereas copying text leaves it in the document. You can paste text from the clipboard multiple times if necessary until you copy or cut other text.

Edit Text and Use Cut, Copy, and Paste

Open Gmail and Edit Text

1 Open Gmail and begin a new message by following the first steps in the previous task.

2 Type some text.

3 Touch where you want to position the insertion point.

The arrow for moving the insertion point ( ) appears.

4 If necessary, drag the arrow ( ) to move the insertion point.

5 Edit the text as needed.

Select Text and Use Cut, Copy, and Paste

1 Touch and hold a word.

Android highlights the word and displays selection handles, the start handle ( ) and the end handle ( ), before and after it.

2 Drag the start handle ( ) or the end handle ( ) to extend the selection as needed.

Ⓐ You can touch **Select All** ( ) to select all the text.

3 Touch **Copy** ( ) to copy the text to the clipboard.

Ⓑ Touch **Cut** ( ) to cut the text and place it on the clipboard.

Ⓒ Touch **End Selection** ( ) to turn off selection mode.

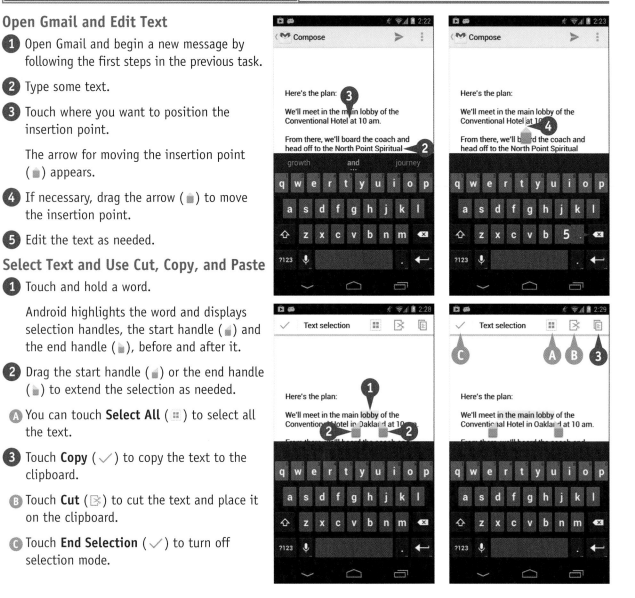

④ Touch where you want to paste the copied or cut text.

Note: If you want the text you paste to replace existing text, select that text and then paste.

⑤ Double-tap the arrow for moving the insertion point (⬛).

The Paste button appears.

⑥ Touch **Paste**.

The copied or cut text appears in the document.

Replace a Word

① Touch and hold the word.

Android selects the word.

A toolbar appears.

② Touch **Replace**.

A list of suggested replacements appears.

③ Touch the appropriate word.

TIPS

How many items can I put on the clipboard?
The Android clipboard contains only a single item. Each time you cut or copy text, it replaces the current contents of the clipboard. You can continue to paste the contents of the clipboard as many times as needed until you place another item on the clipboard.

Can I transfer the contents of the clipboard to my computer?
You cannot access the Android clipboard directly from your computer; however, you can easily transfer the contents of the clipboard using workarounds. For example, begin a new message in the Gmail app or the Email app and address it to yourself. You can then paste in the contents of the clipboard and send the message.

Give Commands with Voice Actions

Android's powerful Voice Actions feature enables you to take essential actions by using your voice to tell your phone or tablet what you want. Voice Actions requires an Internet connection, because the speech recognition runs on Google's servers. You can use Voice Actions either with your device's built-in microphone or with the microphone on a headset or another hands-free device. Unless you are in a quiet environment, or you hold your phone or tablet close to your face, a headset microphone gives much better results than the built-in microphone.

Open Voice Actions

Before you can start using Voice Actions to control your phone or tablet, you must open Voice Actions. You can do this in several ways. In most cases, the easiest way is to touch Home ( ) to display the Home screen, then touch the Google box at the top. If you are working on the Google Now screen, you can also say, "Google" to make Android start receiving voice input. When you are using the Chrome app, touch the omnibox at the top of the screen and then touch the microphone icon ( ).

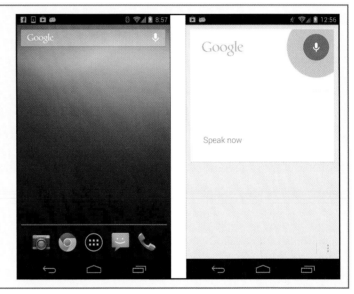

Open a Web Page

One of the most useful Voice Actions is to open a web page using only your voice. You can use this feature to browse the web more easily on your phone or tablet. To open a web page using your voice, first open Voice Actions. You can then say, "Go to" and the web page's address. Android launches your default browser — for example, Chrome — and displays the web page. For example, say, "Go to capitalone.com."

Send an E-Mail Message

You can use Voice Actions to send an e-mail message to a contact. This feature is great for composing and sending messages quickly. To send an email message, open Voice Actions. You can then say, "Send e-mail" and the contact's name, then "subject" and the subject, followed by "message" and the message. Android creates an e-mail message to the contact and enters the text. Review the message, and then touch Send Email to send it.

send email to Chris Smith
subject strategic planning
meeting message hi Chris,

Chris Smith
chris__smith@mac.com
MOBILE

Strategic planning meeting

Hi Chris,

Send a Text Message

You can use Voice Actions to send a text message to a contact. This feature is especially helpful when you do not have time to type a message. To send a text message, open Voice Actions. Say, "Send text to" and the contact's name, then say, "message" and the message. Android creates a text message to the contact, enters the text, and presents it for your review. Touch Send message to send it.

send text to donald wilson
message I'm stuck in traffic but
I'll be with you in an hour.

Donald Wilson
21 3555 1212
MOBILE

I'm stuck in traffic but I'll be with you in an hour

➤ Send message

Send Yourself a Reminder

Another helpful use of Voice Actions is to send yourself a reminder. Open Voice Actions, then say, "Note to self" and the reminder. Android listens to what you say and creates a text note that it sends to your e-mail account along with an audio recording of the note. If the text is correct, allow Android to finish creating and sending the note. If not, touch Cancel (×) to cancel the note.

note to self take my tablet to
Acme industries tomorrow
morning

Take my tablet to Acme industries
tomorrow morning

➤ Save note   ×

Set an Alarm

You can use Voice Actions to set an alarm without needing to open the Clock app. To set an alarm, open Voice actions, then say, "Set an alarm" followed by the time; optionally, add "label" and a name for the alarm. Verify the time as Android sets the alarm. If it is correct, allow Android to finish setting the alarm, which takes a few seconds. If not, touch Cancel (×) to cancel the alarm.

set alarm for 530 a.m.

5:30 AM

🕐 Set alarm   ×

Dictate Text into Apps

Android can transcribe your speech quickly and accurately into correctly spelled and punctuated text. Using your phone or tablet, you can dictate into any app that supports the keyboard so you can dictate e-mail messages, notes, documents, and more. To get the most out of dictation, it is helpful to know the standard terms for dictating punctuation and layout.

Dictate Text into Apps

Open an App That Allows Text Input

Note: This example uses the Gmail app, but you can use another app that allows text input.

① Touch **Home** (▭).

② On the Home screen, touch **All Apps** (▦).

③ On the Apps screen, touch **Gmail** (✉).

④ In Gmail, touch **New Message** (✉).

A new message opens.

Dictate Text

① Touch in the **Compose email** field in the new message.

② Touch the **microphone** icon (🎤) on the keyboard.

The speech-recognition panel replaces the keyboard.

A The red microphone icon (🎤) and "Speak now" prompt indicate that Android is listening for voice input.

③ Speak the text you want to dictate.

B The text appears as you speak.

Note: After a few seconds of silence, Android stops listening (🎤 changes to 🎤).

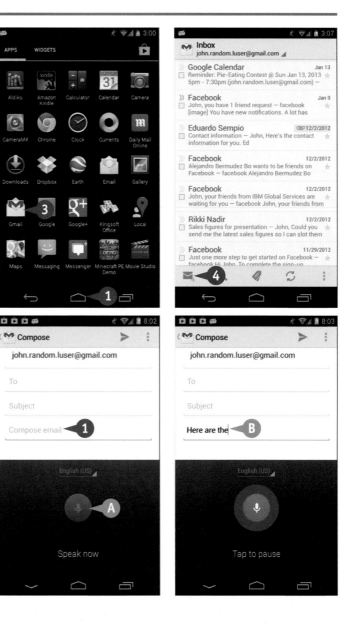

76

When you pause, a Delete button appears for a few seconds.

C If needed, tap **Delete** to delete the last section of text you dictated.

4 If Android has mistranscribed part of the text, touch the appropriate underlined word or phrase.

A list of suggestions appears.

5 Touch the word or phrase you want to insert.

6 Touch the **microphone** icon (🎤) when you are ready to begin dictating again.

7 Touch the red **microphone** icon (🎤) if you need to pause dictation.

Note: You can say standard punctuation terms including "comma," "period," "colon," "exclamation point" or "exclamation mark," and "question mark."

Note: Say "new paragraph" to end the current paragraph and create a new one.

8 Touch ⌨ when you want to display the keyboard again.

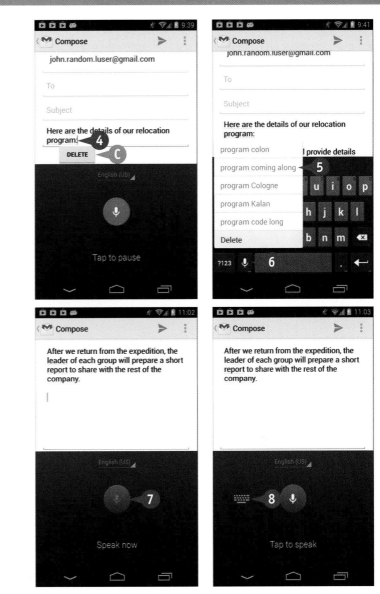

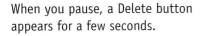

TIP

How can I get dictation as accurate as possible?
To obtain accurate results when dictating text, follow these suggestions:

• Use a headset microphone rather than your phone's or tablet's built-in microphone.

• Speak clearly.

• Pause at the end of each sentence so that Android can catch up with you.

• Make sure the pop-up menu above the microphone icon (🎤) shows your language and localization. If not, change the setting.

Gather Information with Voice Search

Android's capability to accept voice input enables you to use your voice to research a wide variety of information online. By using Voice Search, you can quickly and easily request information about sports, find showtimes for movies, and identify the location of ZIP codes. You can also locate restaurants, get flight information, and learn the time in another place. Voice Search works with natural-language queries, so you do not have to structure your questions and requests in a set format. However, you can get more accurate search results by using suitable keywords.

Find Information about Sports

You can use Voice Search to find information about sports, such as the result of a recent game by a particular team or the date of a future event. To find information about sports, first activate Google Search by touching Home (▬) and then touching the microphone icon (🎤) in the Google box. You can then ask a question such as "Did the Lakers win their last game?" or "When is the next White Sox game?"

Find Showtimes for Movies

You can use Voice Search to find out the current showtimes for a movie in a particular city or location. To find out movie showtimes, first activate Google Search by touching Home (▬) and then touching the microphone icon (🎤) in the Google box. You can then say, "Movie" followed by the movie's name and the city or location. For example, say, "Movie *Django Unchained* Chicago."

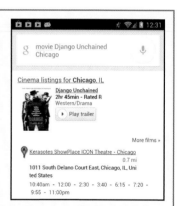

Identify the Location of Area Codes and ZIP Codes

You can use Voice Search to identify the location for a particular telephone area code or a ZIP code. To find out this information, first activate Google Search by touching Home (▬) and then touching the microphone icon (🎤) in the Google box. You can then say, "area code" followed by the area code — for example, "area code 707" — or "ZIP code" followed by the ZIP code.

Get Flight Information

You can use Voice Search to get information about flights. This capability can be useful when you need to check whether the flight you are hoping to take or meet is on time or has suffered a delay. To get flight information, first activate Google Search by touching Home (⌂) and then touching the microphone icon (🎤) in the Google box. You can then say the airline's name, the word "flight," and then the flight number. For example, say, "Air Canada flight AC794."

Locate a Restaurant

You can use Voice Search to get information about restaurants in a specified location. This capability is useful when you want to find a particular type of food. To get restaurant information, first activate Google Search by touching Home (⌂) and then touching the microphone icon (🎤) in the Google box. Say the type of food you want and the keyword "food," and then give the location. For example, say, "Japanese food in Phoenix, Arizona."

Find Out the Time in Another Location

You can use Voice Search to find out the time in another location. This capability is useful for making sure you place phone calls or set appointments during waking hours rather than sleeping hours. To find out the time in another location, first activate Google Search by touching Home (⌂) and then touching the microphone icon (🎤) in the Google box. Then say, "Time" followed by the location. For example, say, "Time Tokyo" to find out the time in Tokyo, Japan.

CHAPTER 4

Setting Up Communications

In this chapter, you learn how to add your e-mail accounts to your phone or tablet. You also learn to choose options for your contacts and calendars.

Set Up Your Gmail Account

Your Android phone or tablet gives you easy access to Gmail, Google's e-mail service, enabling you to access your e-mail messages from anywhere. Normally, you set up your main Gmail account during initial setup of your device. However, if you have other Gmail accounts, such as business or organization accounts, you can add them later by working in the Settings app. To set up a Gmail account, you need your e-mail address and your password. You do not need to know the details of the mail servers involved.

Set Up Your Gmail Account

1 Touch the **Home** button (⬛).

The Home screen appears.

2 Touch the **All Apps** button (⬛).

The Apps screen appears.

Note: If the Widgets tab is displayed on the Apps screen, touch the **Apps** tab.

3 Touch **Settings** (⬛).

Note: If Settings is not on the Apps screen that appears first, scroll left or right until you find Settings.

The Settings screen appears.

4 Touch **Add account**.

Note: On a phone, you may need to scroll down to reach the Accounts section of the Settings screen.

The Add an account screen appears.

5 Touch **Google**.

The Add a Google Account screen appears.

6 Touch **Existing**.

The Sign in screen appears.

7 Type your e-mail address.

8 Type your password.

9 Touch ▶.

A dialog box opens.

10 Touch the **Keep me up to date with news and offers from Google Play** check box (■ changes to ✔).

11 Touch **OK**.

Android signs your device in to your Gmail account.

The Entertainment screen appears.

12 Touch **Set up credit card** if you want to set up a credit card for Google Play. Otherwise, touch **Not now**.

The Account sign-in successful screen appears.

13 Touch the check boxes to select the services you want (■ changes to ✔).

14 Touch ▶.

The Settings screen appears.

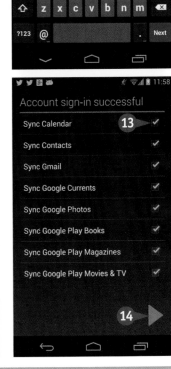

TIPS

Which items should I synchronize with my Gmail account?

To get the most out of your phone and tablet, it is usually a good idea to synchronize most, if not all, of the items that appear on the Account sign-in successful screen. If you want to sync only essential items and not entertainment items, sync Calendar, Contacts, and Gmail with your account.

What are Google Currents?

Google Currents are digital editions of newspapers and magazines. To get started with Google Currents, touch the **Home** button (🏠), touch the **All Apps** button (⊞), and then touch **Currents** (●). On the Choose an account screen, choose the account you want to link to Currents, and then touch **Add account**.

Choose Essential Settings for Gmail

The Gmail app offers many settings that enable you to make it work the way you prefer. To get the most out of Gmail on your phone or tablet, it is a good idea to spend a few minutes exploring the settings that you can change and choosing options that suit you. When customizing the Gmail app, you can start with the General settings category, which contains settings that apply to all your accounts. You can then choose account-specific settings for each of your Gmail accounts.

Choose Essential Settings for Gmail

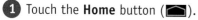

1 Touch the **Home** button (⬛).

The Home screen appears.

2 Touch the **All Apps** button (▦).

The Apps screen appears.

Note: If the Widgets tab is displayed on the Apps screen, touch the **Apps** tab.

3 Touch **Gmail** (✉).

Note: If Gmail is not on the Apps screen that appears first, scroll left or right until you find Gmail.

Your Inbox appears.

4 Touch the **Menu** button (⋮).

The menu opens.

5 Touch **Settings**.

The Gmail screen appears.

6 Touch **General settings** to display the General settings screen.

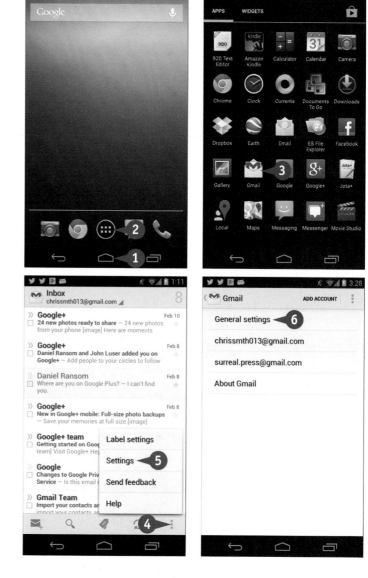

7 Touch the **Confirm before deleting** check box (☐ changes to ☑) if you want confirmation of deletions.

8 Touch the **Confirm before archiving** check box (☐ changes to ☑) if you want confirmation of archiving.

9 Touch the **Confirm before sending** check box (☐ changes to ☑) if you want confirmation of sending.

10 Touch **Swiping conversation list** and then touch the action you want swiping to have.

11 On a phone, swipe up to scroll down.

12 Touch **Hide pictures in messages** and then touch **OK** if you want to hide pictures.

13 Touch the **Gmail** button (✉).

14 On the Gmail screen, touch the account you want to configure.

15 Touch the **Priority Inbox** check box (☐ changes to ☑) if you want to make it your default Inbox.

16 Touch the **Notifications** check box (☐ changes to ☑) to receive notifications in the status bar.

17 On a phone, swipe up to scroll down.

18 Touch the **Download attachment**s check box (☐ changes to ☑) to download attachments automatically.

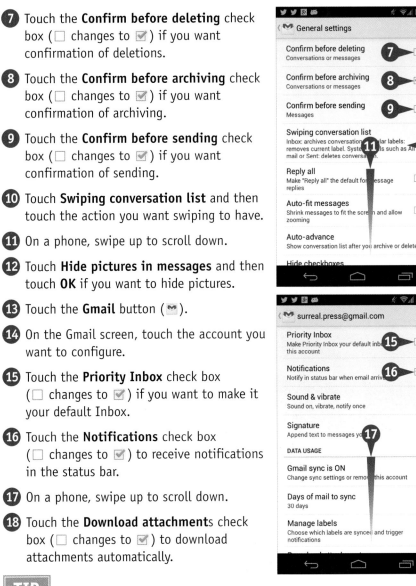

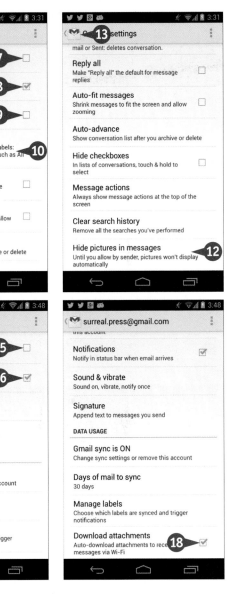

TIP

Why may I want to hide pictures in messages?

A picture in a message can deliberately compromise your privacy. In such an attack, the sender includes in the message a reference to an image on a remote server. When you open the message and image, the e-mail app downloads the image from the remote server. In doing this, marketers can learn information about you and track your surfing habits across the Internet. If you hide pictures in messages, the picture areas appear as placeholder boxes. When you establish a message is harmless and want to see a picture, touch the placeholder to download the picture.

Set Up Your Other E-Mail Accounts

Your Android device's Gmail app is designed only for use with Google's Gmail service. For e-mail accounts with other services, you can use the Email app that Android also includes. Before you can use the Email app, you must set up each account you want to use in it and choose account settings. You can set up many accounts using only the appropriate e-mail address and associated password for each account. For other accounts, you may need more information, such as the names of the incoming and outgoing mail servers.

Set Up Your Other E-Mail Accounts

1 Touch the **Home** button (⬜).

The Home screen appears.

2 Touch the **All Apps** button (▦).

The Apps screen appears.

Note: If the Widgets tab is displayed on the Apps screen, touch the **Apps** tab.

3 Touch **Email** (▢).

Note: If you have not yet set up an account for the Email app, the app automatically displays the Account setup screen when you launch it. Go to step **7**.

Your Inbox appears.

4 Touch the **Menu** button (⋮).

The menu opens.

5 Touch **Settings**.

The Settings screen appears.

6 Touch **Add Account**.

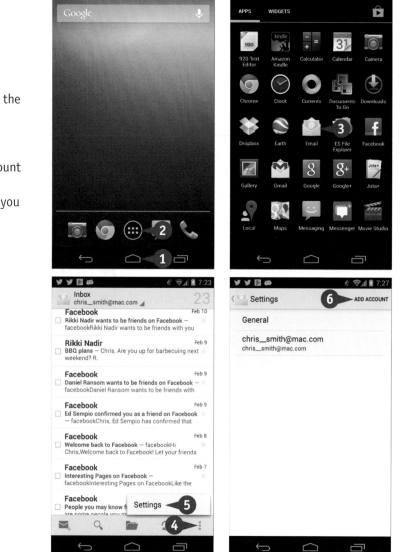

The first Account setup screen appears.

⑦ Type your e-mail address.

⑧ Type your password.

⑨ If you want to send e-mail from this account by default, select the **Send email from this account by default** check box (☐ changes to ☑).

⑩ Touch **Next**.

The Email app verifies your details.

The Account settings screen appears.

⑪ Touch the **Inbox checking frequency** pop-up menu and touch **Automatic (Push)**, **Never**, or a time interval such as **Every 15 minutes**.

⑫ Touch the **Days to sync** pop-up menu and then touch the amount of e-mail to sync: **Automatic**, a length of time such as **One week**, or **All**.

⑬ Touch the check boxes of choice in the list (☐ changes to ☑).

⑭ Touch **Next**.

⑮ Edit the account name as needed.

⑯ Touch **Next**.

Your Inbox appears, and you can work with the messages it contains.

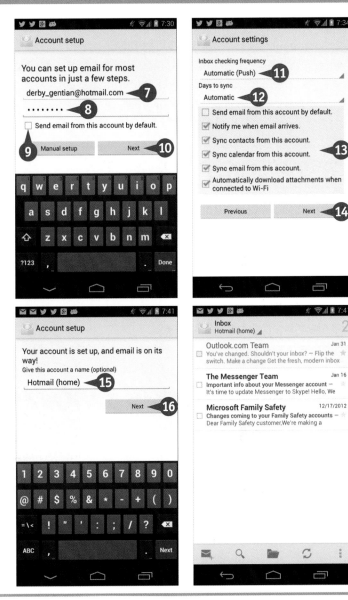

TIP

How do I use the Manual Setup option for the Email app?
If you are unable to set up your account using just the e-mail address and password, touch **Manual setup** on the first Account setup screen. Touch **POP3**, **IMAP**, or **Exchange** on the next screen. You can then enter the server details and security type for the incoming mail server and the outgoing mail server.

IMAP server
imap.surrealmacs.com
Port
993
Security type
SSL/TLS (Accept all certificates)
IMAP path prefix
Optional

Previous   Next

Connect to Exchange Server

Microsoft Exchange Server is widely used server software that provides e-mail, contact management, and scheduling. If your company or organization uses Microsoft Exchange Server, you can connect your Android phone or tablet to it so that you can work with your e-mail messages, contacts, and calendars. To connect to Exchange Server, you set up an account in the Email app. If you want to send e-mail messages from this account by default, you can set this account to be your default account.

Connect to Exchange Server

1 Touch the **Home** button (⬛).

The Home screen appears.

2 Touch the **All Apps** button (▦).

The Apps screen appears.

Note: If the Widgets tab is displayed on the Apps screen, touch the **Apps** tab.

3 Touch **Email** (▣).

Your Inbox appears.

Note: If you have not yet set up an account for the Email app, the app automatically displays the Account setup screen when you launch it. Go to step **7**.

4 Touch the **Menu** button.

The menu opens.

5 Touch **Settings**.

The Settings screen appears.

6 Touch **Add Account**.

The Account setup screen appears.

7 Type your e-mail address.

8 Type your password.

9 If you want to make this your default e-mail account, touch the **Send email from this account by default** check box (☐ changes to ☑).

10 Touch **Manual setup**.

The second Account setup screen appears.

11 Touch **Exchange**.

The third Account setup screen appears.

12 Type the domain name if it is needed.

13 Edit the server name if necessary.

14 If your account requires a secure connection, touch **Use secure connection (SSL)** check box (☐ changes to ☑).

15 Touch the **Accept all SSL certificates** check box (☐ changes to ☑) if your Exchange account requires your device to accept all certificates.

16 On a phone, touch the **Hide Keyboard** button (◥▬◤) to hide the keyboard.

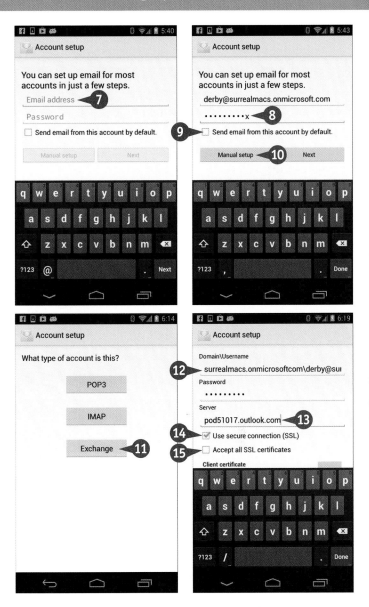

Connect to Exchange Server (continued)

When setting up your Exchange account on your phone or tablet, you need to know your e-mail address, password, and Exchange domain name. You may also need to know the name of the Exchange server to use. You can get this information from your Exchange administrator or systems administrator. Some connections to Exchange servers require your phone or tablet to use a digital certificate, a section of encrypted computer code used to identify a computer or device. Normally, if you need to use a digital certificate, an administrator will provide it and install it on your phone or tablet.

17 If your device must use a certificate to connect to the server, touch **Select**. If not, go to step **20**.

The Choose certificate dialog box opens.

18 Touch the certificate you want to use (■ changes to ◉).

19 Touch **Allow**.

The third Account setup screen appears again.

20 Change the port if necessary.

Note: The default port is 443. Consult your Exchange administrator to find if you need to use a different port.

21 Touch **Next**.

The Remote security administration dialog box opens.

22 Touch **OK**.

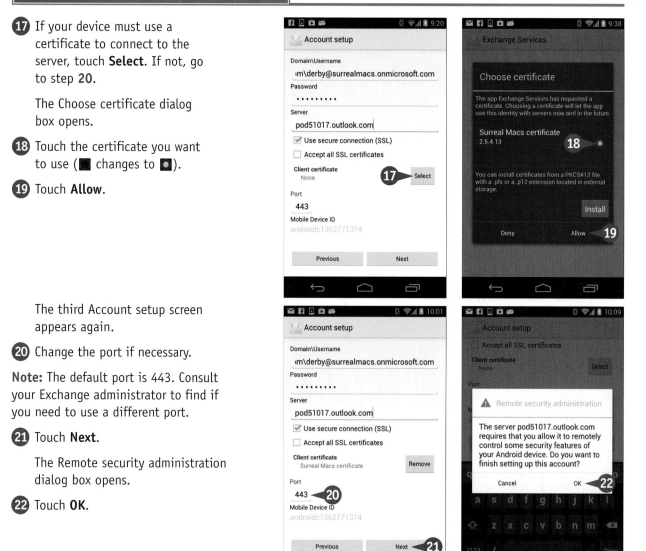

90

The Account settings screen appears.

23 Touch the **Inbox checking frequency** pop-up menu and touch **Automatic (Push)**, **Never**, or a time interval such as **Every 15 minutes**.

24 Touch the **Days to sync** pop-up menu and then touch the amount of e-mail to sync: **Automatic**, a length of time such as **One week**, or **All**.

25 Select the check boxes in the list as needed (☐ changes to ☑).

26 Touch **Next**.

The fourth Account setup screen appears.

27 Change the default account name to your preferred name.

28 Touch **Next**.

The Activate device administrator? screen appears.

Note: The Activate device administrator? screen explains the remote-control features that Exchange can exercise over your phone or tablet. For example, an Exchange administrator can remotely erase all the data from your device.

29 Touch **Activate**.

Your Inbox appears, and you can start using your Exchange account.

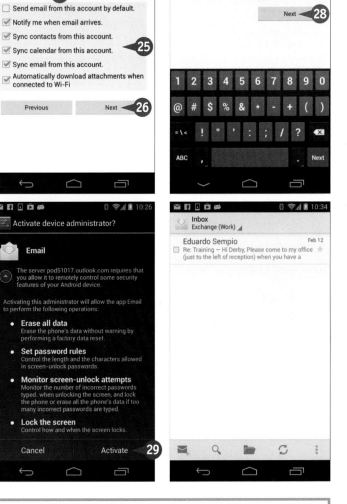

Is there a disadvantage to choosing Automatic for the Inbox checking frequency?
The Automatic setting causes the Email app to use a technology called *Push*, in which the server notifies your device whenever new mail is available. Using Push, you receive your messages more quickly, but your device uses more battery power.

What is SSL and which SSL certificates should my device accept?
SSL is the abbreviation for *Secure Sockets Layer*, a communications technology for establishing secure connections. You will probably need to select the **Use secure connection (SSL)** check box (☐ changes to ☑), but you may not need to select the **Accept all SSL certificates** check box.

Set Your Default Account and Signatures

You can set up multiple e-mail accounts in the Email app to enable yourself to access all your non-Gmail accounts. When you do this, you should set the appropriate e-mail account to be the default account. This is the account from which the Email app sends messages unless you choose another account. To help make your e-mail messages complete without you having to type the same information repeatedly, you can create e-mail signatures. A *signature* is text, such as your name and contact information, that the app automatically adds to the end of each message you create.

Set Your Default Account and Signatures

1 Touch the **Home** button (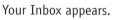).

The Home screen appears.

2 Touch the **All Apps** button (⊞).

The Apps screen appears.

Note: If the Widgets tab is displayed on the Apps screen, touch the **Apps** tab.

3 Touch **Email** (📧).

Note: If Email is not on the Apps screen that appears first, scroll left or right until you find Email.

Your Inbox appears.

4 Touch the **Menu** button (⋮).

The menu opens.

5 Touch **Settings**.

The Settings screen appears.

6 Touch the account you want to affect.

The configuration screen for the account opens.

7 Touch the **Default account** check box (☐ changes to ☑) to make this account the default account.

8 Touch **Signature**.

The Signature dialog box opens.

9 Type the text of the signature.

Note: Touch **Return** (◀▬) on the keyboard to create a new line in the signature.

Note: Although you can create long signatures, Internet etiquette recommends keeping them to four lines or fewer.

10 Touch **OK**.

The configuration screen for the account appears.

11 Touch the **Email** button (◾).

The Settings screen appears.

12 Touch another account to set a signature for it.

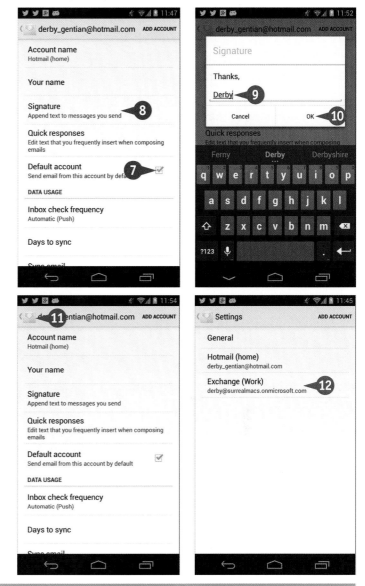

How do I create signatures in the Gmail app?

In the Gmail app, touch the **Settings menu** button (⋮) and touch **Settings**. On the Gmail screen, touch the account you want to affect. Touch **Signature** (Ⓐ) to display the Signature dialog box, type the signature, and then touch **OK**.

Choose When and How to Get Your E-Mail

The Email app can get your e-mail messages by using two different technologies: Push and Fetch. With Push, the e-mail server pushes your new messages to the app as soon as the server receives them. With Fetch, the app checks in periodically with the server and downloads the new messages it discovers. Push is normally more convenient than Fetch, but some e-mail providers do not support Push. In this case, you must use Fetch instead. You can configure the interval at which Fetch retrieves your e-mail. You can also check manually for e-mail at any point.

Choose When and How to Get Your E-Mail

1 Touch the **Home** button (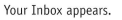).

The Home screen appears.

2 Touch the **All Apps** button (▦).

The Apps screen appears.

Note: If the Widgets tab is displayed on the Apps screen, touch the **Apps** tab.

3 Touch **Email** (▨).

Note: If Email is not on the Apps screen that appears first, scroll left or right until you find Email.

Your Inbox appears.

4 Touch the **Menu** button (⋮).

The menu opens.

5 Touch **Settings**.

The Settings screen appears.

6 Touch the account you want to affect.

The configuration screen for the account opens.

7 Touch **Inbox check frequency**.

The Inbox check frequency dialog box opens.

8 Touch the radio button next to the setting you want to select (○ changes to ◉): **Automatic (Push)**, **Never**, or an interval in the range of **Every 5 minutes** to **Every hour**.

Note: Automatic retrieval using Push tends to use more power and may shorten battery life.

The Inbox check frequency dialog box closes.

9 Touch **Days to sync**.

A dialog box opens.

10 To select a setting, touch the radio button next to the setting you want (○ changes to ◉): **Automatic**, **One day**, **Three days**, **One week**, **Two weeks**, **One month**, or **All**.

The dialog box closes.

11 Touch the **Email** button (▣).

The Settings screen appears.

12 Touch the **Email** button (▣).

Your Inbox appears.

TIPS

How many days of e-mail should I sync?
This is entirely up to you. If you receive few messages, choose **All** so that you can carry all your e-mail with you. If you receive many messages, choose a sync interval such as **Three days** or **One week** to make sure sync times do not grow too long.

Can I choose between Push and Fetch for Gmail?
No. At this writing, Gmail does not enable you to choose between Push and Fetch.

Use the Quick Responses Feature

When you compose new messages and replies in the Email app, you may find you type the same phrases — or the same sentences, or even whole paragraphs — over and over again. In this case, you may be able to save time and effort by using the Quick Responses feature. This feature enables you to set up canned replies that you can insert into your messages with minimal effort. To set up your Quick Responses, you work from the Settings screen in the Email app. After creating your Quick Responses, you can use them in messages whenever you need to.

Use the Quick Responses Feature

1 Touch the **Home** button ().

The Home screen appears.

2 Touch the **All Apps** button (▦).

The Apps screen appears.

Note: If the Widgets tab is displayed on the Apps screen, touch the **Apps** tab.

3 Touch **Email** (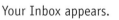).

Note: If Email is not on the Apps screen that appears first, scroll left or right until you find Email.

Your Inbox appears.

4 Touch the **Menu** button (⋮).

The menu opens.

5 Touch **Settings**.

The Settings screen appears.

6 Touch the account you want to affect.

7 Touch **Quick responses**.

The Quick responses screen appears.

8 Touch **Create new**.

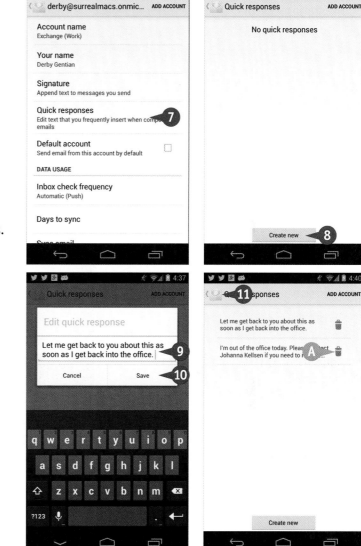

The Edit quick response dialog box opens.

9 Type the quick response.

10 Touch **Save**.

The quick response appears on the Quick responses screen.

Note: You can repeat steps **8** to **10** to create as many quick responses as you need.

Ⓐ Touch the **Delete** button (🗑) to delete a quick response.

11 Touch the **Email** button (📧).

The Settings screen appears.

12 Touch the **Email** button (📧).

Your Inbox appears.

TIP

How do I use my Quick Responses?
Start a reply to a message, or start a new message and address it. With the Compose email field selected, touch the **Menu** button (⋮) and touch **Insert quick response**. In the Insert quick response dialog box, touch the quick response (Ⓐ) that you want to insert.

Insert quick response

Let me get back to you about this as Ⓐ
soon as I get back into the office.

I'm out of the office today. Please
contact Johanna Kellsen if you need t...

Cancel

Set Up and Use the Priority Inbox

If you receive many e-mail messages, you can use Gmail's Priority Inbox feature to identify the messages that need your attention urgently. Priority Inbox tries to identify your important messages so it can present them to you separately from your less important messages. To use Priority Inbox, turn the feature on in Gmail's settings. You can then display your Priority Inbox in Gmail and work through its contents.

Set Up and Use the Priority Inbox

Turn on the Priority Inbox Feature

1 Touch the **Home** button ().

The Home screen appears.

2 Touch the **All Apps** button (▦).

The Apps screen appears.

Note: If the Widgets tab is displayed on the Apps screen, touch the **Apps** tab.

3 Touch **Gmail** (✉).

Note: If Gmail is not on the Apps screen that appears first, scroll left or right until you find Gmail.

Your Inbox appears.

4 Touch the **Menu** button (⋮).

The menu opens.

5 Touch **Settings**.

The Gmail screen appears.

6 Touch the account for which you want to set up Priority Inbox.

The configuration screen for the account appears.

7 Touch the **Priority Inbox** check box (☐ changes to ☑).

8 Touch the **Gmail** button (📧).

The Gmail screen appears.

Note: You can touch another account to set up Priority Inbox for it.

9 Touch the **Gmail** button (📧).

Your Inbox appears.

View Your Priority Inbox

1 In Gmail, touch the pop-up menu at the top of the screen.

The pop-up menu opens.

2 Touch the **Priority Inbox** you want to display.

The Priority Inbox appears, and you can work with the messages it contains.

How does Priority Inbox work?

Priority Inbox collects any messages in conversations you and Gmail have labeled as important. You can mark a message as important by touching the **Menu** button (⋮) and touching **Mark important**. Gmail automatically labels messages as important for various reasons, such as messages that come from people you contact frequently, or messages that are part of a conversation you have labeled as important. Priority Inbox is a clever and helpful feature, but it is not foolproof. Even if Priority Inbox seems to be catching all your important messages, be sure to check your other messages in case any vital ones have ended up with your less-important messages.

Choose Which Contacts to Display

Android provides the People app to manage your contacts. The People app syncs contacts from your Google Account, so your Google Contacts automatically show up in the People app. You can also sync contacts from other e-mail accounts or import contacts manually. If you have many contacts, you may want to display only one group of them — for example, only your Facebook contacts or only your Corporate contacts. You can do this easily, but you can also create a custom display group that contains exactly the contacts you want to see.

Choose Which Contacts to Display

1 Touch the **Home** button (🔲).

The Home screen appears.

2 Touch the **All Apps** button (▦).

The Apps screen appears.

Note: If the Widgets tab is displayed on the Apps screen, touch the **Apps** tab.

3 Touch **People** (🔲).

Note: If People is not on the Apps screen that appears first, scroll left or right until you find People.

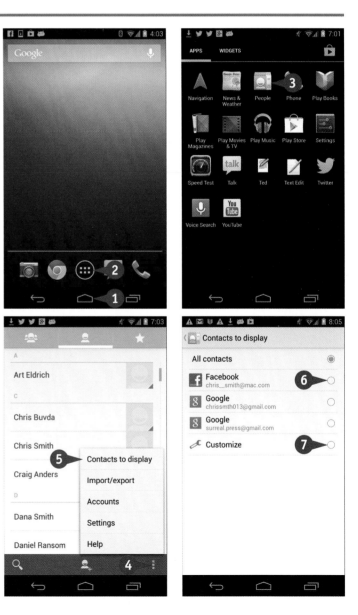

4 Touch the **Menu** button (⋮).

The menu opens.

5 Touch **Contacts to display**.

The Contacts to display screen appears.

6 To use an existing group, select its radio button (○ changes to ◉) and skip the remaining steps in this list.

7 To create a custom group, select the **Customize** radio button (○ changes to ◉).

The Define custom view screen appears.

8 Touch an account's heading.

The account's contact groups appear.

9 Select the check box for each group you want to include (☐ changes to ☑).

10 Touch **OK**.

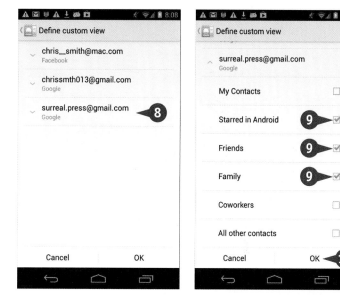

The Contacts In Custom View screen appears, showing the contacts in the groups you chose.

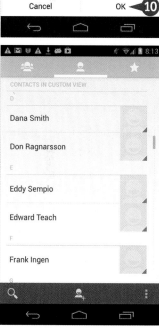

TIPS

What are the icons at the top of the Contacts screen for?
Touch the **Groups** button (🖾) to display the list of contact groups within the displayed accounts. Touch the **Favorites** button (★) to display your list of favorite contacts. Touch the **Contacts** button (🖳) to display the list of contacts again.

How do I display all my contacts again?
In the People app, touch the **Menu** button (⋮), and then touch **Contacts to display**. On the Contacts to display screen, select the **All contacts** option button (○ changes to ◉). The full list of contacts then appears.

Import Your Contacts into the People App

Your phone or tablet can sync contacts with your Google Account or with other e-mail accounts that you set up, such as Exchange Server. However, if you have contact data stored elsewhere, you will need to import it into your device. You can import contact information from vCard files, a widely used format, by sending the files to your device or placing the files on it. If your device takes a SIM card, you can import contacts stored on a compatible SIM card — for example, from your old phone.

Import Your Contacts into the People App

Import Contacts Attached to an E-Mail Message

1 Touch the vCard file attached to the message. Touch the main part of the button, not the Menu button (⋮) at its right end.

2 If the Complete action using dialog box opens, touch **Contacts** and **Always**.

Note: In the Complete action using dialog box, you can touch **Just once** if you want to open vCard files with other apps in the future. However, it is normally more helpful to set Android to open vCard files with the Contacts app.

The Create contact under account dialog box opens.

3 Touch the account into which you want to import the contact data.

Ⓐ Android displays an acknowledgment and then imports the contact data.

Note: If your contact data is stored in a spreadsheet such as Microsoft Excel, save it as a comma-separated values, or CSV, file. You can then import that file into Google Contacts online and sync the contacts to your phone or tablet.

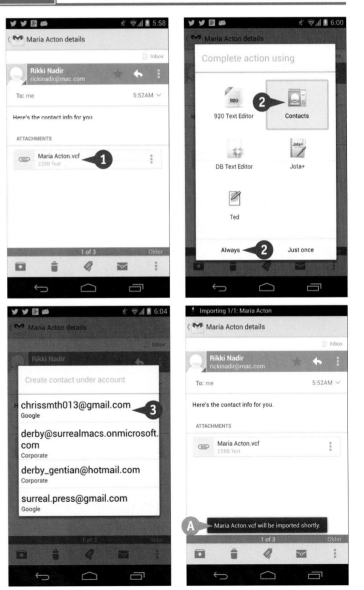

Import Contacts from a File

1 Copy the file to the Download folder on your phone or tablet using an app such as Windows Explorer or Android File Transfer.

2 In the People app, touch the **Menu** button (⋮).

The menu opens.

3 Touch **Import/export**.

The Import/export contacts dialog box opens.

4 Touch **Import from storage**.

Note: To import contacts from a SIM card you have inserted in your device, touch **Import from SIM card**.

The Create contact under account dialog box opens.

5 Touch the account in which you want to store the contact data.

Ⓑ The Contacts app searches for the file and then imports the data.

Note: After importing the data from the vCard file, delete it from the Download folder so that you can import further files from there without importing the contact data again. You can delete the file using Windows Explorer on your PC, Android File Transfer on your Mac, or an app such as ES File Explorer on your device.

TIP

How do I create vCard files containing my contacts?

On Windows, click **Start**, click your username, and then click **Contacts**. Select the contacts to export, and then click **Export** on the toolbar. In the Export Windows Contacts dialog box, click **vCards (folder of .vcf files)** and **Export**. On the Mac, click **Contacts** if it appears on the Dock; otherwise, click **Launchpad** on the Dock, and then click **Contacts** on the Launchpad screen. In the Contacts app, select the contacts to export, and then drag them to the desktop.

Choose Calendar Notifications and Reminders

Android's Calendar app is a great way to track your time commitments on your phone or tablet. You can easily add your appointments to the calendar, send invitations to other people for meetings and shared appointments, and accept invitations to events other people have created. To help you remember your appointments, the Calendar app can notify you of upcoming appointments by playing sounds, vibrating, and displaying pop-up messages. You can choose your notifications and control when they appear by working on the Settings screen in the Calendar app.

Choose Calendar Notifications and Reminders

1 Touch the **Home** button (▬).

The Home screen appears.

2 Touch the **All Apps** button (▦).

The Apps screen appears.

Note: If the Widgets tab is displayed on the Apps screen, touch the **Apps** tab.

3 Touch **Calendar** (▦).

Note: If Calendar is not on the Apps screen that appears first, scroll left or right until you find Calendar.

The Calendar app opens.

4 Touch the **Menu** button (⋮).

The menu opens

5 Touch **Settings**.

The Settings screen appears.

6 Touch **General settings** to display the General Settings screen.

Note: On a phone, scroll down to display the Notifications & reminders section.

7 Touch the **Notifications** check box (☐ changes to ☑) if you want to receive notifications.

8 Touch the **Vibrate** check box (☐ changes to ☑) if you want the device to vibrate for reminders.

Note: The Vibrate option appears only if your device has a vibration motor.

9 Touch the **Pop-up notification** check box (☐ changes to ☑) if you want to receive pop-ups.

10 Touch **Sound**.

The Sound dialog box opens.

11 Touch a sound radio button (○ changes to ◉) to hear the sound.

12 Touch **OK**.

The General settings screen appears.

13 Touch **Default reminder time**.

The Default reminder time dialog box opens.

14 Touch the interval you want (○ changes to ◉).

15 Touch the **Calendar** button (🗓).

The Settings screen appears.

16 Touch the **Calendar** button (🗓).

Your calendars appear.

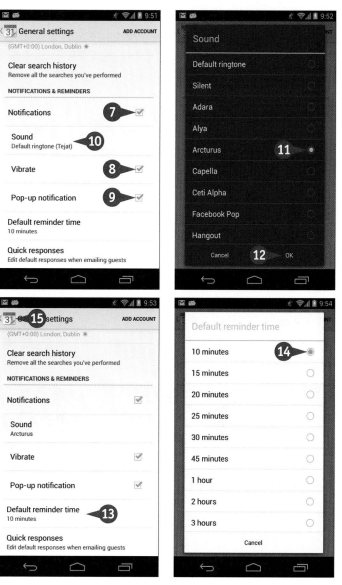

TIP

What are Quick responses in the Calendar?
Quick responses are pieces of boilerplate text you can insert quickly in your replies to calendar invitations. To set up your quick responses, touch **Quick responses** on the General settings screen, and then work on the Quick responses screen.

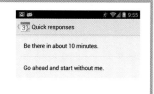

Choose Week and Time Zone Settings

The Calendar app lets you choose whether to display the week number in the year from Week 1 to Week 52. You can also choose which day to use as the start of the week: Saturday, Sunday, or Monday.

If you travel to different time zones, you may need to specify in which time zone to show event dates and times. Otherwise, Calendar uses the time zone for your current location.

Choose Week and Time Zone Settings

1 Touch the **Home** button (⬭).

The Home screen appears.

2 Touch the **All Apps** button (▦).

The Apps screen appears.

Note: If the Widgets tab is displayed on the Apps screen, touch the **Apps** tab.

3 Touch **Calendar** (📅).

Note: If Calendar is not on the Apps screen that appears first, scroll left or right until you find Calendar.

The Calendar app opens.

4 Touch the **Menu** button (⋮).

The menu opens

5 Touch **Settings**.

The Settings screen appears.

6 Touch **General settings**.

The General settings screen appears.

7 Touch the **Show week number** check box (☐ changes to ☑) if you want to show week numbers.

8 Touch **Week starts on**.

The Week starts on dialog box opens.

9 Touch the day on which you want your week to start (○ changes to ◉).

You can also select Locale default (○ changes to ◉) to start the week on the default day for that place.

The Week starts on dialog box closes.

10 Touch the **Use home time zone** check box if you want to use time zones (☐ changes to ☑).

11 Touch **Home time zone**.

The Home time zone dialog box opens.

12 Touch the time zone to use (○ changes to ◉).

The Home time zone dialog box closes.

13 Touch the **Calendar** button (📅).

The Settings screen appears.

14 Touch the **Calendar** button (📅).

Your calendar appears.

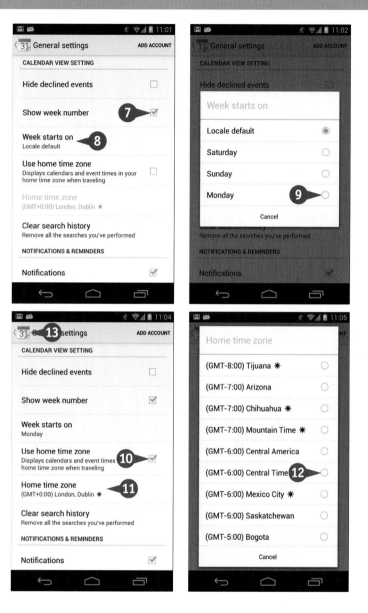

What does the Hide declined events setting do?

Select **Hide declined events** (☐ changes to ☑) if you want to prevent events to which you have been invited but which you have declined from appearing in your calendar. Depending on your business life and social life, you may find it helpful to see events you have declined as well as those you have accepted; if so, deselect **Hide declined events** (☑ changes to ☐).

CHAPTER 5

Networking and Communicating

In this chapter, you learn to control your Android device's cellular, Bluetooth, and wireless connections; share your device's Internet connection; and transfer data and make purchases wirelessly.

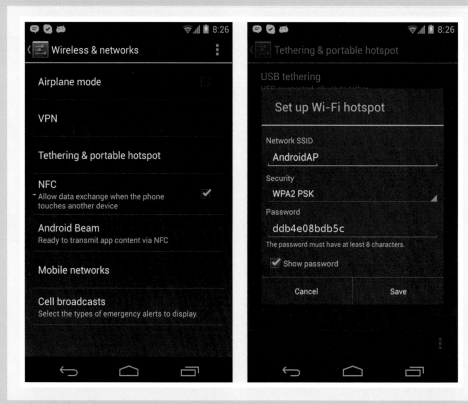

Control Wi-Fi, Bluetooth, and Cellular Access

I f your Android device has cellular capability, you will normally want to keep it connected to the cellular network so that you can make or receive calls and access the Internet when no Wi-Fi connection is available. However, when you do not need or may not use the cellular network, you can turn on Airplane mode to cut off all connections. Turning on Airplane mode turns off Wi-Fi and Bluetooth connections as well. However, you can also turn Wi-Fi and Bluetooth on and off separately when you need to.

Control Wi-Fi, Bluetooth, and Cellular Access

Open the Settings App

1 Touch the **Home** button (⬟).

The Home screen appears.

A The Wi-Fi icon (📶) shows the strength of the Wi-Fi signal.

B The Cellular icon (📶) shows the strength of the cellular signal.

2 Touch the **All Apps** button (⊞).

The Apps screen appears.

Note: If the Widgets tab is displayed on the Apps screen, touch the **Apps** tab.

3 Touch **Settings** (⚙).

Note: If Settings is not on the Apps screen that appears first, scroll left or right until you find Settings.

Turn On Airplane Mode

1 On the Settings screen, touch **More**.

The Wireless & networks screen appears.

2 Touch the **Airplane mode** check box (☐ changes to ☑).

C The Airplane mode icon (✈) appears in the status bar. The Wi-Fi icon (📶) and the Cellular icon (📶) disappear from the status bar.

3 Touch the **Settings** button (⚙).

The Settings screen appears.

110

Turn Wi-Fi On or Off

1 Touch the **Wi-Fi** switch to set it to On.

Your phone or tablet connects to a known Wi-Fi network if one is available.

D The Wi-Fi icon () appears in the status bar.

Turn Bluetooth On or Off

1 Touch the **Bluetooth** switch to set it to On.

E The Bluetooth icon (▓) appears in the status bar.

When should I use Airplane mode?
Airplane mode is designed for use on airplanes, but you can also use it any other time you want to take your device offline. For example, you may want to use Airplane mode while in the movie theater or in important meetings.

Should I turn Bluetooth on or leave it off?
Turn Bluetooth on if you want to use Bluetooth devices with your phone or tablet. When you are not using Bluetooth, turn it off to save battery power.

Connect Bluetooth Devices

To extend the functionality of your phone or tablet, you can connect devices to it that communicate using the wireless Bluetooth technology. Bluetooth is a networking protocol that is limited to short distances, typically up to about 30 feet. For example, you can connect a Bluetooth headset and microphone so that you can listen to music and make and take phone calls. Alternatively, you can connect a Bluetooth keyboard so that you can quickly type e-mail messages, notes, or documents.

Connect Bluetooth Devices

1 Touch the **Home** button (⬛).

The Home screen appears.

2 Touch the **All Apps** button (⬛).

The Apps screen appears.

Note: If the Widgets tab is displayed on the Apps screen, touch the **Apps** tab.

3 Touch **Settings** (⬛).

Note: If Settings is not on the Apps screen that appears first, scroll left or right until you find Settings.

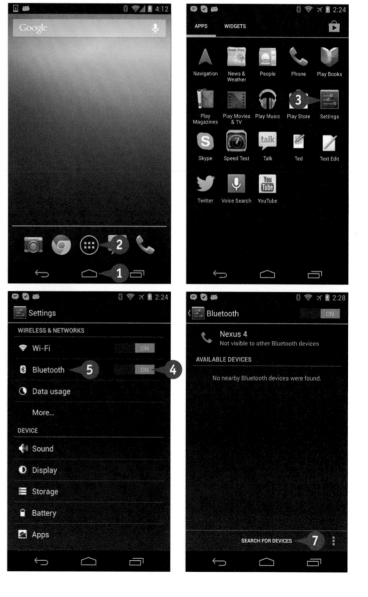

The Settings screen appears.

4 Make sure the **Bluetooth** switch is set to On.

5 Touch the left side of the **Bluetooth** button, not the switch.

The Bluetooth screen appears.

Note: By default, your Android device is not visible to other Bluetooth devices. You can make it visible for two minutes by touching its entry at the top of the Bluetooth screen.

6 Turn on the Bluetooth device and make it visible.

7 Touch **Search for devices**.

Your phone or tablet searches for Bluetooth devices and displays a list of those it finds.

8 Touch the button for the device you want to connect.

9 When connecting a keyboard, type the code shown in the Bluetooth pairing request dialog box.

Android pairs the device.

A The device appears in the Paired devices list.

10 Touch **Options** (▦).

The Paired Bluetooth device screen appears.

11 Optionally, touch **Rename** and type a new name for the device.

Note: Renaming lets you give a device a descriptive name rather than a make or model number.

B When you no longer need to use the paired device, touch **Unpair** to remove the pairing.

What else can I do with Bluetooth?
You can connect your phone or tablet to your Bluetooth-enabled computer or another Bluetooth-enabled device via Bluetooth and transfer files back and forth. File transfer is slow compared to Wi-Fi, but it can be highly convenient.

Where do I find the files I receive via Bluetooth?
From the Bluetooth screen in the Settings app, touch the **Menu** button (▤) to open the menu, and then touch **Show received files**. The Bluetooth received screen appears, showing a list of the files your device has received.

Control Data Roaming and Cellular Usage

When you need to use your phone or cellular-capable tablet in a location where your carrier does not provide Internet service, you can turn on the Data roaming feature. Data roaming enables you to access the Internet using the networks of other carriers. You can incur extra charges when using data roaming, especially when you use it in another country. For this reason, you may prefer to keep data roaming off most of the time and turn it on only when you need it. Normally, you will want to use data roaming only when no wireless network connection is available.

Control Data Roaming and Cellular Usage

1 Touch the **Home** button ( ).

The Home screen appears.

2 Touch the **All Apps** buttons ( ).

The Apps screen appears.

Note: If the Widgets tab is displayed on the Apps screen, touch the **Apps** tab.

3 Touch **Settings** ( ).

Note: If Settings is not on the Apps screen that appears first, scroll left or right until you find Settings.

The Settings screen appears.

4 Touch **More**.

The Wireless & networks screen appears.

5 Touch **Mobile networks**.

The Mobile networks settings screen appears.

6 Touch the **Data enabled** check box to select (☑) or deselect (■) the option.

7 To use data roaming, select **Data roaming** (■ changes to ☑).

The Attention dialog box opens.

8 Touch **OK**.

The Attention dialog box closes.

9 Touch **Phone** (📞).

The Wireless & networks screen appears.

10 Touch **Settings** (⚏).

The Settings screen appears.

11 Touch **Data usage**.

The Data usage screen appears.

12 Touch the **Set mobile data limit** check box to select the option (■ changes to ☑).

13 Touch **Data usage cycle** and set the cycle's dates.

14 Drag the **Limit bar** (◼️◻️) up or down to set the data limit.

15 Drag the **Warning bar** (◻️◼️) up or down to set the warning level.

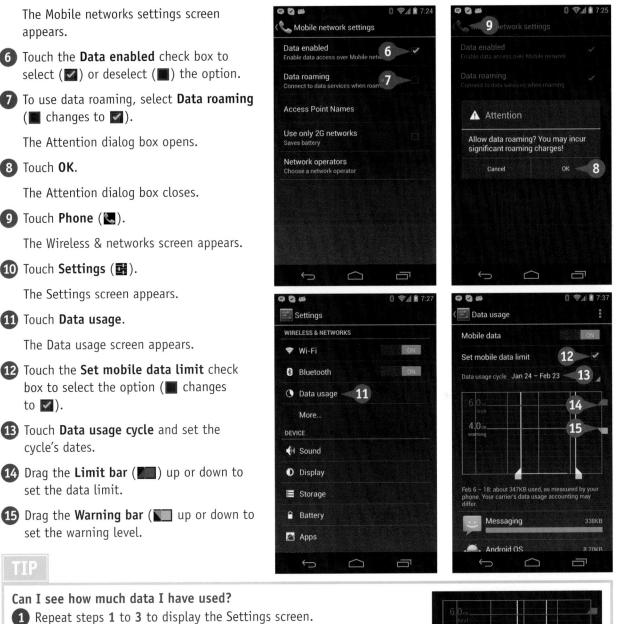

TIP

Can I see how much data I have used?

1 Repeat steps **1** to **3** to display the Settings screen.

2 Touch **Data usage** to display the Data usage screen.

3 Drag **Start** (◤) left or right to set the start of the period.

4 Drag **End** (◥) left or right to set the end of the period.

5 Look at the usage figure.

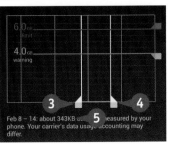

Connect Your Device to a Different Carrier

The SIM card makes your phone or cellular-capable tablet connect automatically to a particular carrier's network, such as the AT&T network or the Verizon network. When you go outside your carrier's network, you can connect the phone or tablet manually to a different carrier — for example, when you travel abroad. To connect to a different carrier, you may need to set up an account with that carrier or pay extra charges to your standard carrier.

Connect Your Device to a Different Carrier

 Touch the **Home** button (⬠).

The Home screen appears.

2 Touch the **All Apps** button (⊞).

The Apps screen appears.

Note: If the Widgets tab is displayed on the Apps screen, touch the **Apps** tab.

3 Touch **Settings** (⊞).

Note: If Settings is not on the Apps screen that appears first, scroll left or right until you find Settings.

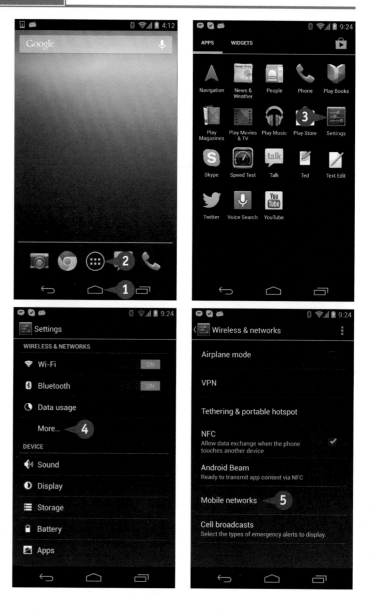

The Settings screen appears.

4 Touch **More**.

The Wireless & networks screen appears.

5 Touch **Mobile networks**.

The Mobile network settings screen appears.

6 Touch **Network operators**.

The Available networks screen appears.

7 Touch the network you want to use.

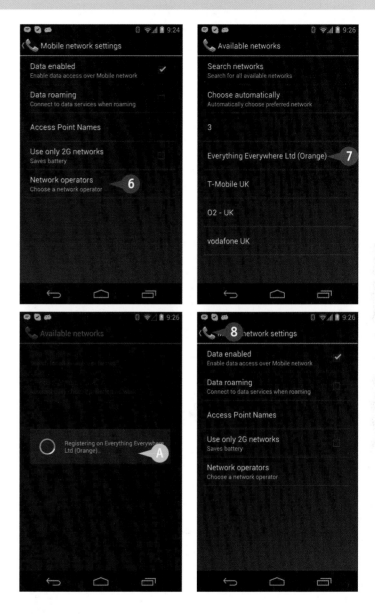

Ⓐ Android registers your device with the carrier.

The Mobile network settings screen appears.

8 Touch **Phone** (📞).

The Wireless & networks screen appears.

9 Touch **Settings** (⚙).

The Settings screen appears.

How do I return to my regular carrier?
To return to your regular carrier, display the Available networks screen following steps **1** to **6**, and then touch **Choose automatically**.

Is there another way to change my carrier?
If your phone or cellular-capable tablet has an easily accessible SIM card and your device is not locked to a particular carrier, you can remove the existing SIM card and replace it with one for the carrier to which you want to switch.

Connect to Your Work Network via VPN

I f you use your phone or tablet for work, you may need to connect it to your work network. By using the settings, username, and password that the network's administrator provides, you can connect via *virtual private networking*, or VPN, across the Internet. VPN uses encryption to create a secure connection across the Internet. By using VPN, you can connect securely from anywhere you have an Internet connection. Before you create a VPN connection, you must set a lock screen PIN or password on your phone or tablet.

Connect to Your Work Network via VPN

1 Touch the **Home** button ().

The Home screen appears.

2 Touch the **All Apps** button (⊞).

The Apps screen appears.

Note: If the Widgets tab is displayed on the Apps screen, touch the **Apps** tab.

3 Touch **Settings** (⊞).

Note: If Settings is not on the Apps screen that appears first, scroll left or right until you find Settings.

The Settings screen appears.

4 Touch **More**.

The Wireless & networks screen appears.

5 Touch **VPN**.

Note: If you have not yet set a lock screen PIN or password, an Attention dialog box appears when you touch **VPN**. Touch **OK** to display the Unlock selection screen, then touch either **PIN** or **Password** and set up the security mechanism.

On the VPN screen, touch **Add** (■).

7 In the Edit VPN profile dialog box, type a descriptive name for the connection.

8 Choose the VPN type. See the first tip for more information.

9 Type the server address.

10 Type the security information.

11 Touch **Save**.

12 Touch the VPN's name.

13 In the Connect to dialog box, type your username.

14 Type your password.

15 Touch the **Save account information** check box to select (☑) or deselect (■) the option.

16 Touch **Connect**.

A The Connected readout appears. You can now work with network resources such as e-mail and network folders.

17 When you are ready to disconnect, touch the VPN's name.

18 In the VPN is connected dialog box, touch **Disconnect**.

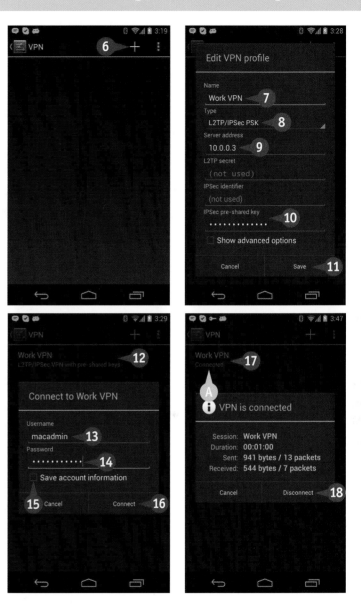

TIPS

What VPN type should I choose?
You must use the type of connection the VPN server uses. Ask the VPN's administrator which VPN type this is. PPTP, the Point-to-Point Tunneling Protocol, and L2TP, the Layer 2 Tunneling Protocol, are the most widely used VPN types, but it is hard to guess what type you need.

What is the pre-shared key?
The pre-shared key, also called a *shared secret*, is a group password for the VPN. The pre-shared key, or PSK, is shared among a group of users rather than being dedicated to a single user.

Use the Tethering Feature

Your phone or cellular-capable tablet can share its cellular connection with your computer or other devices. This feature enables you to connect your computer or Wi-Fi–only devices to the Internet through the cellular connection your phone or tablet has established. You can share the Internet access in two ways. The first way is tethering, in which you connect your Android device to your computer via USB and share the connection across the USB cable. The second way is by turning your Android device into a portable Wi-Fi hotspot.

Use the Tethering Feature

Turn Tethering On or Off

1 Connect your phone or tablet to your computer via the USB cable.

2 Touch the **Home** button (⬟).

The Home screen appears.

3 Touch the **All Apps** button (▦).

The Apps screen appears.

Note: If the Widgets tab is displayed on the Apps screen, touch the **Apps** tab.

4 Touch **Settings** (▤).

Note: If Settings is not on the Apps screen that appears first, scroll left or right until you find Settings.

The Settings screen appears.

5 Touch **More**.

The Wireless & networks screen appears.

6 Touch **Tethering & portable hotspot**.

The Tethering & portable hotspot screen appears.

7 Touch the **USB tethering** check box (■ changes to ✅).

Ⓐ The USB tethering button shows the readout "Tethered."

Your computer starts using the phone's or tablet's Internet connection across the USB cable.

8 When you finish using the connection, deselect **USB tethering** (✅ changes to ■).

Set Your Mac to Use the Tethered Connection

1 On your Mac, click **System Preferences** (▥) on the Dock.

The System Preferences window opens.

2 Click **Network**.

The Network preferences pane appears.

3 In the left pane, click the entry for your Android device.

4 Click **Apply**.

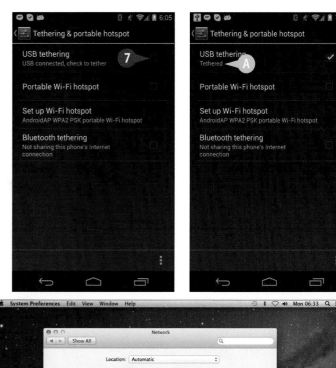

Why does my Android device not appear in my Mac's Network preferences?
You may need to install a driver, a piece of software that enables the Mac to use the Android device's USB connection. The HoRNDIS driver available at http://joshuawise.com/horndis enables OS X to use many Android devices this way.

To install HoRNDIS, you must allow applications downloaded from anywhere. Click **System Preferences** (▥) on the Dock, click **Security & Privacy**, click **General**, and then click **Anywhere** in the Allow applications downloaded from area. You may need to click the lock icon and type your password to make these changes.

Set Up Your Portable Hotspot Feature

Your Android phone or cellular-capable tablet can access the Internet from anywhere that has a suitable connection to the cell network, and it can act as a Wi-Fi hotspot to share that Internet access with your computer and other devices. This feature is called *Portable Hotspot*. For you to use Portable Hotspot, your cellular carrier must permit you to use it. Many carriers charge an extra monthly fee for using Portable Hotspot. Verify your carrier's policy for Portable Hotspot and be careful not to exceed your cellular data allowance.

Set Up Your Portable Hotspot Feature

1 Touch the **Home** button ().

The Home screen appears.

2 Touch the **All Apps** button (■).

The Apps screen appears.

Note: If the Widgets tab is displayed on the Apps screen, touch the **Apps** tab.

3 Touch **Settings** (■).

Note: If Settings is not on the Apps screen that appears first, scroll left or right until you find Settings.

The Settings screen appears.

4 Touch **More**.

The Wireless & networks screen appears.

5 Touch **Tethering & portable hotspot**.

The Tethering & portable hotspot screen appears.

6 Touch **Set up Wi-Fi hotspot**.

The Set up Wi-Fi hotspot dialog box appears.

7 Type the name for the hotspot.

8 Touch **Security** and choose the security type. See the tip for a recommendation.

9 Touch **Password** and type a password of eight characters or more.

A Touch **Show password** if you need to verify the password (■ changes to ☑).

10 Touch **Save**.

The Set up Wi-Fi hotspot dialog box closes.

B The hotspot's details appear on the Set up Wi-Fi hotspot button.

11 Touch **Portable Wi-Fi hotspot** (■ changes to ☑).

C ☜ appears in the status bar to indicate portable hotspot is active.

You can now connect your computers or devices to the portable hotspot's Wi-Fi network.

TIPS

What security type should I choose for my Wi-Fi hotspot?
WPA2 PSK is the most secure type. Use WPA2 PSK unless any of the devices you need to connect to the hotspot does not support this security method. Do not use Open, because any device within Wi-Fi range will be able to connect freely to your hotspot.

Are there disadvantages to using Portable Hotspot?
Because the devices share the Internet connection, the more devices you use, the slower the connection speed will appear to be on each device. You must also be careful not to exceed your cellular data allowance, which could run up extra costs.

To conserve your cellular data allowance, connect your phone or cellular-capable tablet to the Internet via Wi-Fi networks whenever possible. If your tablet is Wi-Fi–only, you must always use Wi-Fi networks. Your device can connect to both infrastructure wireless networks and ad hoc wireless networks. An infrastructure network uses a wireless access point, whereas an ad hoc network is hosted by a device. The first time you connect to a Wi-Fi network, you provide the network's password. After that, your phone or tablet stores the password for future connections. You can make the device forget a network you no longer use.

Manage Your Wireless Networks

Connect to an Infrastructure Wireless Network

1 Touch the **Home** button (⬛).

The Home screen appears.

Ⓐ The Wi-Fi signal icon (📶) in the status bar and on the Wi-Fi screen shows the strength of the Wi-Fi signal. The more bars that appear, the stronger the signal is.

2 Touch the **All Apps** button (⊞).

The Apps screen appears.

Note: If the Widgets tab is displayed on the Apps screen, touch the **Apps** tab.

3 Touch **Settings** (⚙).

Note: If Settings is not on the Apps screen that appears first, scroll left or right until you find Settings.

The Settings screen appears.

4 Make sure the **Wi-Fi** switch is set to On.

5 Touch the left part of the **Wi-Fi** button, not the switch.

The Wi-Fi screen appears.

6 Touch the network to which you want to connect.

Note: If the network has no password, your phone or tablet connects to it without prompting you for a password.

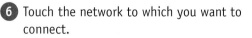

A dialog box for connecting to the network opens.

7 Type the password.

8 Touch **Connect**.

Your device connects to the network.

B The Connected readout appears below the network's name.

Connect to an Ad Hoc Wireless Network

1 Display the Wi-Fi screen by following steps **1** to **5** in the previous subsection.

2 Touch the **Menu** button (**▮**).

The menu opens.

3 Touch **Wi-Fi Direct**.

The Wi-Fi Direct screen appears.

4 In the Peer devices list, touch the device to connect to.

When the peer device accepts the invitation to connect, Android establishes the network.

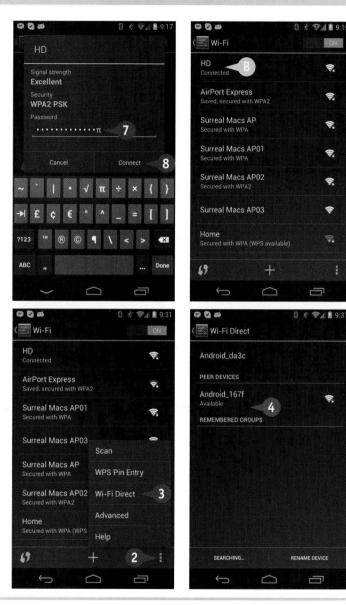

How do I stop my phone or tablet from using a wireless network?
Tell the device to forget the network. On the Wi-Fi screen, touch the network's name, and then touch **Forget** in the dialog box for the network.

I get the message "Authentication problem" when I try to connect to a network. How do I solve this?
The message "Authentication problem" usually means you have mistyped the password. On the Wi-Fi screen, touch the network's name, and then touch **Forget** in the dialog box for the network. Touch the network's name again and retype the password. Touch the **Show password** check box (**■** changes to **☑**) so you can see the characters.

Log In to Wi-Fi Hotspots

hether you are in town or on the road, you can log in to Wi-Fi hotspots to enjoy fast Internet access without using your phone's or cellular tablet's data allowance. You can find Wi-Fi hotspots at many locations, including coffee shops and restaurants, hotels, and airports. Some municipal areas, and even some parks and highway rest stops, also provide public Wi-Fi. Some Wi-Fi hotspots charge for access, whereas others are free. If you travel extensively, it is worth signing up for a plan that provides long-term access to Wi-Fi hotspots.

Log In to Wi-Fi Hotspots

1 Touch the **Home** button ().

The Home screen appears.

2 Touch the **All Apps** button (⊞).

The Apps screen appears.

Note: If the Widgets tab is displayed on the Apps screen, touch the **Apps** tab.

3 Touch **Settings** (⚙).

Note: If Settings is not on the Apps screen that appears first, scroll left or right until you find Settings.

The Settings screen appears.

4 Touch **Wi-Fi**.

The Wi-Fi screen appears.

5 Touch the network to which you want to connect.

Note: If your phone or tablet prompts you to enter a username and password, enter those the hotspot operator has given you. Many Wi-Fi hotspots use a login page instead of a username and password.

Your phone or tablet joins the hotspot. The Wi-Fi screen displays Connected next to the hotspot.

6 Touch the **Home** button ().

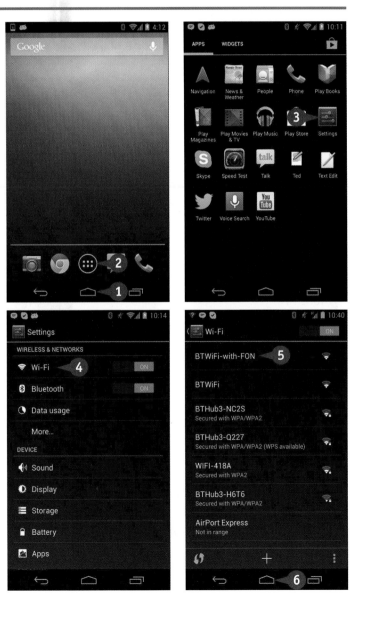

126

The Home screen appears.

7 Touch the **Chrome** button ().

The Chrome app opens and displays a login page for the hotspot.

8 Type the login information for the hotspot.

9 Touch the button for logging in.

After connecting to the hotspot, you can use the Internet. For example, you can browse the web using Chrome or send and receive e-mail using the Gmail app or the Email app.

10 When you finish using the hotspot, touch the **Recent Apps** button (▭).

The Recent apps menu opens.

11 Touch **Settings**.

The Wi-Fi screen in the Settings app appears.

12 Touch the Wi-Fi network's name.

The network's dialog box opens.

13 Touch **Forget**.

Your Android device forgets the network.

What precautions should I take when using Wi-Fi hotspots?
The main danger is that you may connect to a malevolent network. To stay safe, connect only to hotspots provided by reputable establishments — for example, national hotel chains or restaurant chains — instead of hotspots run by unknown operators. Even then, it is best not to transmit any private information that may interest eavesdroppers. When you finish using a Wi-Fi hotspot that you do not plan to use again, tell your phone or tablet to forget the network. To forget the network, touch the Wi-Fi network's name on the Wi-Fi screen, and then touch **Forget**.

Transfer Data Using Android Beam

ndroid includes a feature called Android Beam that lets you transfer data wirelessly between Android devices. Android Beam uses a technology called *Near Field Communication*, or NFC, which enables NFC-enabled smartphones and tablets to automatically establish a radio connection when you bring them within a few inches of each other. If your phone or tablet includes an NFC chip, you can transfer data to another NFC-enabled device by bringing them back-to-back briefly. This feature is great for transferring contacts, photos, and other data you want to share quickly and effortlessly.

Transfer Data Using Android Beam

Turn On Android Beam

1 Touch the **Home** button (⬠).

The Home screen appears.

2 Touch the **All Apps** button (▦).

The Apps screen appears.

Note: If the Widgets tab is displayed on the Apps screen, touch the **Apps** tab.

3 Touch **Settings** (▦).

Note: If Settings is not on the Apps screen that appears first, scroll left or right until you find Settings.

The Settings screen appears.

4 Touch **More**.

The Wireless & networks screen appears.

5 Touch **NFC** (■ changes to ✔).

6 If Android Beam shows Off, touch **Android Beam**. Otherwise, skip the remaining steps in this list.

The Android Beam screen appears.

7 Move the **Android Beam** switch to On.

8 Touch **Settings** (⊞).

The Wireless & networks screen appears.

Ⓐ The Ready to transmit app content via NFC readout appears.

Transfer Data via Android Beam

1 Open the app that contains the data you want to transfer. For example, touch the Home button (⬛), touch the All Apps button (⊞), and then touch People (🖼) to open the People app. Then touch a contact to display the record.

2 Position your phone or tablet back-to-back with another NFC-enabled phone or tablet.

When the NFC chips connect, your device vibrates, the screen image shrinks, and the Touch to beam prompt appears.

3 Touch the **Touch to beam** prompt.

Your phone or tablet beams the data to the other device.

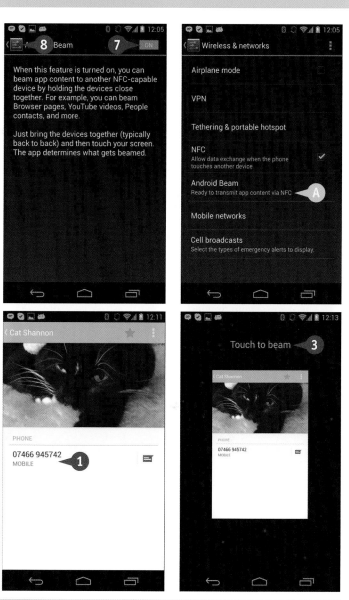

TIPS

Why can my phone and tablet not connect via Android Beam?

If you have turned on NFC and enabled Android Beam on both devices, the problem is most likely that you have not brought the NFC chips close enough to each other. Hold the phone and tablet back-to-back and move the phone around the tablet until the devices vibrate. You will then have found the right location to use for Android Beam connections.

What happens when my device receives data via Android Beam?

Your device accepts the data, but it may prompt you to decide where to place it. For example, if the People app receives a contact, it may prompt you to choose in which account to place the new contact.

If your Android device contains a Near Field Communication chip, you can use NFC to make payments with contactless payment systems. To make a payment, you bring your phone or tablet to within a few inches of the NFC payment terminal and then confirm the transaction by touching a prompt on the screen. This payment system can be fast, convenient, and practical, eliminating the need to bring your wallet out into the open, take physical money from it, and receive and put away change. Contactless payment systems are currently available in various major chains and major public locations, such as airports and stations. Experts expect contactless payment systems to become widely used in the coming years.

Create a Google Wallet Account

Before you can make an NFC payment, you must set up a Google Wallet account. Google Wallet is a secure digital payment technology developed and promoted by Google. After setting up a Google Wallet account and adding a means of payment, you can use Google Wallet to make payments online or with your Android device. To create a Google Wallet account, type **https://www.google.com/wallet/** in the address box in your web browser and then click Sign up. With the account created, you can add a means of payment: a credit card, a debit

card, or a voucher. You can add multiple means of payment and switch among them as needed. If you lose your Android device, or if someone steals it, you can log into your Google Wallet account using another computer and disable Google Wallet on the device to prevent anyone else from making payments with it.

Install Wallet on Your Phone or Tablet

After creating a Google Wallet account, you can set up your phone or tablet to use the account so that you can make payments with the device. To do so, you set up the Wallet app on your device. If your phone or tablet does not have the Wallet app installed, you can install it by touching Play Store on the Apps screen, touching Apps, and then searching for Wallet. After you locate the Wallet app, download and install it, and then sign in to it.

Enable NFC on Your Android Device

To make NFC payments using your Android phone or tablet, you must enable NFC on your device. To do so, touch the Home button ( ), then touch All Apps ( ) to display the Apps screen. Touch Settings ( ) to open the Settings app, touch More to display the Wireless & networks screen, and then touch NFC (changes to).

Learn Where You Can Make NFC Payments

At this writing, you can make NFC payments at hundreds of thousands of stores in the United States. Major merchants who accept NFC payments include Banana Republic, Foot Locker, Macy's, OfficeMax, ToysRUs, and Old Navy. The list of stores that accept NFC payments is increasing rapidly, and Google plans to introduce Google Wallet in other countries in the near future. Most stores that accept NFC payments display signs near their checkout terminals. If you do not see a sign, ask a member of the staff if the store accepts NFC payments.

Make a Payment via NFC

When you have set up your Android phone or tablet with Google Wallet and enabled NFC, you can make payments using NFC at establishments that accept contactless payments. To make a payment with NFC, first unlock your phone or tablet. Touch the Home button (⬡) to display the Home screen, and then touch All Apps (⬛) to display the Apps screen. Touch Wallet to launch the Wallet app. On the screen of payment options that Wallet displays, touch the card or voucher you want to use. Touch the back of your phone or tablet to the payment terminal.

Take Other Actions with NFC

NFC is a powerful and flexible technology that is currently finding new uses in both business and home settings. As well as making payments, you may be able to use your phone or tablet to authorize you to enter buildings or zones controlled by contactless terminals. If your work or play involves such areas, find out whether your phone or tablet can substitute for a pass card that you would normally carry. If so, you can use your Android device to access controlled areas.

CHAPTER 6

Making Calls and Instant Messaging

With your Android phone, you can make phone calls and conference calls anywhere you go. With either a phone or a tablet, you can also enjoy instant messaging and video calling with your contacts.

Make Phone Calls

With your Android phone, you can make phone calls anywhere you have a connection to the cellular network. You can make a phone call by dialing the phone number using the keypad, but you can place calls more easily by tapping the appropriate phone number for a contact or by using your call logs. When you need other people near you to be able to hear both ends of the phone call you are making, you can switch on your phone's speaker.

Make Phone Calls

Open the Phone App

1 Touch the **Home** button (■).

The Home screen appears.

2 Touch **Phone** (■).

The Phone app opens and displays the screen you used last — for example, the Contacts screen.

Note: You can also place a call to a phone number that your phone has identified — for example, by tapping an underlined phone number that represents a link on a web page.

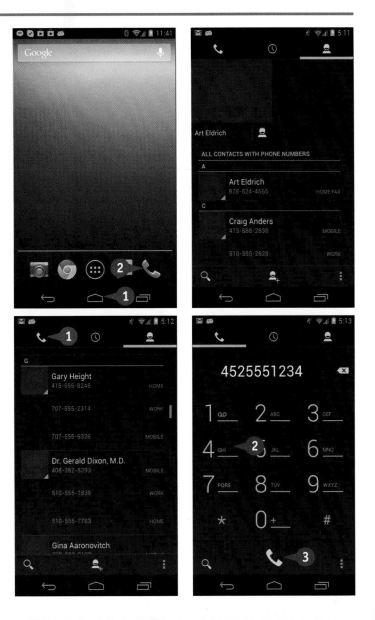

Dial a Call Using the Keypad

1 In the Phone app, touch the **Keypad** button (■) at the top of the screen.

The Keypad screen appears.

2 Touch the number keys to dial the number.

3 Touch the **Dial** button (■) at the bottom of the Keypad screen.

Your phone makes the call.

Dial a Call to a Contact

1 In the Phone app, touch the **Contacts** tab (👤).

The Contacts list appears.

2 Touch the contact you want to call. If the contact has multiple numbers, touch the appropriate number.

Your phone makes the call.

End a Phone Call

1 Touch the **End Call** button (📞).

Your phone ends the call.

Ⓐ The Call Ended message appears for a moment.

Your phone then displays the screen from which you placed the call — for example, the Contacts screen.

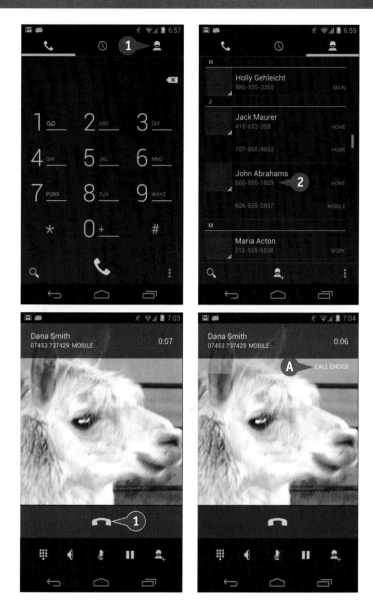

TIP

Can I use my phone as a speakerphone?

Yes, as long as your phone has a speaker, which most do. All you need to do is touch the **Speaker** icon (🔊) on the control panel that appears while you are making a phone call. Your phone starts playing the call through the main speaker rather than the ear speaker, turning your phone into a speakerphone. Touch the **Speaker** icon (🔊) again when you want to switch off the speaker.

Make Phone Calls with a Headset

If you have a headset with a microphone and built-in controls, you can use it to listen to music and to make and receive phone calls. Using the headset is convenient both when you are out and about and when you are listening to music, because you can accept an incoming call using the headset controls without even looking at your phone's screen. Your phone automatically pauses the music when you answer a phone call and resumes it after the call ends.

Make Phone Calls with a Headset

Make a Call Using the Headset

1 Connect the headset to your phone if it is not already connected.

Note: You can dial a call by activating Voice Actions and speaking the number or the contact's name. See Chapter 3 for instructions on using Voice Actions.

2 Touch the **Home** button ().

The Home screen appears.

3 Touch **Phone** (📞).

The Phone app opens.

4 Dial the call.

5 If you need to change the volume, press the Volume Up button or the Volume Down button on either the headset or the phone.

6 Press the clicker button on the headset to mute or unmute the call.

7 Touch the **End call** button (📞) to end the call.

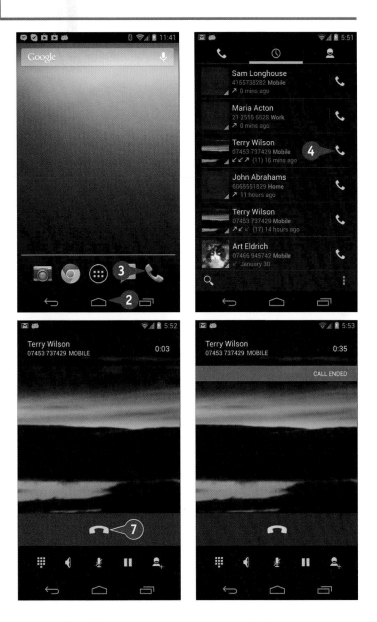

Take a Call Using the Headset

1 Connect the headset to your phone if it is not already connected.

When you receive an incoming call, the phone ringtone plays in the headset and the screen comes on if it is off.

A The lock screen shows the caller's name and phone details — for example, Mobile or the phone number.

Note: If you are listening to music or watching a video when you receive a call, your phone automatically fades and pauses the music.

2 Press the clicker button on the headset to take the call.

The lock screen shows the caller's name and the call's duration.

3 If you need to change the volume, press the Volume Up button or the Volume Down button on the headset.

4 Press the clicker button on the headset to mute or unmute the call if necessary.

B A blue line appears under the Mute icon (🎤) when the call is muted.

5 Touch the **End Call** button (📞) when you are ready to end the call.

The Phone app appears, showing the screen you last used.

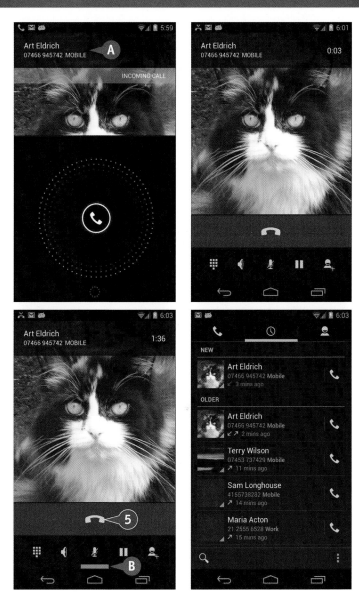

TIP

Can I take further actions using the headset?
This depends on the model of headset and how tightly it is integrated with your phone. Many headsets include volume buttons that you can press to increase or decrease the audio volume during a call. Some headsets have extra functionality — for example, you can press a button to end a call. Explore your headset's controls or even read its documentation to find out all it can do.

Make a Conference Call

When you need to talk to more than one person at a time, you can make a conference call using your Android phone. This capability is great for both business and social calls. To make a conference call, you do not need to set it up with an operator in advance; instead, you call the first participant, and then add each other participant in turn. During a conference call, you can talk in private to individual participants. You can also drop a participant from the call without affecting the other participants.

Make a Conference Call

Establish a Conference Call

1 Touch the **Home** button (▭).

The Home screen appears.

2 Touch **Phone** (📞).

The Phone app opens.

3 Touch the **Contacts** tab (🔲).

The Contacts screen appears.

Note: You can also call a contact by using the keypad or the call log.

4 Touch the phone number for the contact you want to call first.

Your phone makes the call.

5 After the contact answers the call, touch the **Make another call** button (🔲).

The Keypad screen appears.

6 Touch the **Contacts** tab (🔲).

The Contacts screen appears.

7 Locate the contact and touch the phone number to use.

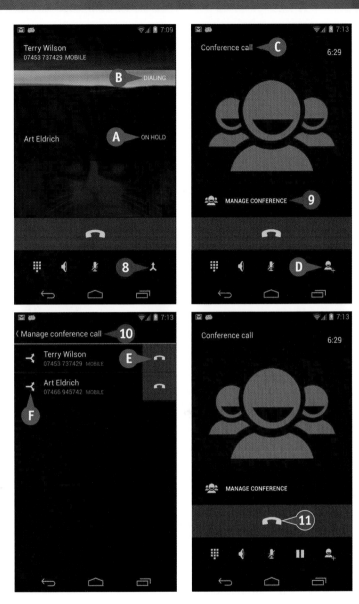

Ⓐ Your phone places the first call on hold.

Ⓑ Your phone makes the new call.

❽ Touch the **Merge calls** button (🤼).

Ⓒ The Phone app merges the calls and displays "Conference call" at the top of the screen.

You can now speak to both participants.

Ⓓ You can add further participants by touching the **Make another call** button (👤), touching the contact's number, and then touching the **Merge calls** button (🤼).

❾ To speak privately to or end the call with one participant, touch **Manage Conference**.

The Manage conference call screen appears.

Ⓔ Touch the **End call** button (📞) to end a call with a participant.

Ⓕ Touch the **Split calls** button (◀) to speak privately to a participant, putting the other participants on hold.

❿ Touch **Manage conference call** to return to the call.

⓫ Touch the **End call** button (📞) to end the call.

TIPS

How do I get back to my conference call after leaving it?
You can leave the conference call and work with other apps by touching the **Home** button (⬭) or the **Recent Apps** button (▤) and then touching the app you want. To return to the call, open the Notification shade and touch **Ongoing call**. You can also touch **Hang Up** in the notification shade to end the call without returning to the Phone app.

How many participants can I include in a conference call?
The number of participants depends on your cellular carrier rather than on Android. Contact your carrier's support department to find out the limit.

Using your Android phone, you can make calls quickly and easily in several ways. You can dial a phone number from your Contacts list with a single touch, but you can save even more time and effort by using your call logs and your Frequently called list. Your call logs track the phone numbers that you have called and that have called you. You can filter a call log so that it shows only calls you have missed, only outgoing calls, or only incoming calls. The Frequently called list automatically gathers the contacts to whom you phone and from persons whom phone you most often.

Call with Call Logs and Frequently Called

Call Using the Call Logs

1 Touch the **Home** button (▬).

The Home screen appears.

2 Touch **Phone** (◣).

The Phone app opens.

3 Touch the **Call log** tab (◔).

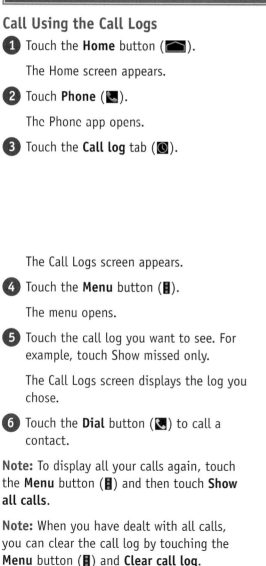

The Call Logs screen appears.

4 Touch the **Menu** button (▤).

The menu opens.

5 Touch the call log you want to see. For example, touch Show missed only.

The Call Logs screen displays the log you chose.

6 Touch the **Dial** button (◣) to call a contact.

Note: To display all your calls again, touch the **Menu** button (▤) and then touch **Show all calls**.

Note: When you have dealt with all calls, you can clear the call log by touching the **Menu** button (▤) and **Clear call log**.

Call Using Your Frequently Called List

1 Touch the **Home** button (▢).

The Home screen appears.

2 Touch **Phone** (📞).

The Phone app opens.

3 Touch the **Contacts** tab (🔲).

The Contacts screen appears.

4 Scroll up to the top.

The Frequently called list appears.

Note: The Frequently called list shows the contacts and phone numbers you have called, and from which you have received calls, most often.

5 Touch the number you want to call.

How can I remove a contact from the Frequently Called list?
You cannot remove an individual number from the Frequently Called list, but you can clear the entire list. To do so:

1 Touch the **Menu** button (⋮).

2 Touch **Clear frequents**.

3 Touch **OK** in the Clear frequently contacted? dialog box.

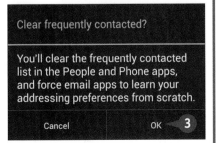

Clear frequently contacted?

You'll clear the frequently contacted list in the People and Phone apps, and force email apps to learn your addressing preferences from scratch.

Cancel   OK ◄ **3**

Send and Receive Instant Messages

When you need to communicate quickly with another phone user, but do not need to speak to him, you can send an instant message instead. The message can use either SMS or MMS. SMS stands for *Short Message Service*; MMS stands for *Multimedia Messaging Service*. An SMS message consists of only text, whereas an MMS message can contain text, videos, photos, sounds, or other data. When you start a message, the Messaging app creates it as an SMS message. If you add a photo, video, or other content, Messaging automatically converts the message to an MMS message.

Send and Receive Instant Messages

① Touch the **Home** button (⬒).

The Home screen appears.

② Touch the **Messaging** button (▣).

Note: If Messaging does not appear on the Home screen, touch the **Apps** button (▦), and then touch **Messaging**.

The Messaging app opens.

③ Touch the **New message** button (▤).

The New Message screen appears.

④ Touch the **To** field and start typing the contact's name or phone number.

Note: You can also start typing the phone number if you remember it or part of it.

A list of matching contacts appears.

⑤ Touch the contact you want.

Ⓐ The contact's name appears in the To field.

⑥ Touch the text field and type the message.

⑦ To add pictures, video, or audio to the message, touch the **Attach** button (📎).

The Attach dialog box opens.

8 Touch the type of item you want to attach. This example uses Pictures.

Note: If the Choose an action dialog box appears, touch the appropriate app. For example, for attaching a photo, touch Gallery.

9 In the Gallery app, touch the album that contains the photos you want to use.

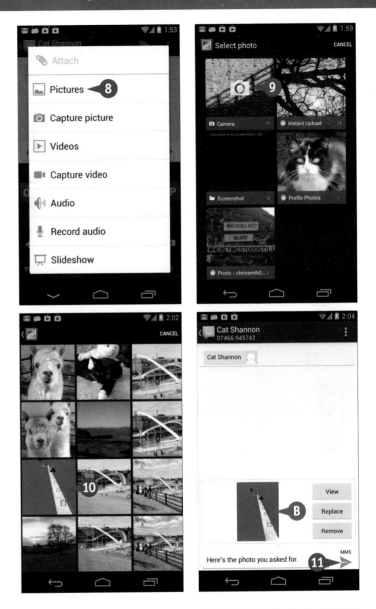

The album opens.

10 Touch the photo you want to attach.

B The photo appears in the message.

11 Touch the **Send** button (➤).

Messaging sends the message.

TIPS

Can I send instant messages on a tablet that does not have cellular connectivity?

Yes, but you must use a different app, such as Google's Messenger app or the Skype app. You can send messages to other users of the same messaging service.

Why do videos I send via MMS look so jerky and grainy?

MMS messages are limited in size, so you can send only a small amount of video that uses a low resolution and high compression. If you record a video, the Camera app limits it to 10 seconds. Android limits audio recordings to 7 minutes.

Manage Your Instant Messages

Messaging is great for communicating quickly and frequently with family, friends, and colleagues. It may not take long before the interface is full of messages and navigating among them becomes difficult. To keep your messages under control, you can forward messages to others and delete messages you do not need to keep. You can either delete messages from a thread, leaving the thread's other messages, or delete an entire thread you no longer want.

Manage Your Instant Messages

Forward or Delete a Message

1 Touch the **Home** button (▬).

The Home screen appears.

2 Touch **Messaging** (▣).

Note: If Messaging does not appear on the Home screen, touch the **All Apps** button (▦), and then touch **Messaging**.

The Messaging app opens.

3 Touch the thread that contains the message you will forward.

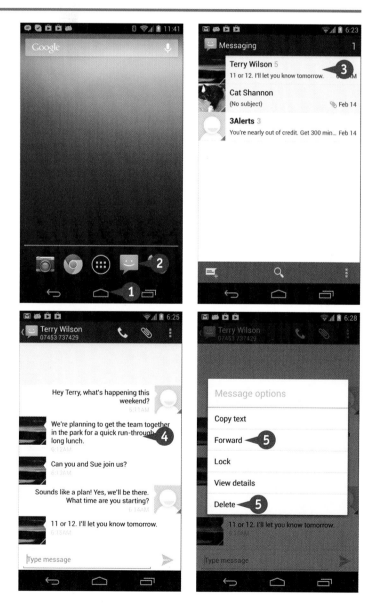

The thread appears.

4 Touch and hold the message you want to forward or delete.

The Message options dialog box opens.

5 Touch **Forward** or **Delete**.

Note: From the Message options dialog box, you can also copy the message's text, lock the message against deletion, or view the message's details.

If you touch **Forward**, Messaging starts a new message containing the forwarded message. You can then address the message and touch the **Send** button (➤) to send it.

Delete Threads

1 Touch the **Home** button (⬭).

The Home screen appears.

2 Touch **Messaging** (💬).

Note: If Messaging does not appear on the Home screen, touch the **All Apps** button (⬜), and then touch **Messaging**.

The Messaging app opens.

3 Touch and hold the thread you want to delete.

The Choose conversations bar appears at the top of the screen.

A The thread shows a blue selection highlight.

4 Touch any other threads you want to delete.

Each thread you touch shows a blue selection highlight.

5 Touch the **Delete** button (🗑).

The Delete? dialog box appears.

6 Touch **Delete**.

Messaging deletes the threads.

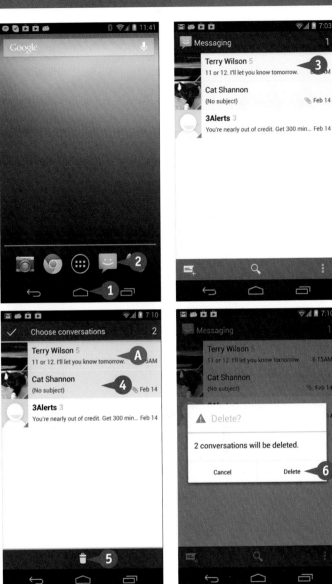

TIP

How can I get rid of all my messages quickly?

1 In the Messaging app, touch the **Menu** button (⋮).

2 On the menu, touch **Delete all threads**.

3 In the Delete? dialog box, touch **Delete**.

Use Video Chat with Google Talk

B y using Google Talk, you can enjoy audio and video chats with your contacts that have Google Accounts. Google Talk runs on Windows PCs as well as Android phones and tablets and can connect to Mac chat clients such as Adium, and Linux clients such as Pidgin, so you can chat with a wide range of people. To use Google Talk, your phone or tablet must be connected to either a wireless network or the cellular network. Using a wireless network is preferable because you typically get better performance and do not use up your cellular data allowance.

Use Video Chat with Google Talk

1 Touch the **Home** button ().

The Home screen appears.

2 Touch the **All Apps** button (▦).

The Apps screen appears.

3 Touch **Talk** ().

Note: If Talk is not on the Apps screen that appears first, scroll left or right until you find Talk.

The Talk app opens. Your contact list appears.

A Your contact entry and status appear at the top of the list. The color indicates your status: green means Available, red means Busy, and gray means Invisible.

4 Touch the **Video call** button (▬◀).

Note: You can also touch an entry in your contact list to see your latest chat with the contact or to send the contact a text message.

Your phone or tablet places a video call to your contact.

B Your video preview appears.

If your contact accepts the call, your contact's video feed appears on-screen.

C Your own video appears in an inset window.

5 To control the call, touch the screen.

D Touch the **Mute** button (🎤) to mute your microphone. Touch the **Unmute** button (🎤) to unmute the audio.

E Touch the **Audio** button (🔊) to switch the audio among the speaker, wired headphone, handset earpiece, and Bluetooth audio.

F Touch the **Switch cameras** button (📷) to switch between the front-facing camera and the rear-facing camera.

6 Touch the **Switch pictures** button (🖼) to display your video large.

G Touch the **Stabilization** button (✋) to apply image stabilization.

H Touch the **Silly Faces** button (😃) to apply a silly face, such as big eyes.

I Touch the **Background** button (🖼) to apply a different background to your video.

7 Touch the **Talk** button (💬) to return to your call.

8 Touch × to end the call.

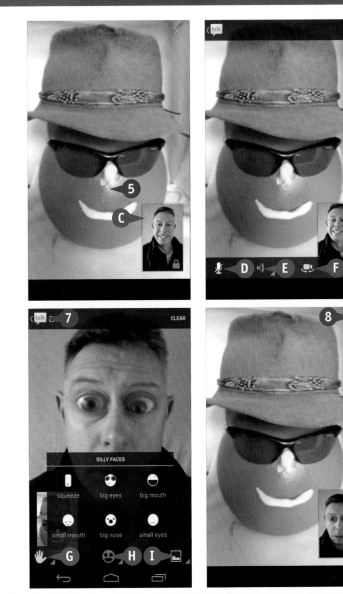

How do I change my status?

1 After opening Talk, touch your entry in the contact list to display the Status screen.

2 Touch the top button and touch **Available**, **Busy**, or **Invisible**.

3 Touch the text box and type the status you want, or touch **Change to a recently-used status** and then touch a recent status on the pop-up menu.

Install Skype on Your Phone or Tablet

I f you want to chat or make either voice or video calls with people who do not have access to Google Talk, you can install the Skype app. Skype is a service that enables you to chat and make both voice and video calls with other Skype users; you can also make voice calls to telephones. To install Skype on your phone or tablet, you open the Play Store app and download the app. To make calls with Skype, you use a Skype account or a Microsoft account.

Install Skype on Your Phone or Tablet

1 Touch the **Home** button (▭).

The Home screen appears.

2 Touch the **All Apps** button (▦).

The Apps screen appears.

Note: Look through the apps on the Apps screen to make sure Skypebook is not already installed.

3 Touch **Play Store** (▶).

Note: If Play Store is not on the Apps screen that appears first, scroll left or right until you find Play Store.

The Google Play screen appears.

4 Touch **Apps**.

The Apps screen appears.

5 Touch the **Search** button (🔍).

The search box appears.

6 Type **skype**.

A list of search results appears.

7 Touch the result with the Skype logo.

148

The Skype screen in the App Store appears.

8 Touch **Install**.

9 On the following screen, touch **Accept & download**.

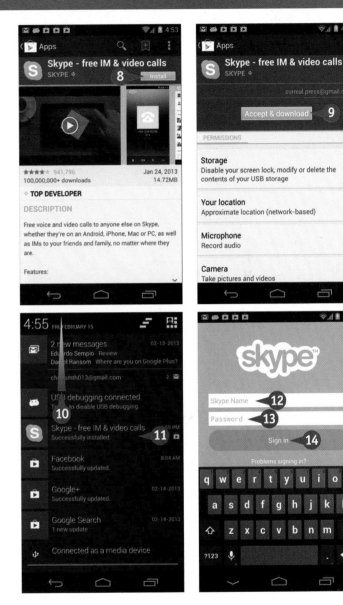

10 Drag down to open the Notification shade.

11 Touch the **Skype: Successfully installed** notification.

The Skype login screen appears.

12 Type your Skype name.

13 Type your password.

14 Touch **Sign in**.

Skype signs you in, enabling you to make and receive calls.

TIP

How do I get a Skype account?
If you are using your phone or tablet, the easiest way to sign up for a Skype account is to touch **Create a Skype account** at the bottom of the Sign in screen. On a phone, you may need to hide the on-screen keyboard to see this button. Skype then walks you through the sign-up process. On a computer, open your web browser, go to http://www.skype.com, click **Join**, and then follow through the sign-up screens.

Make Video Calls with Skype

After installing the Skype app, you can make voice calls or video calls to other Skype users. You can also send instant messages to other Skype users. Using Skype, you can also make voice calls to telephones. Skype charges for this service, so before you can use it, you must put money in your Skype account. To receive calls from telephones on your Android device using Skype, you must buy a Skype number, which callers dial to call you.

Make Video Calls with Skype

1 Touch the **Home** button ().

The Home screen appears.

Note: If the Skype icon appears on the Home screen, touch **Skype** and go to step 4.

2 Touch the **All Apps** button ().

The Apps screen appears.

3 Touch **Skype** (🅂).

Note: If Skype is not on the Apps screen that appears first, scroll left or right until you find Skype.

The Skype home screen appears.

Ⓐ You can touch **Tell friends what you're up to**, type a status message, and touch **Share**.

4 Touch **Contacts**.

The Contacts screen appears.

5 Touch the contact you want to call.

The contact's details appear.

6 Touch **Video call**.

Your phone or tablet places the call.

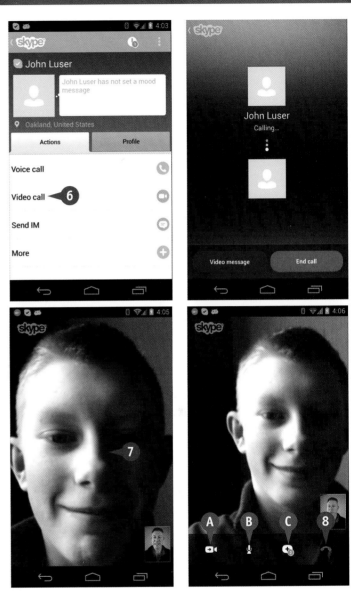

If your contact accepts the call, the contact's video feed appears with your video inset. You can start conversing.

7 Touch the screen to display the controls.

A Touch the **Video** button (⏹) to switch to your device's other camera or turn the video off.

B Touch the **Mute** button (🎤) to mute the audio (🎤 changes to 🚫). Touch the **Unmute** button (🚫) to unmute the audio (🚫 changes to 🎤).

C Touch the **Messages** button (➕) to display a menu for showing your messages.

8 Touch the **End call** button (📞) to end the call.

TIPS

How do I put money on my Skype account?
On the Skype Home screen, touch **Profile**. On the Account tab of the Profile screen, touch **Skype Credit**. In the Skype Credit dialog box, touch **Buy Credit** and follow the prompts.

How do I buy a Skype number to receive phone calls?
On the Skype Home screen, touch **Profile**. On the Account tab of the Profile screen, touch **Skype Number**. In the Skype Number dialog box, touch **Buy now** and follow the prompts.

CHAPTER 7

Enjoying Social Networking

With your Android phone or tablet, you can log in to Google+, Facebook, and Twitter, and enjoy social networking all day long anywhere you can access the Internet.

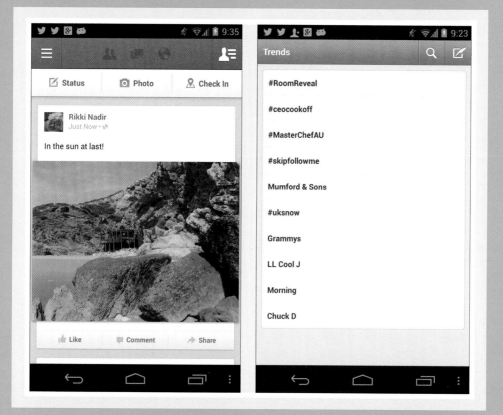

Set Up Google+

Google+ is Google's social network. With your Android phone or tablet, you can easily log in to Google+ and stay connected to your social network wherever you go. Before you can use Google+, you must set it up by connecting it to your Google account. Google+ includes a range of social-networking features. You can use the Google Circles feature to organize your contacts into different groups for easy communication; share your photos in moments using the Instant Upload feature; and chat with your family, friends, and colleagues using the Messenger feature.

Set Up Google+

1 Touch the **Home** button (⬛).

The Home screen appears.

2 Touch the **All Apps** button (⬛).

The Apps screen appears.

Note: If the Widgets tab is displayed on the Apps screen, touch the **Apps** tab.

3 Touch **Google+** (⬛).

Note: If Google+ is not on the Apps screen that appears first, scroll left or right until you find Google+.

The Choose an account dialog box appears.

4 Select the radio button for the account you want to use (⬛ changes to ⬛).

Note: If the correct account does not appear, touch **Add account** and follow the prompts to add the account.

5 Touch **OK**.

The Google Profiles screen appears.

6 If necessary, edit your first name so it appears the way you prefer.

7 Touch **Next**.

8 If necessary, edit your last name.

9 Touch **Continue**.

10 On the Add people screen, touch **Follow** to add a person or entity to the list of people you are following.

Note: Scroll down to see more categories. Scroll sideways to see more items within a category.

Ⓐ Google+ adds the person or entity to your Following circle.

11 Touch **Next**.

12 On the Enrich your contacts screen, touch the **Add your Google+ connections to Android contacts** check box to select (☑) or deselect (☐) it.

13 Touch the **Let Google make suggestions based on who you communicate with most often on this phone** check box to select (☑) or deselect (☐) this option.

14 Touch **Next**.

15 On the Turn on Instant Upload screen, touch one of the following options: **Over Wi-Fi or mobile network, Over Wi-Fi only,** or **Turn off Instant Upload** (○ changes to ◉).

16 Touch **Done**.

 TIP

What are Google circles?

Circles are separate groups within your social network. Google+ provides circles called Friends, Family, Acquaintances, and Following to get you started, so you can associate your contacts with different groups. You can also access the What's hot and Nearby circles, create your own custom circles, and share data only with particular circles. For example, you may want to share some items with your friends but not with your acquaintances.

Navigate Google+

After setting up Google+ on your phone or tablet, you can enjoy social networking on it. From the Circles screen that Google+ displays when you launch the app, you can easily view the posts for one or more circles, comment on posts, or post your own photos. You can write posts, share moods, and even shoot new videos and post them at once.

Navigate Google+

1 Touch the **Home** button ( ).

The Home screen appears.

2 Touch the **All Apps** button ( ).

The Apps screen appears.

Note: If the Widgets tab is displayed on the Apps screen, touch the **Apps** tab.

3 Touch **Google+** ( ).

Note: If Google+ is not on the Apps screen that appears first, scroll left or right until you find Google+.

Google+ displays the Circles screen.

4 Touch the **Circles** pop-up menu.

5 Touch the circle you want to display. For example, touch Friends.

The posts for the circle you touched appear.

6 Touch **Photo** to share a photo.

A From a posts screen, you can also touch **Check in** (📍) to share your location, touch **Mood** (😊) to share a mood, or touch **Write** (✏) to write a post. Touch an existing post to comment on it.

The Select to share screen appears.

7 Touch the photo or photos to share.

B You can touch the **Video** button (📹) to record a video.

C You can touch the **Photo** button (📷) to take a photo.

8 Touch the **Use Photo** button (➡).

9 Touch the pop-up button and choose with which circle you want to share the picture.

10 Type any text.

11 Touch the **Remove** button (✕) if you want to remove your location.

12 Touch **Share**.

Google+ shares the picture.

TIP

How do I control which notifications I receive?

Touch the **Menu** button (⋮) and then touch **Settings**. On the Settings screen, touch **Notifications** to display the Notifications screen. You can then turn notifications on and off (Ⓐ), choose your ringtone (Ⓑ), turn vibration on or off (Ⓒ), and choose whether to get notifications for mentions (Ⓓ), shares, comments, and other Google+ events involving you.

Install the Facebook App and Log In

If you use Facebook, you will likely want to access Facebook using your phone or tablet. You can access Facebook via Chrome or another web browser, but for a presentation tailored to your mobile device, you can install the Facebook app. After installing the Facebook app, you open the app and log in. The app then keeps you logged in so that you can easily get updates.

Install the Facebook App and Log In

1 Touch the **Home** button (⬠).

The Home screen appears.

2 Touch the **All Apps** button (⊞).

The Apps screen appears.

Note: If the Widgets tab is displayed on the Apps screen, touch the **Apps** tab.

Note: Look through the apps on the Apps screen to make sure Facebook is not already installed.

3 Touch **Play Store** (▷).

Note: If Play Store is not on the Apps screen that appears first, scroll left or right until you find Play Store.

The Google Play screen appears.

4 Touch **Apps**.

The Apps screen appears.

5 Touch the **Search** button (🔍).

The search box appears.

6 Type **facebook**.

A list of search results appears.

7 Touch the result with the Facebook logo.

The Facebook screen in the App Store appears.

8 Touch **Install**.

9 On the following screen, touch **Accept & download**.

10 Drag down to open the Notification shade.

11 Touch the **Facebook: Successfully installed** notification.

The Facebook login screen appears.

12 Type your e-mail address or phone number.

13 Type your password.

14 Touch **Log In**.

Facebook logs you in, and you can network.

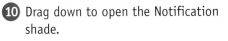

TIP

How do I log out of Facebook?

You do not need to log out. You can simply stay logged in so that you can quickly access your social network. However, if you decide to log out, touch the **Menu** button () to display the menu panel, and then touch **Log Out**. In the Log Out dialog box, touch **Confirm** (**A**).

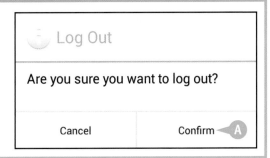

Navigate Facebook

After installing the Facebook app, you can open the app and use it for social networking. On your Facebook home page, you can see what is new in your social network and quickly access other pages. On these, you can take other actions, such as accepting or refusing friend requests, reading your messages, and reviewing your notifications. You can also easily post updates to let your friends know your news and submit friend requests to people with whom you want to become friends.

Navigate Facebook

1 Touch the **Home** button (▢).

The Home screen appears.

2 Touch the **All Apps** button (▦).

The Apps screen appears.

Note: If the Widgets tab is displayed on the Apps screen, touch the **Apps** tab.

3 Touch **Facebook**.

The Facebook app opens.

Your home page appears.

Ⓐ You can touch **Like** to like an item.

Ⓑ You can touch **Comment** to comment on an item.

4 Touch a person's name to display the person's profile.

Ⓒ You can touch **Message** to send a message to the person.

Ⓓ You can touch **About** to see more about the person.

5 Touch the **Friends Request** button (▦).

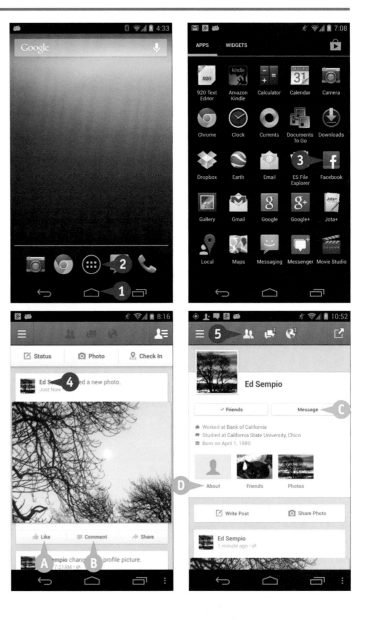

Your friend requests appear.

Ⓔ You can touch **Confirm** to confirm a friend.

Ⓕ You can touch **Not Now** to postpone the decision about a friend request.

⑥ Touch the **Messages** button (🖼).

Your messages appear.

Ⓖ You can touch the **Compose** button (📝) to write a new message.

⑦ Touch the **Notifications** button (🌐).

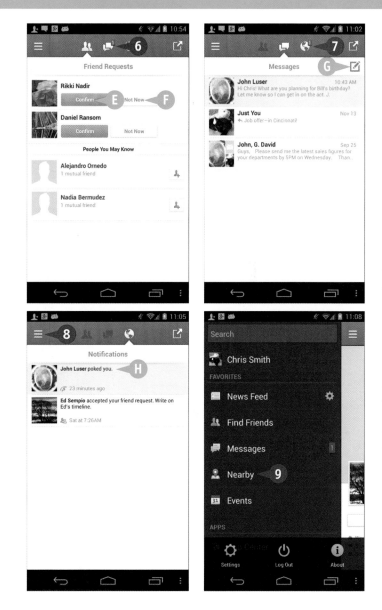

Your notifications appear.

Ⓗ You can touch a notification to open it. You can then take actions such as responding to a poke.

⑧ Touch the **Menu** button (☰) in the upper-left corner of the screen.

The menu panel appears.

⑨ Touch the area of Facebook you want to display.

TIP

How can I make the Facebook app work my way?

In the Facebook app, touch the **Menu** button (▤) to display the menu, and then touch **Settings** to display the Settings screen. Here you can choose General settings including your chat availability, the Facebook refresh interval, whether to give your location, and whether to sync photos. You can also choose a wide range of Notification settings, including whether your device vibrates or flashes its phone LED when you receive a notification.

Install the Twitter App and Log In

If you like tweeting on the Twitter microblogging service, reading other people's tweets, or both, you will likely want to install the Twitter app on your phone or tablet so you can enjoy Twitter anywhere. If you do not install the Twitter app, you can still use Twitter through the Chrome app or another web browser. In general, the Twitter app is easier and offers some extra features, such as switching easily among multiple Twitter accounts.

Install the Twitter App and Log In

1 Touch the **Home** button (⬛).

The Home screen appears.

2 Touch the **All Apps** button (▦).

The Apps screen appears.

Note: If the Widgets tab is displayed on the Apps screen, touch the **Apps** tab.

3 Touch **Play Store** (▷).

Note: If Play Store is not on the Apps screen that appears first, scroll left or right until you find Play Store.

The Google Play screen appears.

4 Touch **Apps**.

The Apps screen appears.

5 Touch the **Search** button (🔍).

The search box appears.

6 Type **twitter**.

A list of search results appears.

7 Touch the result with the Twitter logo.

The Twitter screen in the App Store appears.

8 Touch **Install**.

9 On the following screen, touch **Accept & download**.

10 Drag down to open the Notification shade.

11 Touch the **Twitter: Successfully installed** notification.

The Welcome to Twitter screen appears.

12 Touch **Sign In**.

Note: If you do not yet have a Twitter account, touch **Sign Up** and follow through the sign-up screens.

The Sign In screen appears.

13 Type your Twitter username or e-mail address.

14 Type your password.

15 Touch **Sign In**.

The Twitter app signs you into Twitter, and you can start using the service.

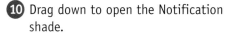

TIP

Should I allow Twitter to use my current location?
This is entirely your choice. By allowing Twitter to use your location, you can let your followers know exactly where you are tweeting from; this is sometimes helpful, but it can also be a security risk. You can also receive location-specific tweets, which are useful when you need information related to where you are.

Twitter would like to use your current location to customize your experience.

| Don't allow | OK |

Send Tweets

After you install the Twitter app, you can use it to send tweets from your phone or tablet. Your tweet can consist of nothing but text, but you can also add a new photo you take or an existing photo on your device. You can also add one or more hashtags, such as #animals or #cute, to help readers locate your tweets. In addition, you can add your location to your tweets when you want to share it with others.

Send Tweets

① Touch the **Home** button ().

The Home screen appears.

② Touch the **All Apps** button (⬚).

The Apps screen appears.

Note: If the Widgets tab is displayed on the Apps screen, touch the **Apps** tab.

③ Touch **Twitter** ().

Note: If Twitter is not on the Apps screen that appears first, scroll left or right until you find Twitter.

Your Twitter home screen appears, showing the latest posts from the people you are following.

④ Touch the **Compose** button (✎).

The dialog box for creating a tweet appears.

⑤ Type the text of your tweet.

Ⓐ The counter shows the number of characters left.

Note: You can take a photo with the Camera app and add it to your tweet. To do so, touch the **Camera** button (📷), and then take the photo.

⑥ To add a photo that is already on your phone or tablet, touch the **Photo** button (🖼).

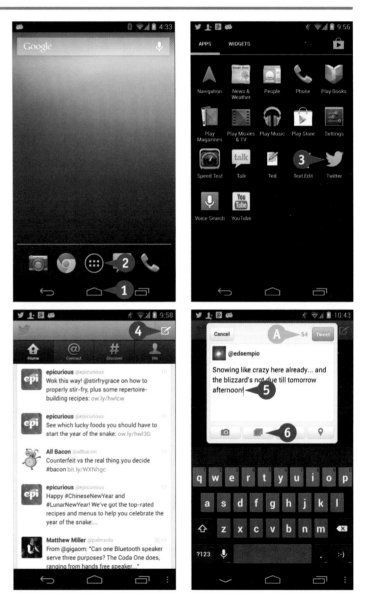

The Select photo screen appears.

7 Touch the album or collection that contains the photo you want to use. For example, touch Camera.

8 Touch the photo you want to use.

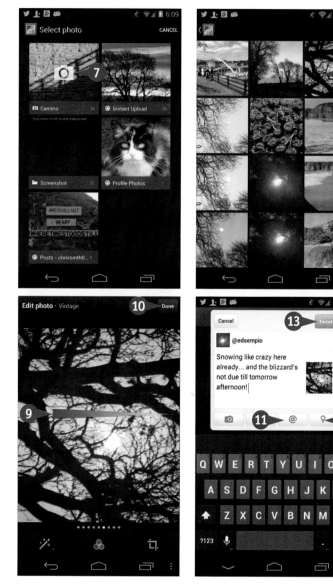

9 Swipe left one or more times to apply a different effect to the photo. Your choices include Black & white, Warm, and Gritty.

10 Touch **Done**.

The photo appears in your tweet.

11 To add a hashtag, touch the **Hashtag** button (@), and then type the text of the hashtag.

12 Touch the **Location** button (♀) (♀ changes to ♀) to add your location to the tweet.

13 Touch **Tweet** to post the tweet.

What do the three buttons at the bottom of the picture screen do?
Touch the **Effects** button (▨) to view thumbnails of the effects so you can compare them. Touch the **Enhance** button (▨) to enhance the photo's colors. Touch the **Crop** button (▣) to display the Move and Scale screen, and then crop the photo, as you want.

Is there another way to start a tweet?
Yes. You can also start a tweet from a photo. In the Gallery app, touch the photo you want to use, and then touch the **Share** button (◂). On the pop-up menu, touch **See all**, and then touch **Twitter** to start a tweet.

CHAPTER 8

Working with Apps

Apps are software that provide specific functionality to your phone or tablet. Android comes with some apps built in, and you can install further apps to make your device perform the tasks you need. You can download apps from Google's Play Store or other sources, run them as needed, and switch quickly among them. To keep apps running well, you can update them manually or automatically.

Run Apps and Switch Quickly among Them

When you need to use an app on your Android device, you run it. You can run any app from the Apps screen, but you can also put apps on the Home screen or on the Favorites bar so that you can run them directly from the Home screen. You can run multiple apps at once. Each app appears full screen, so you work in a single app at a time, but you can switch from one app to another as needed. You can switch apps quickly by using the Recent Apps list.

Run Apps and Switch Quickly among Them

Launch Multiple Apps

1 Touch the **Home** button (⬛).

The Home screen appears.

2 Touch the **All Apps** button (▦).

The Apps screen appears.

Note: If the Widgets tab is displayed on the Apps screen, touch the **Apps** tab.

Note: If necessary, swipe left to display more apps.

3 Touch the first app you want to launch.

The app opens.

4 Touch the **Home** button (⬛).

The Home screen appears.

5 Touch the **All Apps** button (▦).

The Apps screen appears.

Note: If necessary, swipe left to display more apps.

6 Touch the second app you want to launch.

The app opens.

Switch Quickly among Running Apps

1 From a running app, touch the **Recent Apps** button ( ).

Note: You can also display the Recent Apps list by touching the **Recent Apps** button ( ) from the Home screen.

The Recent Apps list appears.

The apps at the bottom of the list are the ones you have used most recently.

2 If necessary, scroll up to reach other apps.

3 Touch the app you want to display.

The app's screen appears, and you can start using the app.

TIP

Can I do anything else from the Recent Apps list?

You can also display an app's information or remove the app from the Recent Apps list. To display the app's information, touch and hold its icon in the Recent Apps list, then touch **App info**. To remove an app, either drag it left or right off the list, or touch and hold, and then touch **Remove from list**.

Explore Google Play

Your Android phone or tablet includes apps you can use for everyday tasks. For example, you can surf the web using the Chrome app, send and receive e-mail messages on Google's Gmail service using the Gmail app, and keep your schedule using the Calendar app. When you need to perform tasks that your existing apps do not cover, you can add other apps. To get apps, you can run the Play Store app, which gives you access to the Google Play service. The Google Play service contains apps that Google has approved for use on Android devices.

Explore Google Play

1 Touch the **Home** button (▱).

The Home screen appears.

2 Touch the **All Apps** button (▦).

The Apps screen appears.

Note: If the Widgets tab is displayed on the Apps screen, touch the **Apps** tab.

3 Touch **Play Store** (▣).

Note: If the Play Store icon does not appear on the first Apps screen, swipe left to display the next Apps screen.

The Play Store app opens and displays the Google Play screen.

4 Touch **Apps**.

The Apps screen appears, showing the Featured list.

Ⓐ Touch **Staff Picks** to see apps recommended by the Google Play staff.

Ⓑ Touch **Editors' Choices** to see apps selected by the Google Play editors.

Ⓒ Touch **Games** to display the Games screen.

Ⓓ Touch the **Back** button (◁) to return from any of the above screens to the Apps screen.

5 To browse Google Play by categories, touch **Categories** or swipe right.

The Categories screen appears.

6 Touch the category you want to browse, for example, touch Business.

The category's screen appears.

7 Touch the **Play Store** button (⊡) or touch the **Back** button (⬅) to return to the Categories screen.

8 Swipe left twice.

The Top Paid screen appears, showing the top apps for which people pay.

9 Swipe left once more.

The Top Free screen appears, showing the top free apps.

Note: Swipe left again to reach other screens: Top Grossing, Top New Paid, Top New Free, and Trending. Swipe right to go back to the other screens.

TIP

How can I see which apps I have previously bought on Google Play?
From the Google Play screen or anywhere in the Apps screens, touch the **Menu** button (▤) and then touch **My Apps**. The My Apps screen appears, showing your Installed list first. From here, you can quickly get any available updates for your apps.

Find the Apps You Need on Google Play

Browsing the Google Play service is a good way to get an idea of the many types of apps available for your Android device. However, when you need to find a particular app, you can search Google Play instead. Searching returns a list of matches that you can explore in detail. When you find an app you want, you can download and install it. As part of the installation process, you can review the permissions the app requires on your phone or tablet. If you are prepared to grant these permissions, you can complete the installation; if not, you can cancel it.

Find the Apps You Need on Google Play

1 Touch the **Home** button (▬).

The Home screen appears.

2 Touch the **All Apps** button (▦).

The Apps screen appears.

Note: If the Widgets tab is displayed on the Apps screen, touch the **Apps** tab.

3 Touch **Play Store** (▷).

Note: If the Play Store icon does not appear on the first Apps screen, swipe left to display the next Apps screen.

The Play Store app opens and displays the Google Play screen.

4 Touch **Apps**.

The Apps screen appears, showing the Featured list.

5 Touch the **Search** button (🔍).

The Search box appears.

A The pop-up menu shows your recent searches, if any.

Note: You can also speak your search terms. Touch the **microphone** button (🎤) and then speak the terms when the "Speak now" prompt appears.

6 Type your search terms.

B The pop-up menu displays suggestions. If one of them is what you want, touch it. Otherwise, finish typing your search terms.

7 Touch the **Search** button (🔍).

A screen of search results appears.

8 Touch the result you want to view.

The app's screen appears.

9 Touch the **Play** button (▶) to view the video of the app.

10 Read the description and, below it, the user reviews.

11 If you want to install the app, touch **Install**.

You can proceed with reading and accepting the permissions and then downloading the app. You can then launch the app from the Apps screen.

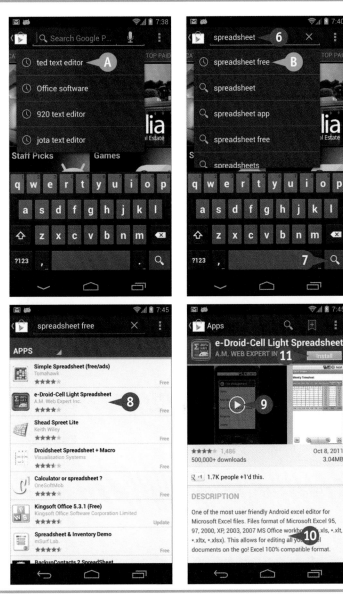

TIP

What permissions should I accept for an app?
You must decide depending on what the app does. For example, an app that creates files needs the Modify or delete the contents of your USB storage permission; an app that can open e-mail attachments needs the Read email attachments permission. However, you should be suspicious of any app that wants to access sensitive data such as your contacts but does not have a good reason to do so.

Update Your Apps

Android developers often update their apps to remove bugs and to add new features. To keep your apps running well, you should install app updates when they become available. Most updates for paid apps are free, but you must usually pay to upgrade to a new version of the app. You can update all your apps at once or update a single app at a time. Normally, updating all your apps is most convenient, but you may sometimes need to update a single app without downloading all available updates.

Update Your Apps

1 Touch the **Home** button (⬭).

The Home screen appears.

2 Touch the **All Apps** button (▦).

The Apps screen appears.

Note: If the Widgets tab is displayed on the Apps screen, touch the **Apps** tab.

3 Touch **Play Store**.

Note: If the Play Store icon does not appear on the first Apps screen, swipe left to display the next Apps screen.

The Play Store app opens and displays the Google Play screen.

4 Touch **Apps**.

The Apps screen appears.

Note: If the Widgets tab is displayed on the Apps screen, touch the **Apps** tab.

5 Touch the **Menu** button (▤).

The menu opens.

 Touch **My Apps**.

The My Apps screen appears.

Note: If the My Apps screen does not show the Installed list at first, swipe right or touch **Installed** to display the Installed list.

7 Touch the **Update** button. This button shows the Update icon (FPO) and the number of updates — for example, FPO Update 18.

Android downloads the updates and installs them.

A The Update Installed icon (📲) indicates that an update has been installed.

8 If the Manual updates list appears, touch an app's button, and then touch **Update** on the app's screen.

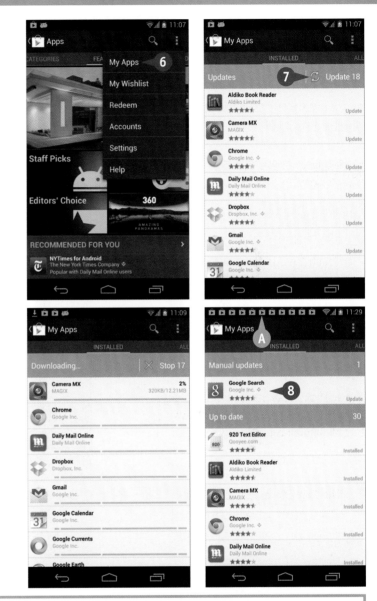

TIP

How do I update a single app?
Display the Installed list by following steps **1** to **6** in the main text. Touch the app's button to display the screen for the app, then touch **Update** (**A**).

Remove an App You No Longer Need

Each app you install takes up some of your device's storage space and appears on the Apps screen. When you no longer need an app you have installed, you can remove it from your device. The app remains available to you on Google Play, so you can easily reinstall it if you change your mind. You can remove an app either by using the Apps screen or by using the App info screen for the app, whichever you find easier. You cannot remove the apps that come built in to Android, only the apps you have installed.

Remove an App You No Longer Need

Remove an App by Using the Apps Screen

1 Touch the **Home** button (⬒).

The Home screen appears.

2 Touch the **All Apps** button (▦).

The Apps screen appears.

Note: If the Widgets tab is displayed on the Apps screen, touch the **Apps** tab.

3 Touch and hold the icon for the app you want to remove.

The Home screen appears.

Ⓐ The app icon you are holding appears in the main part of the screen.

Ⓑ The Uninstall button and the App info icon appear at the top of the screen.

4 Drag the app to the Uninstall button.

Ⓒ The app icon and the Uninstall button turn red.

5 Release the app icon.

A confirmation dialog box appears.

6 Touch **OK**.

Android removes the app.

Remove an App by Using Its App Info Screen

1 Touch the **Home** button ().

The Home screen appears.

2 Touch the **All Apps** button (▦).

The Apps screen appears.

Note: If the Widgets tab is displayed on the Apps screen, touch the **Apps** tab.

3 Touch **Play Store**.

Note: If the Play Store icon does not appear on the first Apps screen, swipe left to display the next Apps screen.

The Play Store app opens and displays the Google Play screen.

4 Touch the **Menu** button (▐).

The menu opens.

5 Touch **My Apps**.

The My Apps screen appears.

6 Touch the app you want to remove.

The app's screen appears.

7 Touch **Uninstall**.

A confirmation dialog box appears.

8 Touch **OK**.

Android removes the app.

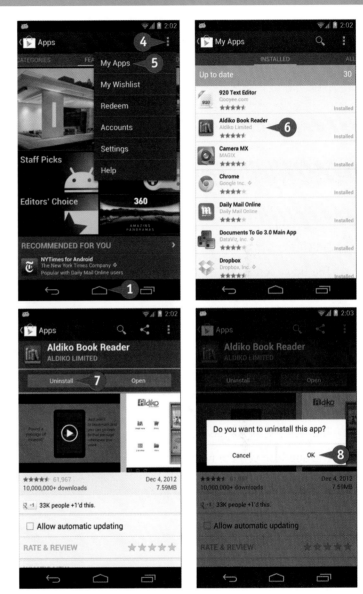

TIP

How do I reinstall an app I have removed?

You can easily reinstall an app by using the My Apps list on the Play Store. Touch the **Home** button () to display the Home screen, then touch the **All Apps** button (▦) to display the Apps screen. Touch **Play Store**, touch the **Menu** button (▐), and then touch **My Apps**. Touch **All** or swipe left to display the All list, then touch the app. On the app's screen, touch **Install**.

Choose Which Apps to Update Automatically

Keeping your Android apps up to date enables you to take advantage of bug fixes and new features that developers add to the apps. You can easily apply updates manually, but you can also set your phone or tablet to update its apps automatically. You can choose to update all apps or just some apps automatically. Automatic updates can be very helpful, but they may involve transferring large amounts of data. To prevent automatic updates from consuming your cellular data plan, you can set your phone or cellular-capable tablet to download updates only when it is connected to a Wi-Fi network.

Choose Which Apps to Update Automatically

Open the My Apps Screen in the Play Store

 Touch the **Home** button (▬).

The Home screen appears.

 Touch the **All Apps** button (▦).

The Apps screen appears.

Note: If the Widgets tab is displayed on the Apps screen, touch the **Apps** tab.

 Touch **Play Store**.

Note: If the Play Store icon does not appear on the first Apps screen, swipe left to display the next Apps screen.

The Play Store app opens and displays the Google Play screen.

 Touch the **Menu** button (▤).

The menu opens.

 Touch **My Apps**.

The My Apps screen appears.

Set All Your Apps to Update Automatically

1 On the My Apps screen, touch the **Menu** button (⁝).

2 Touch **Settings**.

The Settings screen appears.

3 Touch **Auto-update apps** (■ changes to ✅).

4 On a phone or cellular-capable tablet, select **Update over Wi-Fi only** (■ changes to ✅) if you want to update apps only over Wi-Fi connections.

5 Touch the **Play Store** button (▶).

The My Apps screen appears.

Control Automatic Updates for an Individual App

1 On the My Apps screen, touch the app you want to affect.

The App info screen for the app opens.

2 Touch **Allow automatic updating** to select (✅) or deselect (■).

3 Touch the **Play Store** button (▶).

The My Apps screen appears, and you can set automatic updating for other apps.

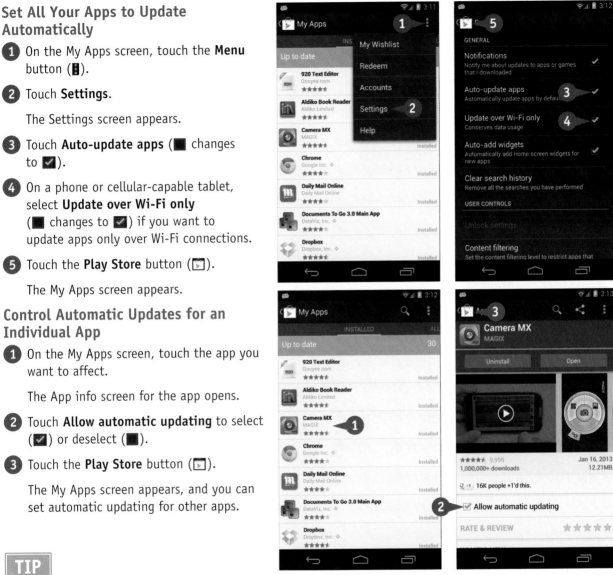

TIP

Is there a quicker way to reach the App info screen?
If an app is running, you can display its App info screen like this: Touch the **Recent Apps** button (▭) (**A**) to display the Recent Apps list, then touch and hold the appropriate app (**B**). When the pop-up menu appears, touch **App info** (**C**).

Manually Install an App

The normal way to install an app on your Android phone or tablet is by downloading it from the Google Play service using the Play Store app. But you can also load an app onto your device manually by using a technique called *sideloading*. In sideloading, you acquire a package file containing the app you want to install. You then transfer the package file to your phone or tablet, enable installation of apps from unknown sources, and install the app.

Understanding What Manual Installation Is Useful For

Sideloading is primarily useful for installing apps that are not available on Google Play. For example, you may need to sideload an app that your company or organization provides. Sideloading can also be useful for installing an app that is available for other Android devices but not for your phone or tablet. Be aware that apps you download from sources other than Google Play may contain malevolent code. It is wise to search the web for reviews of an app before installing it.

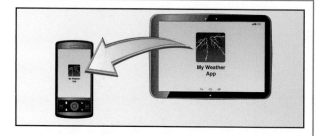

Install an App You Can Use to Sideload

By sideloading an app, you can add functionality to your Android device. The sideloading process requires a file-management app on your Android device. You use this app to install the app you are sideloading. To get your device ready to sideload an app, open the Play Store app and install a file-management app from Google Play. Two good choices are ES File Explorer, shown here, and Astro File Manager. Both these apps are free and are easy to use.

Get the App Package File You Need

You can find many apps for sideloading on your Android device to add functionality. Each app comes in a distribution file called a *package file* from which you install the app. You can acquire a package file in several ways. If you already have the app on another phone or tablet, use a file-management app such as ES File Explorer or Astro File Manager to copy the file to a backup, creating a package file. For an app provided by your company or organization, download the package file from the company's or organization's site. For other apps, download the package file from an online repository, but be wary of malevolent software.

Transfer the Package File to Your Phone or Tablet

After acquiring the package file for the app you want to sideload, you need to transfer the file to your phone or tablet. You can transfer the file in several ways. If the package file is on your computer, use a tool such as Windows Explorer or Android File Transfer to copy or move the file. Otherwise, use an online storage service such as Dropbox. If the package file is small, you can also use e-mail.

Enable Installation of Apps from Unknown Sources

By default, Android does not permit you to install apps from sources other than Google Play. Therefore, before you can install the app on your phone or tablet, you must set Android to allow the installation of apps from unknown sources. Touch the Home button (⬛) to display the Home screen, touch the All Apps button (⬛) to display the Apps screen, and then touch Settings (⬛). On the Settings screen, touch Security, then select Unknown sources (⬛ changes to ✓). In the warning dialog box that opens, touch OK.

Manually Install the App

After copying the package file to your Android device and setting Android to allow the installation of apps from unknown sources, you can manually install the app. Open the file-management app on your phone or tablet, and then touch the package file. When the screen listing the permissions appears, read the permissions carefully before you decide to complete the installation. After you install the app, you can run it from the Apps screen like any other app.

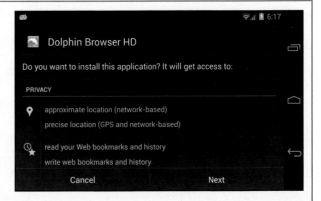

CHAPTER 9

Browsing the Web and E-Mailing

Your Android phone or tablet is fully equipped to browse the web and to send e-mail via either a Wi-Fi connection or a cellular network.

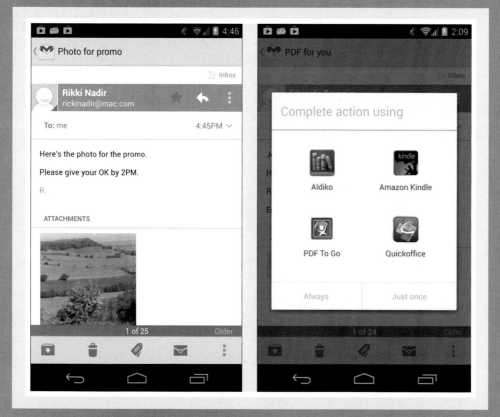

Browse the Web

Your phone or tablet comes equipped with the Chrome app, which you use for browsing the web. The first time you run Chrome, the app displays an introductory screen. Thereafter, Chrome displays the last web page you visited. You can go quickly to a web page by entering its address in the Chrome omnibox or by following a link from another page. Although you can browse quickly by opening a single web page at a time, you may prefer to open multiple pages in separate tabs and switch back and forth among them.

Browse the Web

Open Chrome and Navigate to Web Pages

1 Touch the **Home** button (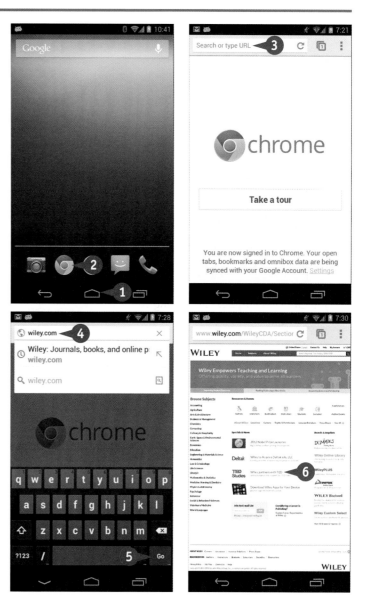).

The Home screen appears.

2 Touch the **Chrome** icon (◉).

Note: If ◉ does not appear in the Favorites tray, touch the **All Apps** button (▦) and then touch **Chrome**.

Chrome opens.

3 Touch the omnibox. This is a combined address box and search box.

The omnibox expands, and the keyboard appears.

4 Type the address of the page you want to open.

5 Touch **Go**.

Chrome displays the page.

6 Touch a link on the page.

Chrome displays that page.

Note: After going to a new page, touch the **Menu** button (⋮) and then touch the **Back** button (←) to go back to the previous page. You can then touch the **Forward** button (→) to go forward again to the page you just went back from.

184

Open Multiple Web Pages and Switch Among Them

1 Touch the **Pages** button ().

Chrome displays the New tab button.

2 Touch **New tab**.

Chrome displays the Most visited screen.

3 Touch the omnibox, and then go to the page you want. For example, type the address and touch Go.

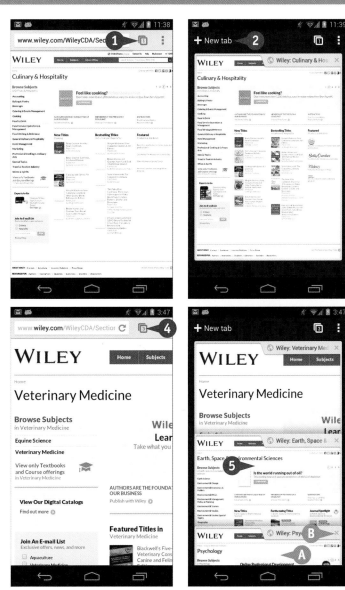

The page appears.

4 To switch to another page, touch the **Pages** button ().

The list of open pages appears.

Ⓐ You can drag up or down to see more of a page before opening it.

Ⓑ You can touch ✕ to close a page, or you can close a page by swiping it left or right.

5 Touch the page you want to display.

Chrome displays the page.

What is the Microphone icon in the Chrome omnibox for?

The Microphone icon (🎤) is for searching by voice. Touch the omnibox to select it. If the omnibox contains an address, touch ✕ to delete it. Then touch the **Microphone** icon (🎤) and say your search terms when the "Speak now" prompt appears.

How do I get the full version of a web page rather than the mobile version?

To acquire the regular version of the web page, touch the **Menu** button (⋮) and then touch the **Request desktop site** check box (☐ changes to ☑). Some sites are programmed to prevent mobiles requesting the desktop versions.

Use Bookmarks, Most Visited, and Other Devices

Typing web addresses can be laborious, so Chrome provides features for reducing the number of addresses you need to enter. Chrome for Android can automatically sync your bookmarks, most-visited sites, and open tabs from Chrome on your computer or other devices via your Google Account, giving your phone or tablet quick access to the same web pages and sites. You can also create bookmarks on your phone or tablet and have Chrome sync them back to your computer.

Use Bookmarks, Most Visited, and Other Devices

Open the Bookmarks Screen

1 Touch the **Home** button (⬛).

The Home screen appears.

2 Touch the **Chrome** icon (🔵).

Chrome opens.

3 Touch the **Menu** button (⋮).

The menu opens.

4 Touch **Bookmarks**.

The Bookmarks screen appears, showing the Mobile Bookmarks folder by default.

Open a Bookmarked Web Page

1 If necessary, navigate to another bookmarks folder by touching **Bookmarks** and then touching the folder.

2 Touch the bookmark.

The web page opens.

Open a Web Page from the Most Visited List

1 On the Bookmarks screen, touch the **Most Visited** button (▦) or **Most visited**.

The Most Visited screen appears.

2 Touch the web page you want to open.

The web page opens.

Open a Web Page from the Other Devices List

1 Touch the **Menu** button (⋮).

The menu opens.

2 Touch **Other devices**.

The Other devices screen appears.

3 If the list you want to use is collapsed to its heading, touch the **Expand List** button (>) to expand it (∨ changes to >).

4 Touch the web page you want to open.

The web page opens.

TIP

How do I make Chrome on my computer sync my data?

Chrome on Windows or OS X automatically syncs your data with your Google Account as long as you are signed in to Chrome. To check whether you are signed in, click the Chrome menu (≡). If "Signed in as" followed by your account name appears on the menu, you are signed in. Otherwise, click **Sign in to Chrome** and provide your Google Account username and password.

Create Bookmarks for Web Pages

While browsing the web on your phone or tablet, you will likely find web pages you want to access again. To access such a web page easily, create a bookmark for it. Chrome automatically makes your bookmarks available to other computers and devices that sign in using the same Google Account, so you can easily access your bookmarked pages on your computer and other devices as well.

Create Bookmarks for Web Pages

Create a Bookmark on Your Phone or Tablet

1. Touch the **Home** button (◻).

2. Touch the **Chrome** (◎) icon.

3. Navigate to the web page you want to bookmark.

4. Touch the **Menu** button (⋮).

   Note: On a tablet, touch the **Favorites** button (☆) at the right end of the Chrome omnibox to open the Add Bookmark screen.

5. Touch the **Bookmark** button (☆).

   The Add Bookmark screen appears.

6. Edit the name as needed.

7. If necessary, edit the address.

Ⓐ If the In box shows the folder in which you want to store the bookmark, touch **Save** and skip the rest of this task.

8. Touch the appropriate folder in the In box.

Ⓑ To use an existing folder, touch it (✓ changes to ✔).

9. To create a new folder, touch **New Folder**.

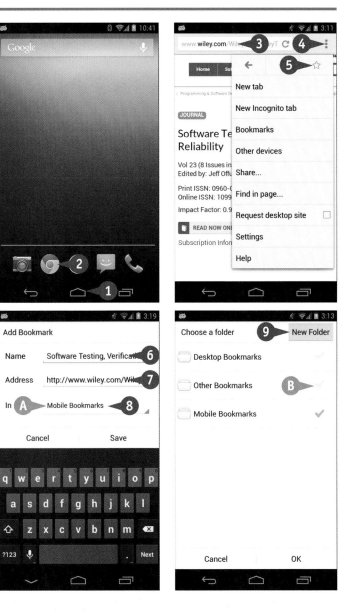

The Add Folder screen appears.

10 Touch **Name**.

The on-screen keyboard appears.

11 Type the name for the folder.

12 Touch the contents of the In box and then touch the folder in which you want to create the new folder.

13 Touch **Save**.

The Choose a folder screen appears.

14 Touch **OK**.

The Add Bookmark screen appears.

15 Touch **Save**.

Chrome creates the bookmark.

The web page appears again.

TIP

How do I delete a bookmark?

Touch the **Menu** button (⋮) to open the menu, and then touch **Bookmarks** to display the Bookmarks screen. Touch and hold the bookmark you want to delete. When the menu appears, touch **Delete bookmark** (**Ⓐ**).

Configure Your Default Search Engine

To find information with Chrome, you often need to search using a search engine. Chrome's default search engine is Google, but you can change to another search engine. Your choices are Google, Yahoo!, and Bing. Google, Yahoo!, and Bing compete directly with one another and return similar results to many searches. However, if you experiment with the three search engines, you will gradually discover which one suits you best.

Configure Your Default Search Engine

1 Touch the **Home** button (⬠).

The Home screen appears.

2 Touch the **Chrome** icon (◉).

Chrome opens.

3 Touch the **Menu** button (⁝).

The menu opens.

4 Touch **Settings**.

The Settings screen appears.

5 Touch **Search engine**.

The Search engine screen appears.

6 Touch the search engine you want to use.

"Currently selected search engine" appears under the search engine you touch.

7 Touch the **Chrome** button (🌐).

The Settings screen appears.

8 Touch the **Chrome** button (🌐).

The web page you were previously viewing appears, and you can continue browsing.

How can I search using a search engine other than Google, Yahoo!, or Bing?
You can search using any search engine you can find on the web. Open a web page to the search engine, and then perform the search using the tools on the page. At this writing, you cannot set any search engine other than Google, Yahoo!, or Bing as the default search engine on an Android device. However, you can easily add the site to your Bookmarks list, and if you use it frequently, it will appear on your Most visited list.

Fill in Forms Using Autofill

I f you fill in forms using your phone or tablet, you can save time by enabling the Autofill feature. Autofill can automatically fill in standard form fields, such as name and address fields, using the information from one or more profiles you enter. Autofill can also automatically store other data you enter in fields, and can store credit-card details to enter them for you automatically. For security, you may prefer not to store your credit-card information in Autofill — but if you do, it can save you time and effort.

Fill in Forms Using Autofill

1 Touch the **Home** button (▭).

The Home screen appears.

2 Touch the **Chrome** icon (◉).

Chrome opens.

3 Touch the **Menu** button (⁝).

The menu opens.

4 Touch **Settings**.

The Settings screen appears.

5 Touch **Autofill forms**.

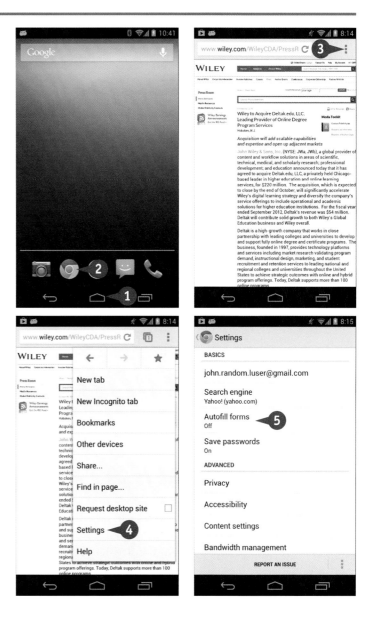

The Autofill forms screen appears.

6 Touch the **Autofill** switch to set it to On if it is Off.

7 Touch **Add profile**.

The Add profile screen appears.

8 Type your name and address details.

9 Touch **Next** to move to the next field.

10 Type your data in the remaining fields.

11 Touch **Save**.

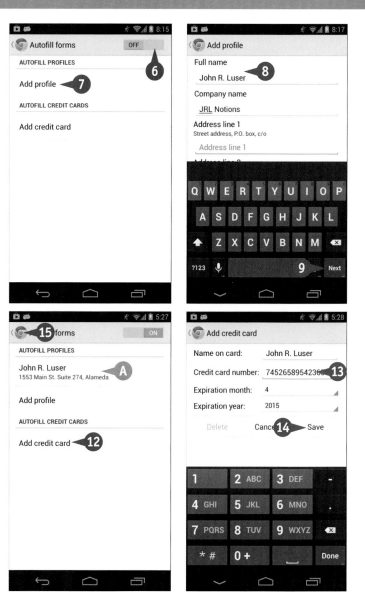

The Autofill forms screen appears.

A The profile you just added appears in the Autofill profiles list.

12 Touch **Add credit card**.

The Add credit card screen appears.

13 Touch each field in turn and enter your details.

14 Touch **Save**.

The Autofill forms screen reappears.

15 Touch the **Chrome** button (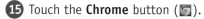).

The Settings screen appears.

16 Touch the **Chrome** button ().

The web page you were viewing before appears.

TIP

How else can Chrome save me time filling in my details on the web?
Chrome can also store your passwords and enter them for you. This feature can save you plenty of complex typing, especially if you use strong and convoluted passwords. To store passwords, touch the **Menu** button (⋮), and then touch **Settings**. On the Settings screen, touch **Save passwords** to display the Save passwords screen, and then touch the **Save passwords** switch to set it to the On position.

Tighten Up Your Browsing Privacy Settings

Along with its many sites that provide useful information or services, the web contains sites that try to infect computers with malevolent software, or *malware*, or lure visitors into providing sensitive personal or financial information. Although Google has built Android to be as secure as possible, it is wise to choose high-security settings. This task shows you how to choose privacy settings, disable JavaScript, and block pop-ups and cookies.

Tighten Up Your Browsing Privacy Settings

1 Touch the **Home** button (⬛).

The Home screen appears.

2 Touch the **Chrome** icon (◉).

Chrome opens.

3 Touch the **Menu** button (⋮).

The menu opens.

4 Touch **Settings**.

The Settings screen appears.

5 Touch **Privacy**.

The Privacy screen appears.

6 Touch the **Navigation error suggestions** check box to select (☑) or deselect (☐) the option.

7 Touch the **Search and URL suggestions** check box to select (☑) or deselect (☐) the option.

8 Touch the **Network action predictions** check box to select (☑) or deselect (☐) the option.

Note: The Navigation error suggestions feature and Search and URL suggestions feature are usually helpful, but they may occasionally display surprising or unsuitable suggestions.

9 Touch **Usage and crash reports**.

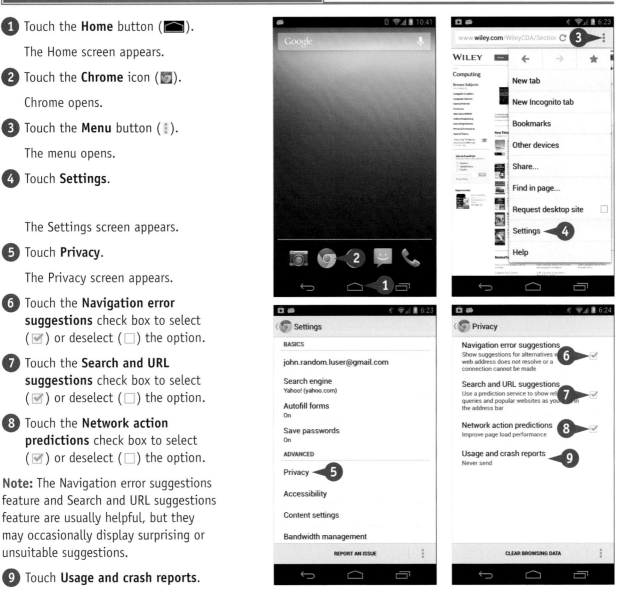

10 In the Usage and crash reports dialog box, touch a check box (○ changes to ◉) to select an option.

11 Touch **Clear Browsing Data** to clear your browsing data,

12 Touch each item you want to clear (□ changes to ☑) in the Clear browsing data dialog box.

13 Touch **Clear**.

14 Touch the **Chrome** button (🔘).

15 On the Settings screen, touch **Content settings**.

16 On the Content settings screen, touch the **Accept cookies** check box to select (☑) or deselect (□) the option.

17 Touch the **Enable JavaScript** check box.

18 Touch the **Block pop-ups** check box.

19 Touch **Google location settings**.

20 Touch the **Let Google apps access your location** switch to set it to On or Off.

21 Touch the **Google** button (🔲).

22 Touch the **Chrome** buttons (🔘) until the last web page you were viewing appears.

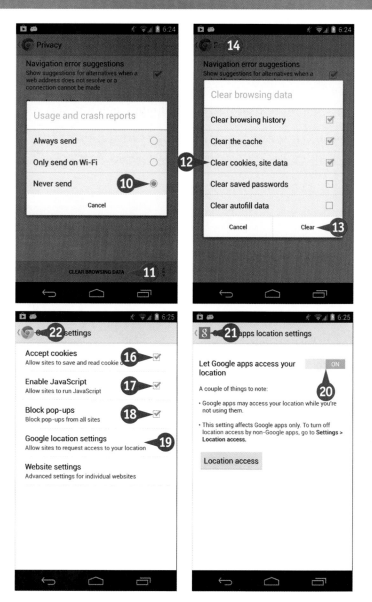

TIP

What are cookies and what threat do they pose?
A cookie is a small text file that a website places on a computer to identify that computer in the future. This is helpful for many sites, such as shopping sites in which you add items to a shopping cart, but when used by malevolent sites, cookies can pose a threat to your privacy. You can set Chrome to refuse cookies, but this prevents many legitimate websites from working properly. Normally it is best to set Chrome to accept cookies.

Read Your E-Mail Messages

A fter you enter the details of your Gmail account, either when first setting up your phone or tablet or subsequently, you are ready to send and receive e-mail messages. You can easily read your incoming e-mail messages, reply to messages you have received, and write new messages as needed. Android devices come with two built-in apps for e-mail: Gmail for use with Google Accounts, and Email for use with other e-mail providers. This chapter shows you how to use Gmail, but the Email app works in a similar way.

Read Your E-Mail Messages

1 Touch the **Home** button ().

The Home screen appears.

2 Touch the **All Apps** button ( ).

The Apps screen appears.

3 Touch **Gmail** ( ).

Note: If Gmail is not on the Apps screen that appears first, scroll left or right until you find Gmail.

Gmail opens, and your Inbox appears.

Ⓐ Each message appears with the sender's name followed by a two-line preview showing the subject line and the first part of the message.

Ⓑ The sender and subject of unread messages appear in boldface on a white background.

Ⓒ Read messages appear on a light-gray background.

Ⓓ This number indicates how many unread messages you have.

4 Touch the message you want to open.

Ⓔ You can touch the **Delete** button ( ) if you want to delete the message.

5 When you want to display the next message, swipe left.

The next message appears.

6 If the message is too wide for the screen, and your device supports landscape orientation, rotate the device to landscape orientation.

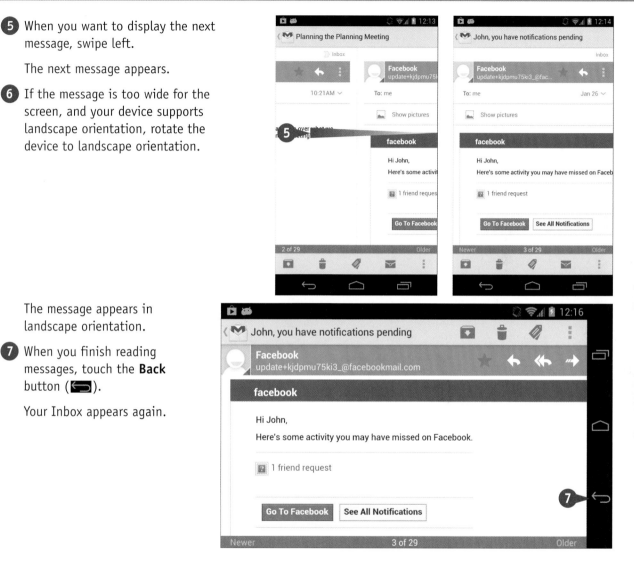

The message appears in landscape orientation.

7 When you finish reading messages, touch the **Back** button (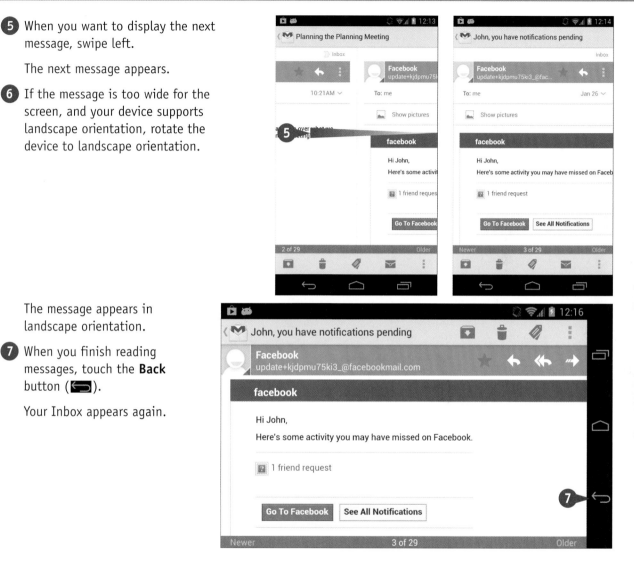).

Your Inbox appears again.

Reply to or Forward an E-Mail Message

After receiving an e-mail message, you often need to reply to it. You can choose to reply only to the sender of the message, or to reply to the sender and all the other recipients in the To field and the Cc field. Your e-mail app adds Re: to the beginning of the subject line to indicate that the message is a reply. Other times, you may need to forward a message you have received to one or more other people. In this case, your e-mail app adds Fwd: to the beginning of the subject line to indicate that the message has been forwarded

Reply to or Forward an E-Mail Message

3 Touch the **Home** button (⬒).

The Home screen appears.

 Touch the **All Apps** button (▦).

The Apps screen appears.

Note: If the Widgets tab is displayed on the Apps screen, touch the **Apps** tab.

 Touch **Gmail** (✉).

Note: If Gmail is not on the Apps screen that appears first, scroll left or right until you find Gmail.

Gmail opens, and your Inbox appears.

Note: If Gmail displays a mailbox other than your Inbox, touch the **Mailbox** pop-up menu and then touch **Inbox**.

4 Touch the message you want to open.

The message opens.

198

Reply to the Message

1 In the open message, touch the **Reply** button (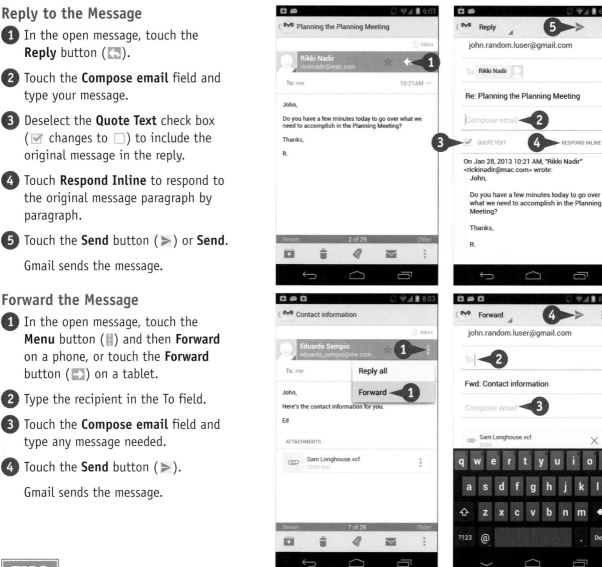).

2 Touch the **Compose email** field and type your message.

3 Deselect the **Quote Text** check box (☑ changes to ☐) to include the original message in the reply.

4 Touch **Respond Inline** to respond to the original message paragraph by paragraph.

5 Touch the **Send** button (➤) or **Send**.

Gmail sends the message.

Forward the Message

1 In the open message, touch the **Menu** button (▮) and then **Forward** on a phone, or touch the **Forward** button (➡) on a tablet.

2 Type the recipient in the To field.

3 Touch the **Compose email** field and type any message needed.

4 Touch the **Send** button (➤).

Gmail sends the message.

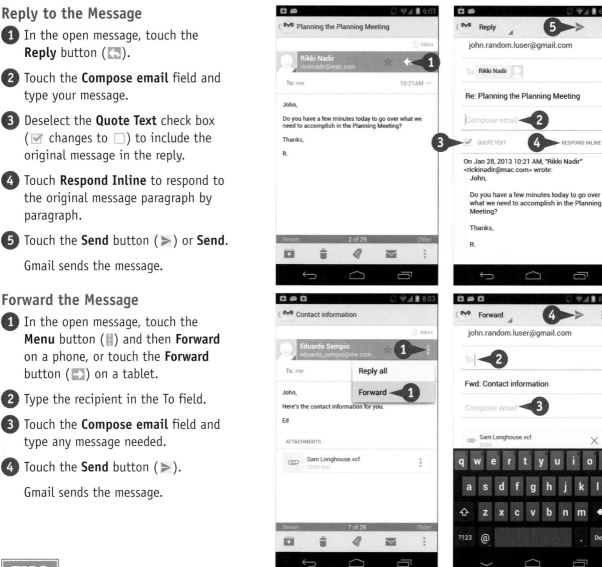

TIPS

What is the point of the Respond Inline feature?
Responding inline is useful when you need to answer an e-mail message one point at a time. When you touch **Respond Inline**, Gmail sets up the reply so that you can edit the original message and add the paragraphs of your reply between the paragraphs of the original for clarity.

How do I reply to all the recipients of a message?
When you need to reply to all recipients of the message, touch the **Menu** button (▮) and **Reply All** on a phone. On a tablet, touch the **Reply All** button (◀◀). You can then compose the reply and touch the **Send** button (➤) to send it.

Label and Archive Your Messages

To keep your Inbox under control, you should archive each message you no longer need in the Inbox and delete any message you do not need to keep. Before archiving a message, you can apply one or more labels to it. Labels help you categorize messages so that you can find them later. You can label, archive, or delete a single message at a time, or you can select multiple messages in your Inbox and label, archive, or delete them all at once.

Label and Archive Your Messages

Open Gmail

1 Touch the **Home** button (■).

The Home screen appears.

2 Touch the **All Apps** button (▦).

The Apps screen appears.

3 Touch **Gmail** (✉).

Note: If Gmail is not on the Apps screen that appears, scroll left or right until you find Gmail.

Gmail opens, and your Inbox appears.

Note: If Gmail displays a mailbox other than your Inbox, touch the **Mailbox** pop-up menu and then touch **Inbox**.

Select Messages, Label Them, and Archive Them

1 Touch the check box to the left of a message (☐ changes to ☑).

Ⓐ The selection bar appears.

2 Touch the check box for each message you want to label or archive (☐ changes to ☑).

Ⓑ The readout shows how many messages you have selected.

3 Touch the **Label** button (🏷).

200

The Change labels dialog box opens.

4 Touch the check box for each label you want to apply (☐ changes to ☑).

5 Touch **OK**.

The Change labels dialog box closes.

C The label or labels you selected appear on the messages.

6 Touch the check box to the left of each message you want to archive (☐ changes to ☑).

7 Touch the **Archive** button (■).

Gmail archives the messages and removes them from the Inbox.

D You can touch **Undo** to undo the archiving.

TIPS

How do I file my messages in folders?
Gmail uses labels instead of folders. Therefore, instead of moving a message to a folder, you apply one or more labels to it, and then archive it. To retrieve the message, you use the label or labels rather than opening the folder as you would in most other e-mail systems.

How can I create new labels for marking my messages?
At this writing, you cannot create new labels directly in the Gmail app. Instead, open Chrome or another browser, log in to your Gmail account, and create the new labels from there.

Write and Send E-Mail Messages

Your phone or tablet is great for reading and replying to e-mail messages you receive, but you will likely also need to write new messages. When you do, you can use the data in the People app to address your outgoing messages quickly and accurately. If the recipient's address is not one of your contacts, you can type the address manually. You can attach one or more files to an e-mail message to send those files to the recipient. This works well for small files, but many mail servers reject files larger than several megabytes in size.

Write and Send E-Mail Messages

1 Touch the **Home** button ().

The Home screen appears.

2 Touch the **All Apps** button (▦).

The Apps screen appears.

Note: If the Widgets tab is displayed on the Apps screen, touch the **Apps** tab.

3 Touch **Gmail** (✉).

Note: If Gmail is not on the Apps screen that appears first, scroll left or right until you find Gmail.

Gmail opens, and your Inbox appears.

Note: If Gmail displays a mailbox other than your Inbox, touch the **Mailbox** pop-up menu then touch **Inbox**.

4 Touch the **Compose** button (✉).

The Compose screen appears, with the insertion point in the To field.

5 Start typing the recipient's name or address.

A pop-up menu displays possible matches from your contacts in the People app.

6 Touch the recipient to whom you want to send the message.

202

The recipient's name appears as a button in the To box.

Note: You can add another recipient by starting to type his or her name or address.

7 To add Cc or Bcc recipients, follow these substeps on a phone:

Ⓐ Touch the **Menu** button (⋮).

Ⓑ Touch **Add Cc/Bcc**, or on a tablet, touch **+CC/BCC**.

Note: On a tablet, touch the +CC/BCC button to reveal the Cc and Bcc fields.

Ⓒ Begin typing the recipient's name.

Ⓓ Touch the correct entry on the pop-up menu.

8 Touch the **Subject** field and type the subject for the message.

9 Touch the **Compose email** field and type the body of the message.

Note: You can also touch the **Microphone** button (🎤) and dictate the contents of the message.

10 Touch the **Send** button (➤).

Gmail sends the message.

TIP

How do I attach a file to a message?

Touch the **Menu** button (⋮) and then touch **Attach picture** or **Attach video** on the menu. If Android gives you a choice of sources, touch the appropriate one — for example, Gallery. Touch the picture or video you want to send, and Gmail attaches it to the message. When attaching a video, remember that mail servers may reject messages with attachments larger than a few megabytes.

To attach a file other than a picture or video, you need to install a third-party add-on such as the Attachments [Gmail Attach] add-on. You can download this add-on for free from Google Play using the Play Store app.

View Files Attached to Incoming Messages

E-mail is not just a great way to communicate, but you can use it to transfer files quickly and easily. When you receive an e-mail message with a file attached to it, you can quickly view the file from the Gmail app. Often, the best approach is to preview the file to get an idea of its contents. Once you know what the file contains, you can choose which app to open the file in.

View Files Attached to Incoming Messages

1 Touch the **Home** button (▭).

The Home screen appears.

2 Touch the **All Apps** button (▦).

The Apps screen appears.

Note: If the Widgets tab is displayed on the Apps screen, touch the **Apps** tab.

3 Touch **Gmail** (✉).

Note: If Gmail is not on the Apps screen that appears first, scroll left or right until you find Gmail.

Gmail opens, and your Inbox appears.

Note: If Gmail displays a mailbox other than your Inbox, touch the **Mailbox** pop-up menu and then touch **Inbox**.

Ⓐ A paperclip icon (📎) indicates that a message has one or more files attached.

4 Touch the message you want to open.

The message opens.

5 Touch the **Menu** button (⋮).

The menu opens.

6 Touch **Preview**.

The preview of the attachment appears.

⑦ When you finish previewing the attachment, touch the **Back** button (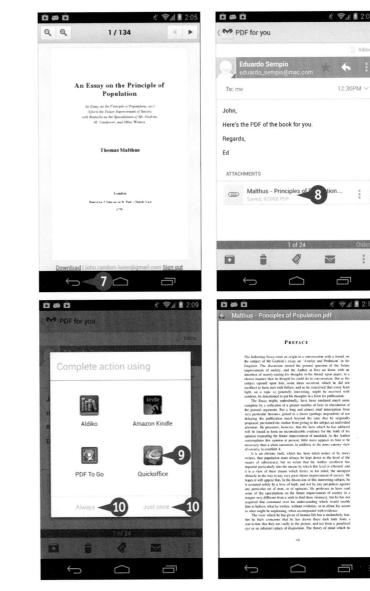).

The message containing the attachment appears again.

Note: If you want to save the attachment, touch the **Menu** button (⋮) and then **Save**. Gmail saves the file, and Saved appears on the attachment's button.

⑧ To open the attachment in a different app, touch the attachment's button.

The Complete action using dialog box appears, listing apps that can open this file type.

⑨ Touch the app you want to use.

⑩ Touch **Always** if you always want to open this file type in this app; otherwise, touch **Just once**.

The file opens in the app.

TIP

How can I delete an attached file from an e-mail message?
You cannot directly delete an attached file from an e-mail message in the Android Gmail app at this writing. You can delete only the message along with its attached file. If you use an e-mail app such as Apple Mail to manage the same Gmail account, you can remove the attached file using that app. When you update your mailbox on your phone or tablet, Gmail deletes the attached file but leaves the message.

Browse by Label and Search for Messages

oogle's Gmail service uses tags called *labels* to categorize messages instead of filing them into folders, as most other services do. You can apply one or more labels to any message as needed. You can then use these labels to browse through your messages to find the ones you need to work with. Browsing is useful when you need to look at a selection of messages to find the right one. Another way to find a particular message is to search for it. Searching is the fastest approach when you can identify one or more keywords contained in the message.

Browse by Label and Search for Messages

1 Touch the **Home** button (▭).

The Home screen appears.

2 Touch the **All Apps** button (▦).

The Apps screen appears.

Note: If the Widgets tab is displayed on the Apps screen, touch the **Apps** tab.

3 Touch **Gmail** (✉).

Note: If Gmail is not on the Apps screen that appears first, scroll left or right until you find Gmail.

Gmail opens, and your Inbox appears.

Note: If Gmail displays a mailbox other than your Inbox, touch the **Mailbox** pop-up menu , and then touch **Inbox**.

4 Touch the **Label** button (🏷).

The Labels screen appears.

5 Touch the label by which you want to browse.

The screen for the label appears, showing the messages that match.

Ⓐ You can touch a message to open it.

⑥ To search, touch the **Search** button (🔍).

Ⓑ The Search mail box appears.

⑦ Type your search term.

Note: If you have searched before, Gmail displays a pop-up menu containing your recent searches below the Search mail box. You can touch a recent search to perform it again.

⑧ Touch the **Search** button (🔍).

Gmail searches and displays matching messages.

Ⓒ You can touch a message to open it.

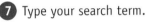

TIP

How can I prevent the Search pop-up menu from showing out-of-date suggestions?

Touch the **Menu** button (⋮) and then **Settings** to display the Settings screen, then touch **General settings**. On the General settings screen, touch **Clear search history** and then touch **OK** (Ⓐ).

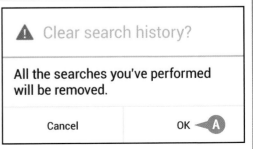

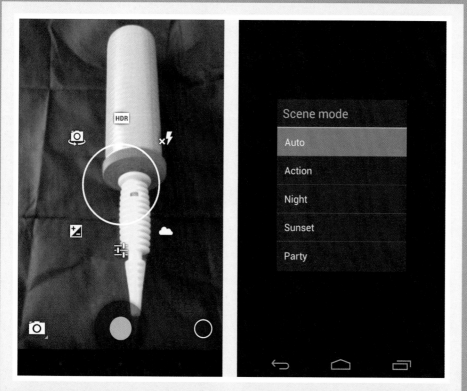

CHAPTER 10

Taking and Using Photos and Videos

Most Android phones and tablets include one or more cameras that enable you to take photos and video using the Camera app. You can edit your photos and share them with other people.

Take Photos with the Camera App

Most Android phones and many Android tablets include a rear camera that you can use to take photos. Most phones and tablets have a front camera facing the same side as the screen that you can use to take photos and videos of yourself or to enjoy video calls. To take photos using the camera, you use the Camera app. This app includes capabilities for zooming in and out and for using a flash for lighting your photos and video clips, plus a *High Dynamic Range*, or HDR, feature for improving the exposure in your photos.

Take Photos with the Camera App

1 Touch the **Home** button (⬛).

   The Home screen appears.

Note: From the lock screen, swipe left to open the Camera app quickly.

2 Touch **Camera** (📷).

Note: If Camera (📷) does not appear on the Home screen, touch the **All Apps** button (▦) to display the Apps screen, touch **Apps** if the Widgets tab is displayed, and then touch **Camera** (📷).

   The Camera app opens.

   The screen shows where the Camera lens is pointing.

3 Aim the phone or tablet so that your subject appears in the middle of the photo area.

Note: If you need to take tightly composed photos, get a tripod that fits your phone or tablet. You can find various models on Amazon, eBay, and photography sites.

4 Touch **Shutter** (◯).

5 Swipe left from the Camera screen.

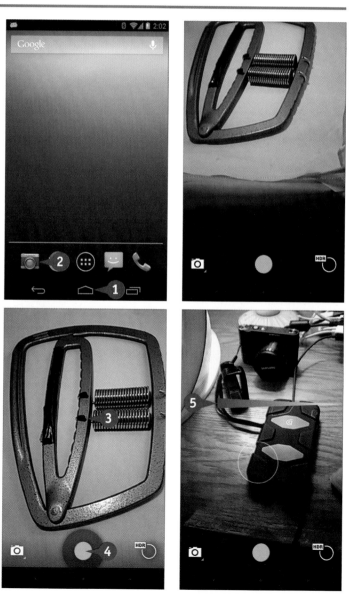

The photo you just took appears in Filmstrip view.

6 Scroll left to see other photos on the Camera.

7 Touch the **View pop-up button**.

The pop-up menu opens.

8 Touch **Grid view**.

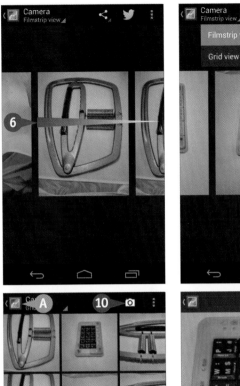

The Camera app displays the photos as a grid.

A In Grid view, you can touch **Gallery** (🖻) to display your full list of photos. You can then navigate among different albums, locations, times, people, or tags.

9 Touch the photo you want to view.

The photo appears full screen.

Note: To return to the Camera from Filmstrip view, swipe right.

10 Touch **Camera** (🔳) when you want to return to the Camera from Grid view.

Note: When viewing a photo, you can touch the **Back** button (◁) to go straight back to the Camera.

TIPS

Why does my phone's Camera app look different from the Camera app shown here?

Some skinned versions of Android include camera apps with different interfaces and other features than those shown here. Consult your device's documentation to learn how to use it and any extra features it offers.

How do I switch to the front-facing camera?

Touch the **Switch Camera** button (🔄) to switch from the rear-facing camera to the front-facing camera. With the front-facing camera, you can zoom, change the focus, and use HDR, but there is no flash on most devices. Touch the **Switch Camera** button (🔄) again to switch back to the rear-facing camera.

Use Zoom and Manual Focus

Ⅰf the camera on your phone or tablet includes zoom capability, you can zoom in so that your subject appears larger. Zoom is useful when you cannot get the camera close enough to make the subject the size you want. After zooming in, you can zoom back out as needed. The cameras on most devices focus automatically on the object in the middle of the picture. This works well for many photos, but when your subject is not in the middle of the picture, you can improve the focus by focusing manually on the subject.

Use Zoom and Manual Focus

Use the Zoom Feature

1 Touch the **Home** button ().

The Home screen appears.

2 Touch **Camera** ().

Note: If Camera () does not appear on the Home screen, touch the **All Apps** button () to display the Apps screen, touch **Apps** if the Widgets tab is displayed, and then touch **Camera** ().

The Camera app opens.

The screen shows where the Camera lens is pointing.

3 If you need to zoom in or out, place two fingers together on the screen and pinch outward.

The zoom indicator appears.

Ⓐ The number in the middle of the zoom indicator shows the zoom level — for example, 1.8× zoom.

4 Touch the **Shutter** button ().

The Camera app takes the photo.

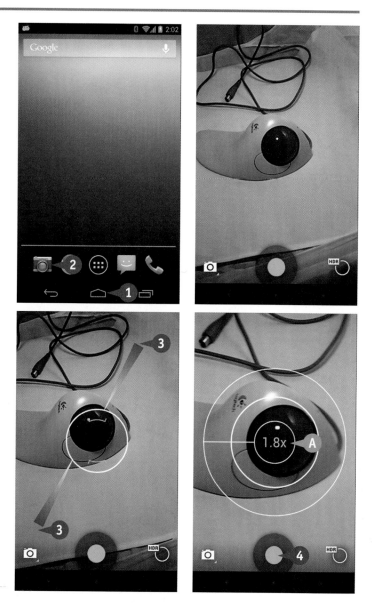

Use Manual Focus

1 Aim the camera lens at your subject.

2 Zoom in as described earlier in the previous subsection if the subject is too far away.

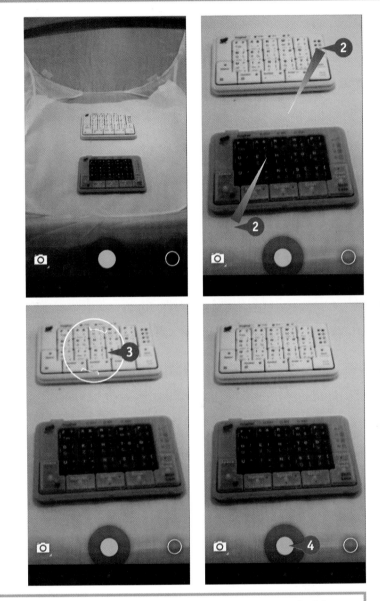

3 Touch the screen where you want to place the focus.

The Camera app focuses on the point you touched.

4 Touch the **Shutter** button ().

The Camera app takes the photo.

TIPS

Why do my pictures become grainy when I zoom in?
The cameras on most smartphones and tablets use digital zoom rather than optical zoom. Digital zoom zooms in by enlarging the pixels that make up the picture, so when you zoom in a long way, the pictures can become grainy as the pixels become larger. By contrast, optical zoom uses moving lenses to zoom in, thus retaining full quality even at extreme zoom.

Can I add optical zoom to my Android device?
Yes, you can add optical zoom by using an external lens. Some lenses come built in to cases, whereas other stick onto your Android device. To find such lenses, look at specialist photography retailers such as Photojojo (http://photojojo.com).

Use the Flash and the HDR Feature

Most phones and many tablets include a flash for lighting your photos. You can choose among three flash settings: On forces the Camera app to use the flash for every photo, Auto lets the Camera app decide whether to use the flash, and Off prevents the Camera app from using the flash. The Camera app includes a feature called *High Dynamic Range*, or HDR. HDR takes three photos in immediate succession with slightly different exposure settings, and then combines them into a single photo that has a better color balance and intensity than a single photo.

Use the Flash and the HDR Feature

Use the Flash

1 Touch the **Home** button (⬠).

The Home screen appears.

2 Touch **Camera** (📷).

Note: If Camera (📷) does not appear on the Home screen, touch the **All Apps** button (⦿) to display the Apps screen, touch **Apps** if the Widgets tab is displayed, and then touch **Camera** (📷).

The Camera app opens showing where the Camera lens is pointing.

3 Touch the **Control** button (◓).

The Control ring appears.

4 Touch **Flash** (⚡, ⚡, or ⚡).

The flash controls appear.

Note: If the Control button displays the HDR badge (📷), touch **Control** (📷) and then touch **HDR** (📷 changes to ◓) to turn off HDR.

5 Touch **On** (⚡) to use the flash, touch **Auto** (⚡) if there is not enough light, or touch **Off** (⚡) to turn the flash off.

6 Touch the **Shutter** button (⬜).

The Camera app takes the photo.

214

Take High Dynamic Range Photos

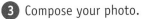 Touch the **Control** button ().

The Control ring appears.

2 Touch the **HDR** button.

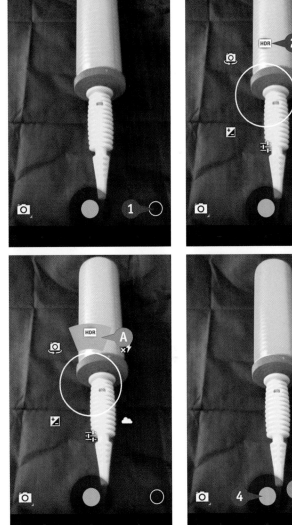

Note: You cannot use the HDR feature and the flash at the same time. If the flash is set to Auto (![]) or to On (![]), turning on HDR turns the flash off (![]).

Ⓐ The HDR button becomes selected.

The Control ring disappears.

Ⓑ The HDR badge appears on the Control button.

3 Compose your photo.

4 Touch the **Shutter** button (![]).

The Camera app takes the HDR photo.

TIPS

Is there any disadvantage to using HDR?
HDR can give better photo quality, but it prevents you from using the flash to light your photos. Taking an HDR photo also takes longer than taking a regular photo, so you cannot shoot photos in rapid succession. When you can, use a tripod for your HDR photos to ensure that each photo has exactly the same alignment.

How can I work more quickly in the Camera app?
Touch and hold the screen to display the Control ring as a pop-up. Still touching the screen, slide your finger to the control you want to change, choose the option you want, and then lift your finger.

Take Panorama and Photo Sphere Photos

As well as taking regular still photos, the Camera app can take panorama photos and Photo Sphere photos. A panorama photo combines a series of photos taken of your surroundings on the same level, giving a long, low photo looking around a single point. A Photo Sphere photo is similar to a panorama photo but goes up and down as well as horizontally. The Camera app guides you through taking the photos for a Photo Sphere photo and then combines them into a single image that gives a 360-degree wraparound view.

Take Panorama and Photo Sphere Photos

Take a Panorama Photo

1 Touch the **Home** button ().

The Home screen appears.

2 Touch **Camera** (◉).

Note: If Camera (◉) does not appear on the Home screen, touch the **All Apps** button (▦) to display the Apps screen, touch **Apps** if the Widgets tab is displayed, and then touch **Camera** (◉).

The Camera app opens.

3 Touch the **Current Mode** button (◉).

The Current Mode pop-up menu appears.

4 Touch **Panorama** (▧).

5 Touch the **Shutter** button (◉).

The Camera app starts taking the panorama.

6 Turn the camera around you, following the green guidance arrow.

When you complete the panorama or touch the **Shutter** button (◉), the Camera app renders it.

Note: If you do not want to capture another panorama photo, touch **Current Mode** (▧) and then touch **Camera** (◉).

216

Take a Photo Sphere Photo

1. Touch the **Current Mode** button (⬜) in the Camera app.

   The Current Mode pop-up menu appears.

2. Touch **Photo Sphere** (⬤).

3. Touch the **Shutter** button (⬤).

   The Align to start prompt appears.

4. Move the white alignment box so that it encompasses the blue dot.

   The Camera app starts taking the Photo Sphere photo.

5. Move the alignment box around the area you want to photograph, placing it around each blue dot that the Camera app displays.

6. Touch the **Shutter** button (⬤) when you finish taking the Photo Sphere photo.

   The Camera app renders the Photo Sphere photo.

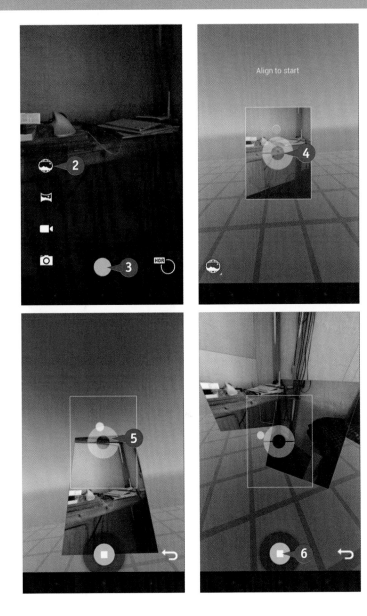

TIPS

Why does Photo Sphere not appear on the Current Mode menu?

Only some cameras can create Photo Sphere photos. Photo Sphere appears on the Current Mode menu only for cameras that support Photo Sphere.

How do I view a Photo Sphere photo?

From the main screen in the Camera app, swipe left to display your last photo. Swipe further if needed until you reach the Photo Sphere photo. Touch the **Photo Sphere** button (⬤) below the photo to start panning automatically through it.

Choose Settings for Taking Photos

To help you shoot correctly exposed photos suitable for your needs, the Camera app includes a range of settings you can configure. You can choose among five scene modes — Auto for regular use, Action for quick shooting, Night for extended exposures, Sunset for enhanced sunset colors, or Party for action photos in low light. You can choose whether to store the location at which you shoot the photo in the photo itself. Finally, you can select among different resolutions. To choose settings, you open the Camera app, display the Settings screen, and then make your choices.

Choose Settings for Taking Photos

1 Touch the **Home** button (▬).

The Home screen appears.

2 Touch **Camera** (📷).

Note: If Camera (📷) does not appear on the Home screen, touch the **All Apps** button (▦) to display the Apps screen, touch **Apps** if the Widgets tab is displayed, and then touch **Camera** (📷).

The Camera app opens.

3 Touch the **Control** button (◐).

The Control ring appears.

4 Touch **Settings** (⊞).

The Settings dialog box opens.

5 Touch **Scene mode**.

The Scene mode dialog box opens.

6 Touch **Auto**, **Action**, **Night**, **Sunset**, or **Party**, as needed.

The Scene mode dialog box closes.

7 Touch the **Store location** switch to set it to On or Off, as needed.

8 Touch **Picture size**.

The Picture size dialog box opens.

9 Touch the resolution you want to use.

The Picture size dialog box closes.

10 Touch the screen outside the Settings dialog box.

The Settings dialog box closes.

You can now take photos with the settings you have chosen.

TIPS

What picture size should I choose for my photos?
Shoot most of your photos at the highest resolution the camera on your phone or tablet supports. You can then create lower-resolution versions of your photos if needed. When you need to shoot lower-resolution photos and then use them directly from your phone or tablet, choose the size you need in the Camera app.

What sizes are VGA and QVGA?
VGA is 640×480 pixels, giving a file size of 0.3 megapixels. QVGA — Quarter VGA — is 160×120 pixels, giving a file size of around 0.02 megapixels. QVGA photos are useful only for viewing at a small size — for example, using as photos on contact records.

219

Edit Your Photos

Android includes powerful tools for editing your photos directly on your phone or tablet. You can apply artistic filters, such as B/W or Punch, to change the overall color balance of the photo. You can apply white or black borders in a variety of designs. You can straighten a photo, crop it, rotate it, flip it, or mirror it. And you can apply a wide range of adjustments, such as correcting the photo's exposure or increasing its sharpness. You can edit your photos starting from either the Camera app or the Gallery app.

Edit Your Photos

1 Touch the **Home** button ().

The Home screen appears.

2 Touch the **All Apps** button ().

The Apps screen appears.

Note: If the Widgets tab is displayed on the Apps screen, touch the **Apps** tab.

3 Touch **Gallery** ().

Note: If Gallery is not on the Apps screen that appears first, scroll left or right until you find Gallery.

The Gallery app opens and displays the Albums screen.

4 Touch the album you want to open.

The photos in the album appear.

5 Touch the photo you want to edit.

The photo opens.

6 Touch the photo.

The controls appear.

7 Touch the **Artistic filters** button ().

The editing tools appear, with the Artistic filters tab at the front.

8 Touch an artistic filter to apply it.

9 Touch the **Borders** tab (▣).

The Borders tools appear.

10 Touch a border to apply it.

11 Touch the **Transforms** tab (▣)

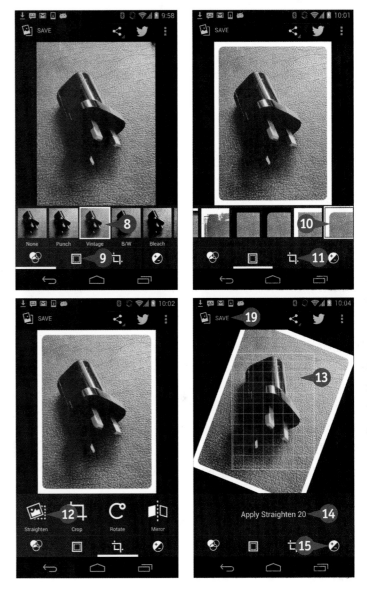

The Transforms tools appear.

12 Touch the transform tool to use.

13 Set the controls as needed.

14 Touch **Apply**.

15 Touch **Adjustments** (▨)

The Adjustments tools appear.

16 Touch the adjustment to use.

17 Set the controls as needed.

18 Touch the **Apply** button.

19 Touch the **Save** button.

The Gallery app saves the edited photo as a new file.

TIPS

How do I undo an edit I have made to a photo?
Touch the **Menu** button (⋮) and then touch **Undo** to undo the edit. You can repeat this move multiple times to undo multiple edits.

How can I see which edits I have made to a photo?
To see a list of the edits you have made, touch the **Menu** button (⋮) and then touch **Show History**. To go straight back to the original photo, touch the **Menu** button (⋮) and then touch **Reset**.

Capture Video

M ost cameras on Android phones and tablets can capture video as well as take photos. Many phones and tablets have rear cameras that can capture high-definition video, also known as HD video, and front cameras that can capture lower-resolution video. To capture video, you use the Camera app. You launch the Camera app as usual, and then switch it to Video mode. After taking the video, you can easily view it on the screen of your phone or tablet. You can also share the video with other people or play it back on your TV, as described later in this chapter.

Capture Video

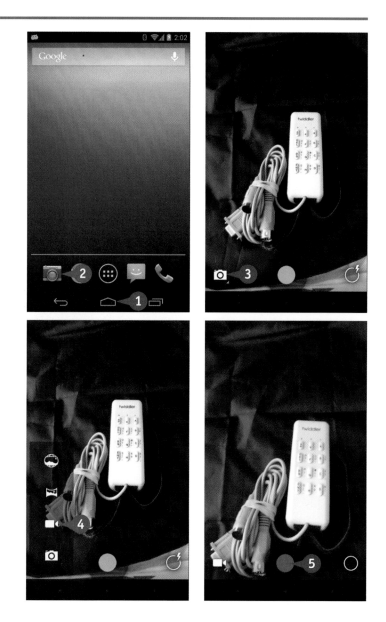

1 Touch the **Home** button (⬡).

The Home screen appears.

2 Touch **Camera** (◉).

Note: If Camera (◉) does not appear on the Home screen, touch the **All Apps** button (▦) to display the Apps screen, touch **Apps** if the Widgets tab is displayed, and then touch **Camera** (◉).

The Camera app opens.

3 Touch the **Current Mode** button (◉).

The Current Mode menu opens.

4 Touch **Video** (▭).

The Camera app switches to Video mode.

5 Touch the **Shutter** button (■).

The Camera app starts recording video.

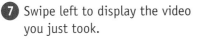 The readout shows the recording time.

6 To stop recording, touch the **Shutter** button (◉).

The Camera app stops recording and displays an animation of the video clip being sent to file.

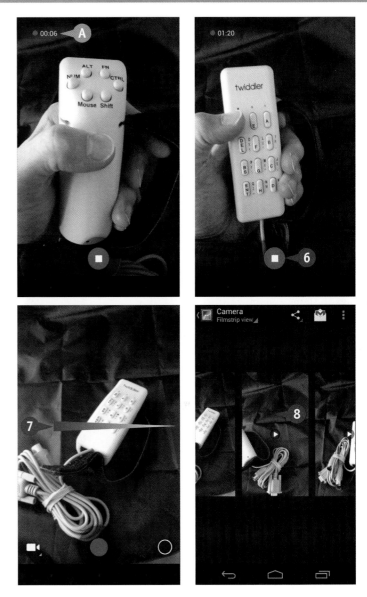

7 Swipe left to display the video you just took.

8 Touch the video to open it.

9 Touch the **Play** button (▶) to start playback.

TIP

What options can I choose for video?
The options vary depending on your device, but typical options include turning the flash on for illumination; changing the white balance among sunny, cloudy, fluorescent, and incandescent; and switching between the front and rear cameras. You can also change the video resolution, set up time-lapse video recording, and choose whether to store the location information in the videos you shoot. To choose options, touch the **Control** button (◉), then touch the icon for the type of option you want to set.

Share Your Photos and Videos

After taking photos and videos with the Camera app on your phone or tablet, you can share them easily with other people. You can also share photos and videos you load on your device from your computer or other sources. Your phone or tablet can share your photos and videos in various ways, depending on which apps you have installed. You can share a photo or video via Twitter, Messaging, Gmail, Email, or Bluetooth. If you have installed other apps that support sharing, such as Facebook or Skype, you can also use them for sharing photos and videos.

Share Your Photos and Videos

Choose a Photo or Video

 Touch the **Home** button ().

The Home screen appears.

2 Touch the **All Apps** button (⊞).

The Apps screen appears.

Note: If the Widgets tab is displayed on the Apps screen, touch the **Apps** tab.

3 Touch **Gallery** (▨).

Note: If Gallery is not on the Apps screen that appears first, scroll left or right until you find Gallery.

The Gallery app opens and displays the Albums screen.

 Touch the album you want to open.

The photos in the album appear.

5 Touch the photo you want to edit.

The photo opens.

6 Touch the photo.

The controls appear.

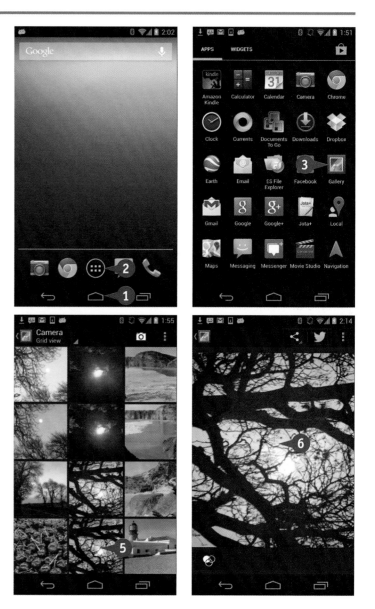

Share a Photo via Twitter

1 Touch **Twitter** ().

A Tweet dialog box opens.

2 Type your message.

3 Touch the **Location** button (◉) if you want to add your location.

4 Touch the **Username** button (@) if you want to add a username.

5 Touch the **Tweet** button.

Twitter posts the tweet.

Share a Photo or Video via Gmail

1 Touch the **Share** button (◄).

The Share menu opens.

2 Touch **Gmail**.

Android starts a new message in Gmail and attaches the photo or video.

3 Add the addressee.

4 Type the subject.

5 Type any body text needed.

6 Touch the **Send** button (➤).

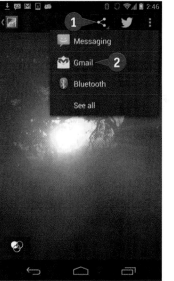

TIP

How do I share a photo or video via other means than Twitter, Gmail, Messaging, or Bluetooth?

1 Open the photo or video.

2 Touch the **Share** button (◄).

3 Touch **See all** to display the full list of sharing apps.

4 Touch the app you want to use.

View Your Photos and Videos on Your TV

You can easily view your photos and videos on the screen of your phone or tablet. But you can also connect your phone or tablet via either a cable or wireless to your TV and display your photos and videos on it instead. Viewing your photos and videos on a large screen is great both for enjoying your media files yourself and for sharing them with others. To connect via wireless, your TV must have either the Android Wireless Display feature built in or an Android Wireless Display adapter connected to its HDMI port or Composite Video port.

View Your Photos and Videos on Your TV

 On your TV, turn on the Android Wireless Display feature. Consult your TV's documentation to find out how to use this feature. If you are using an Android Wireless Display adapter, turn it on.

Note: The technology used for Android Wireless Display is called Miracast. If your TV's documentation does not mention Android Wireless Display, look for Miracast.

2 Touch the **Home** button ( ).

The Home screen appears.

3 Touch the **All Apps** button ( ).

The Apps screen appears.

4 Touch **Settings**.

The Settings screen appears.

5 Touch **Display**.

The Display screen appears.

6 Touch **Wireless display**.

Note: At this writing, Android Wireless Display is a relatively new standard, and only a few manufacturers have released televisions with built-in Android Wireless Display. But the market is growing rapidly, so you should soon find many more Android Wireless Display TVs.

The Wireless display screen appears.

7 Touch the **Wireless display switch** and set it to On.

The Available Devices list shows the Android Wireless Display devices within range.

Ⓐ If the device you want to use does not appear, touch **Search for Displays**.

8 Touch the display you want to use.

Android establishes the connection, and the display begins mirroring your device's screen.

9 Touch the **Home** button (⌂).

The Home screen appears.

10 Touch the **All Apps** button (▦).

The Apps screen appears.

11 Touch the app you will use for sharing. For example, touch Gallery to share photos, or touch Play Movies & TV to share videos.

TIPS

How do I connect my Android device to my TV via a cable?
Get an adapter cable with a SlimPort connector at one end and an HDMI connector at the other end. Plug the SlimPort end of the cable into the SlimPort on the phone or tablet, then plug the HDMI end of the cable into the HDMI port on the TV. Android detects the TV and starts mirroring its screen to the TV.

Can I use a computer monitor instead of a TV?
Yes. You can connect your phone or tablet to a monitor that has an HDMI input by using an adapter cable with a SlimPort connector at one end and an HDMI connector at the other.

Beam a Photo to Another Android Device

When you need to share a photo with another Android phone or tablet, you can beam the photo from your device to the other device. Beaming photos is fast and convenient, because you need only choose the item to beam and then bring the devices into contact. You can also beam other types of files, such as videos, although larger files such as these take longer to transfer between devices. Each device must contain a *Near Field Communication*, or NFC, chip. You must enable both the NFC feature and the Android Beam feature on each device.

Beam a Photo to Another Android Device

Turn On NFC and Android Beam

 Touch the **Home** button (◠).

The Home screen appears.

 Touch the **All Apps** button (▦).

The Apps screen appears.

Note: If the Widgets tab appears on the Apps screen, touch the **Apps** tab.

3 Touch **Settings** (▦).

Note: If Settings is not on the Apps screen that appears first, scroll left or right until you find Settings.

The Settings screen appears.

4 Touch **More**.

The Wireless & networks screen appears.

5 Touch **NFC** (■ changes to ✓).

6 If Android Beam shows Off, touch **Android Beam**. Otherwise, skip the remaining steps in this list.

The Android Beam screen appears.

7 Touch the **Android Beam switch** to set it to On.

8 Touch **Settings** (📠).

The Wireless & networks screen appears.

A The Ready to transmit app content via NFC readout appears.

Transfer a Photo via Android Beam

1 Touch **Home** (⬛).

The Home screen appears.

2 Touch **All Apps** (▦).

The Apps screen appears.

3 Touch **Gallery** (🖼).

The Gallery app opens.

4 Touch the album you want to open.

5 Touch the photo you want to beam.

The photo opens.

6 Place your phone or tablet back-to-back with another NFC-enabled phone or tablet.

When the NFC chips connect, your device vibrates, the screen image shrinks, and the Touch to beam prompt appears.

7 Touch **Touch to beam**.

Your phone or tablet beams the data to the other device.

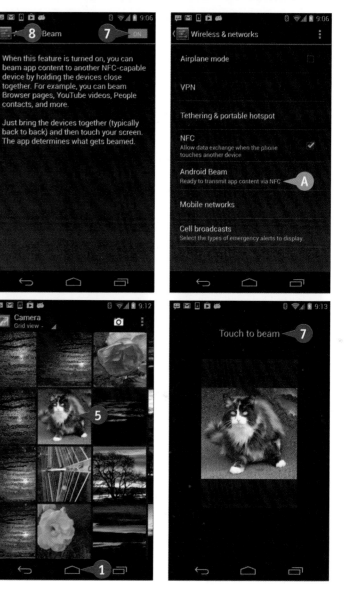

TIP

What happens when my phone or tablet receives a photo via Android Beam?
When your phone or tablet receives a photo via Android Beam, it displays an "Incoming beam" notification over the status bar for a moment. Drag down the status bar to open the Notification shade, then touch **Beam complete**. If the Complete action using dialog box opens, touch **Gallery** and **Always**. The Gallery app opens and displays the photo. The Gallery app places photos you receive via Android Beam in an album called *beam*.

CHAPTER 11

Using Maps, Google Earth, and Clock

Your Android phone or tablet comes equipped with the Maps app for finding your location and directions, the Google Earth app for exploring other places, and the Clock app for telling and measuring the time.

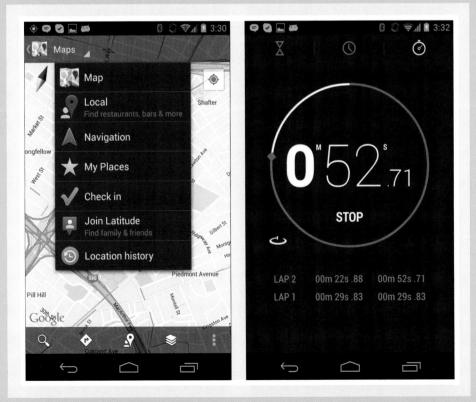

Find Your Location with the Maps App

Your phone or tablet includes a Maps app with which you can pinpoint your location by using the Global Positioning System, known as GPS, or known wireless networks. You can view your location on a road map, a satellite picture, or a terrain map. You can easily switch among map types to find the most useful one for your current needs, and you can add different layers of map information to make the map display exactly what you need. To help you get your bearings, you can rotate the map to match the direction you are facing.

Find Your Location with the Maps App

1 Touch the **Home** button (⬠).

The Home screen appears.

2 Touch the **All Apps** button (▦).

The Apps screen appears.

Note: If the Widgets tab is displayed on the Apps screen, touch the **Apps** tab.

3 Touch **Maps** (🔲).

Note: If Maps is not on the Apps screen that appears first, scroll left or right until you find Maps.

The Maps screen appears.

Ⓐ A blue arrow shows your current location.

4 Place two fingers apart on the screen and pinch in.

The map zooms out, showing a larger area.

5 Touch the **Layers** button (▧).

The Layers dialog box opens.

6 Touch **Satellite**.

The Layers dialog box closes.

The satellite map appears with road names and place names overlaid on it.

7 Touch the **Layers** button () again.

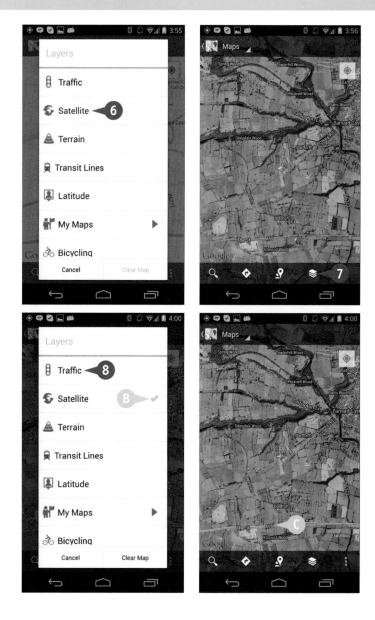

The Layers dialog box opens.

Ⓑ The check mark indicates that Satellite is turned on.

8 Touch **Traffic**.

The Layers dialog box closes.

Ⓒ Colored lines indicating traffic flow appear on the major roads.

TIP

Which is the best view to use in Maps?

That depends on what you are doing. When you need straightforward street navigation, use the regular map without the satellite information or terrain information; you may want to add layers such as Traffic, Transit Lines, or Bicycling, depending on your means of transport. When you want to see a picture of the area, add the Satellite layer. And when you want to see the lay of the land, switch to the Terrain layer.

Find Directions with the Maps App

You can use the Maps app on your phone or tablet to get step-by-step directions to where you want to go. Maps can also show you current traffic information to help you identify the most viable route for a journey and avoid getting stuck in congestion. Maps displays driving directions by default, but you can also display public transit directions and walking directions. It is wise to double-check that public transit direction and schedules are up to date before using them. You can also use the Navigation feature, which gives you directions as you proceed along your route.

Find Directions with the Maps App

1 Touch the **Home** button (⬟).

The Home screen appears.

2 Touch the **All Apps** button (▦).

The Apps screen appears.

Note: If the Widgets tab is displayed on the Apps screen, touch the **Apps** tab.

3 Touch **Maps** (▨).

Note: If Maps is not on the Apps screen that appears first, scroll left or right until you find Maps.

The Maps screen appears.

4 Touch the **Directions** button (◉).

The Directions screen appears.

Ⓐ The upper box shows My Location as the suggested start point.

5 To use another start point, touch the upper box.

6 Type the starting location.

A list of suggestions appears.

7 If a suggestion is correct, touch it. Otherwise, type the entire address.

8 Touch **End point** and enter the end point.

9 Touch the **Driving** button (🚗) for driving directions, the **Public transit** button (🚌) for public transit directions, the **Cycling** button (🚲) for cycling directions, or the **Walking** button (🚶) for walking directions.

Ⓑ If you want turn-by-turn directions, you can touch **Navigation**.

10 Touch **Get directions**.

The route appears on the map.

11 Touch the **Next direction** button (▶) to display the next direction.

Ⓒ Touch the **Previous direction** button (◀) to display the previous direction.

Ⓓ Touch the **Location** button (▲) to display your current location.

12 Touch **Directions list** to display all directions.

13 Tap **Map view** to return to the map.

TIPS

Is there an easy way to find my way back to my start point?

After setting your start point and endpoint in the Maps app, touch the **Menu** button (⋮) to open the menu, then touch **Reverse Start & End**.

How accurate are the directions?

The maps are mostly highly accurate, but you should always follow the directions sensibly rather than slavishly. The Navigation feature is in beta at this writing and traffic data is not real time, so be careful when following the navigation instructions. You may also have to adjust your route for detours caused by construction or special events.

Display Different Layers in the Maps App

The Maps app can display various layers of information about a location. For example, instead of viewing a conventional street map, you can display the Satellite layer so that you see satellite photos as well as the roads. You can then add the Transit Lines layer to see where public transit runs. Some layers, such as Satellite and Transit, can appear at the same time. Other layers are mutually exclusive. For example, if you are viewing the Satellite layer and choose to display the Terrain layer, Maps removes the Satellite layer, because Terrain and Satellite are mutually exclusive.

Display Different Layers in the Maps App

1 Touch the **Home** button (⬟).

The Home screen appears.

2 Touch the **All Apps** button (▦).

The Apps screen appears.

Note: If the Widgets tab is displayed on the Apps screen, touch the **Apps** tab.

3 Touch **Maps** (🗺).

Note: If Maps is not on the Apps screen that appears first, scroll left or right until you find Maps.

The Maps screen appears.

4 Touch the **Layers** button (▤).

The Layers dialog box opens.

5 Touch **Satellite**.

The Layers dialog box closes.

The map appears as a satellite view.

6 Touch the **Layers** button ().

The Layers dialog box opens.

7 Touch **Terrain**.

The Layers dialog box closes.

The map appears as a terrain view with contours in place of the satellite view.

8 Touch the **Layers** button ().

The Layers dialog box opens.

9 Touch **Transit Lines**.

The Layers dialog box closes.

A Transit lines appear.

10 Touch the **Layers** button ().

The Layers dialog box opens.

11 Touch **Bicycling**.

The Layers dialog box closes.

B Designated bicycle paths appear as dotted green lines.

TIPS

What are the Latitude layer, My Maps layer, and Wikipedia layer?

In the Layers dialog box, touch **Latitude** to use Google's Latitude feature for sharing your current location with your friends, not to see lines of latitude. Touch **My Maps** to see your My Maps list of stored maps. Touch **Wikipedia** to display W symbols for places that have entries in Wikipedia.

How can I remove the layers I have added to the map?

Touch the **Layers** button () to display the Layers dialog box. To remove a single layer, touch the layer to remove its check mark. To remove all layers, touch **Clear Map** at the bottom of the Layers dialog box.

Rotate, Zoom, and Tilt the Map

To make the maps easier to use and more helpful, the Maps app lets you rotate, zoom, and tilt the map. Rotating the map enables you to align the map with the direction in which you are looking, which helps you identify your location. Zooming the map lets you move from viewing a large area at a small scale to viewing a small area at a large scale. Tilting the map gives you a better idea of the lay of the land. You can combine the three movements to explore the map in great detail.

Rotate, Zoom, and Tilt the Map

Open the Maps App

1 Touch the **Home** button (▭).

The Home screen appears.

2 Touch the **All Apps** button (▦).

The Apps screen appears.

Note: If the Widgets tab is displayed on the Apps screen, touch the **Apps** tab.

3 Touch **Maps** (▨).

Note: If Maps is not on the Apps screen that appears first, scroll left or right until you find Maps.

The Maps screen appears.

Rotate the Map

1 Place two fingers, or your finger and thumb, apart on the map, and then rotate them in the appropriate direction.

The map rotates.

 The compass arrow, ▮, appears. The red end points north; the white end points south.

2 Touch the **compass arrow** (▮) when you want to make the map point north again.

Zoom the Map

1 Place your thumb and index finger together on the screen and then pinch apart (pinch-out zoom).

The map zooms in to a close-up view of the area.

2 Place your thumb and index finger apart on the screen and then pinch together (pinch-in zoom).

The map zooms out to a wide-aerial view.

Note: You can zoom in by increments by double-tapping the area on which you want to zoom. Double-tap with two fingers to zoom out, again in increments.

Tilt the Map

1 Place two fingers near the top of the screen and draw them down.

The map tilts away from you, giving a flatter perspective instead of a straight-down perspective.

2 When you finish using the tilted map, place two fingers near the bottom of the screen and then draw them up.

The straight-down perspective reappears.

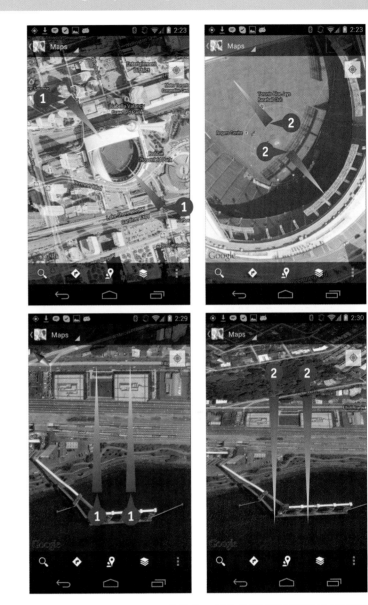

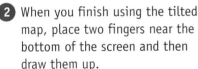

TIPS

How can I see the scale of the map I am viewing?
Touch the **Menu** button (⋮) to display the menu, then touch **Settings** to display the Settings screen. Touch **Display** to open the Display screen. Select the **Scale Bar** check box (■ changes to ☑) to turn on the scale bar.

Are there other hidden display options?
You can also display zoom buttons on the map. Touch the **Menu** button (⋮) to display the menu, then touch **Settings** to display the Settings screen. Touch **Display** to open the Display screen. Select the **Zoom Buttons** check box (■ changes to ☑) to display the zoom buttons.

Make a Map Available Offline

If you know you will need to use the Maps app when your phone or tablet has no Internet connection, you can use Maps' feature for making maps available offline. This feature enables you to save specific sections of a map to your device so you can access them no matter where you go. After saving a map to your device, you access it by going to the My Places screen and touching the **Offline** tab. You can keep offline maps for as long as needed and delete those you no longer need.

Make a Map Available Offline

Open the Maps App

1. Touch the **Home** button (▬).

   The Home screen appears.

2. Touch the **All Apps** button (▦).

   The Apps screen appears.

Note: If the Widgets tab is displayed on the Apps screen, touch the **Apps** tab.

3. Touch **Maps** (▨).

Note: If Maps is not on the Apps screen that appears first, scroll left or right until you find Maps.

   The Maps screen appears.

Make a Map Available Offline

1. Navigate to the area you want to make available offline.

2. Touch the **Menu** button (▤).

   The menu opens.

3. Touch **Make available offline**.

   The Select map area screen appears.

4. Adjust the map by dragging and zooming so that the highlighted area shows all the map you want.

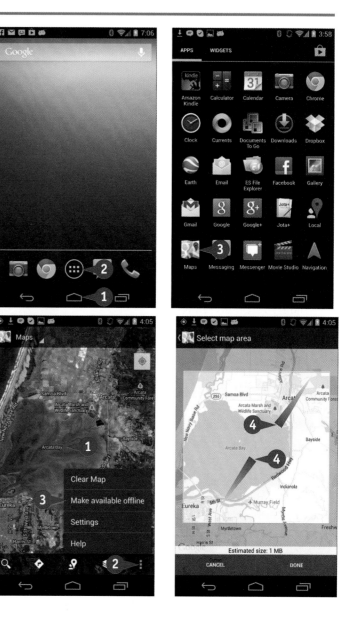

Ⓐ The Estimated size readout shows how big the saved map will be.

5 Touch **Done**.

Ⓑ The Maps app downloads the map.

Display a Saved Map

1 Touch the pop-up menu in the upper-right corner of the Maps screen. The name of the pop-up menu shows the item you have currently selected.

The pop-up menu opens.

2 Touch **My Places**.

The My Places screen appears.

3 Touch **Offline**.

The Offline tab appears.

4 Touch the map you want to display.

How do I rename a downloaded map?

On the Offline tab of the My Places screen, touch the **down arrow** button (▼), then touch **Rename**. Type the new name in the Rename map dialog box, and then touch **OK**.

How do I get rid of the saved maps I no longer need?

On the Offline tab of the My Places screen, touch the **down arrow** button (▼), then touch **Delete**. In the confirmation dialog box, touch **Yes**.

Explore with Street View

The Maps app is not only great for finding out where you are and for getting directions to places, but it can also show you the view at ground level by using Google's Street view feature. Street view displays images from Google's vast database of city streets and rural areas. You can pan around the area at which you enter Street view, enabling you to get a good idea of what a place looks like. You can also move along certain streets almost as if you were walking along them, and you can look up and down.

Explore with Street View

1 Touch the **Home** button (▢).

The Home screen appears.

2 Touch the **All Apps** button (▦).

The Apps screen appears.

Note: If the Widgets tab is displayed on the Apps screen, touch the **Apps** tab.

3 Touch **Maps** (▨).

Note: If Maps is not on the Apps screen that appears first, scroll left or right until you find Maps.

The Maps screen appears.

4 Navigate to the area you want to explore.

5 Touch and hold the place where you want to enter Street view.

An info window appears showing the address and a thumbnail picture.

6 Touch the info window.

The info page for the place appears.

7 Touch **Street view**.

Street view appears.

Note: The images in Street view may be several years old, so what you see in Street view may be significantly different from reality.

8 Drag the Street view figure (![icon]) to move around.

9 Drag down to look up, or drag up to look down.

10 Drag left to look right, or drag right to look left.

11 When you are ready to return to the map, touch the **Street view** button (![icon]).

Maps exits Street view and displays the map instead.

What else can I do in Street view?

You can turn on Compass mode, which lets you control what Street view displays by panning and tilting your phone or tablet. To turn on Compass mode, touch the **Menu** button (![icon]) and **Compass mode**. Repeat the command when you want to turn off Compass mode.

I have found an unsuitable image in Street view. How do I tell Google about it?

If you see something unsuitable or inaccurate in Street view, you can report it to Google. With the offensive image on screen, touch the **Menu** button (![icon]) and **Report image**. Android opens a Chrome window to the page for reporting the image to Google. Fill in the details and touch **Submit**.

Explore Google Earth

G oogle Earth is an information service that shows a virtual globe and detailed maps supplemented by geographical information. The Earth app runs on your Android phone or tablet and accesses Google Earth across the Internet, allowing you to explore many of the places on Earth from your device. After opening the Earth app, you can quickly go to your current location and explore it by zooming, panning, and tilting. You can also use the Earth app's built-in tools for discovering the wealth of information it provides.

Explore Google Earth

Open the Earth App

1 Touch the **Home** button ().

The Home screen appears.

2 Touch the **All Apps** button ().

The Apps screen appears.

Note: If the Widgets tab is displayed on the Apps screen, touch the **Apps** tab.

3 Touch **Earth** ().

Note: If Earth is not on the Apps screen that appears first, scroll left or right until you find Earth.

Explore Your Current Location by Panning and Zooming

1 Touch the **Menu** button (𝗕).

The menu opens.

2 Touch **My location**.

Earth displays the area in which you are currently located.

Ⓐ The blue dot marks your location.

3 Place two fingers together on the screen and pinch outward to zoom in.

Note: You can also zoom in by increments by double-tapping the area of interest. Double-tap with three fingers to zoom out by increments.

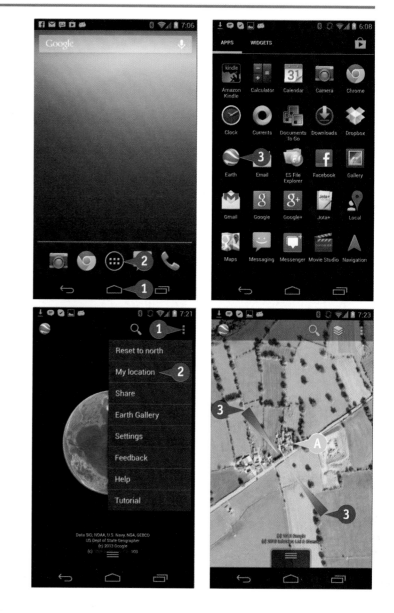

The zoomed area appears.

4 Touch and drag to pan the area shown in the opposite direction. For example, touch and drag right to pan the area to the left.

5 Place two fingers on the screen and rotate them clockwise or counterclockwise.

The view rotates.

B The compass arrow points to north.

6 Place two fingers near the top of the screen and drag down.

The view tilts upward.

7 Place two fingers near the bottom of the screen and drag up.

The view tilts back down.

How can I make Earth point directly to north again?
Touch the **Menu** button (▤) to open the menu, and then touch **Reset to north**.

How can I get an overview of what Google Earth provides?
Touch the **Menu** button (▤) to open the menu, and then touch **Earth Gallery**. The Earth app opens Earth Gallery, which contains various categories of maps. Touch the category you want — for example, touch Terrain & Elevation — and then touch the map you want to view.

continued ▶

The Earth app includes the Places drawer, which suggests places you may want to browse based on your current location. By touching a place in the Places drawer, you can not only virtually visit the location but also view a short video of it. You can also search for locations that you want to visit. Searching is helpful when you know the place's name but do not know where to find it on the map. After finding a place you like, you can easily share it with other people using tools such as Facebook, Gmail, or Email.

Explore Google Earth (continued)

Explore the Places Drawer

1. Touch the **Places drawer handle** (▤).

   The Places drawer opens.

2. Scroll left or right to display other places.

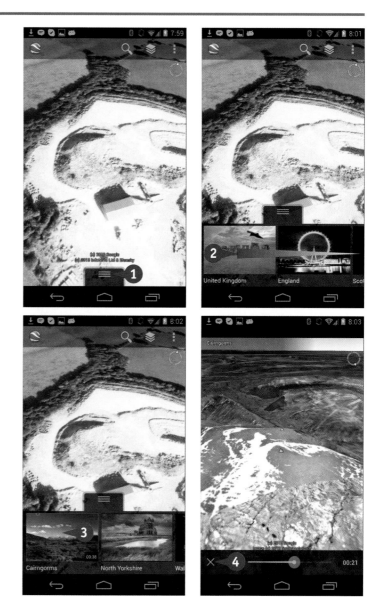

3. Touch the place you want to view.

   A video tour of the place opens and starts playing.

4. Touch × to close the video preview.

Search for a Place

1 Touch the **Search** button ( ).

The search box appears.

2 Type your search term.

3 Touch **Go**.

The Earth app displays a list of search results.

4 Touch the result you want to see.

Ⓐ The Earth app displays the place.

You can continue to explore other places.

TIP

How can I view more information about a place?
You can display different layers, including Places, Businesses, Panoramio Photos, Wikipedia, Borders and Labels, Roads, 3D Buildings, and Oceans. After going to the place, touch the **Layers** button ( ). In the Layers dialog box, select the layer you want to display (changes to). Touch the **Back** button ( ) to display the selected layers.

After finding an interesting place in the Earth app, you can easily share it via e-mail, messaging, or other means such as Facebook or Twitter. When you share a place, the Earth app creates a screenshot showing the place and includes it in the sharing message, so that the recipient can see the place and decide whether to visit it. You can use a similar technique for sharing a place from the Maps app. Maps does not create a screenshot showing the place, but it does include the address and a URL for accessing the place in a web browser.

Share a Location via E-Mail or Messaging

Share a Location from the Earth App

1 In the Earth app, navigate to the place you want to share.

2 Touch the **Menu** button (▤).

The menu appears.

3 Touch **Share**.

The Earth app takes a screenshot of the place.

The Complete action using dialog box appears.

4 Touch the app to use, for example, Gmail.

5 Touch **Just once**.

The app you chose appears. For example, Gmail displays the Compose screen for a new message.

Ⓐ The screenshot appears in the message.

6 Address the message.

7 Type a subject.

8 Type any text needed.

9 Touch **Send** (➤) to send the message.

Share a Location from the Maps App

1 In the Maps app, navigate to the area containing the place you want to share.

2 Touch and hold the place you want to share.

An info window appears.

3 Touch the info window.

The information screen appears.

4 Touch **Share this place**.

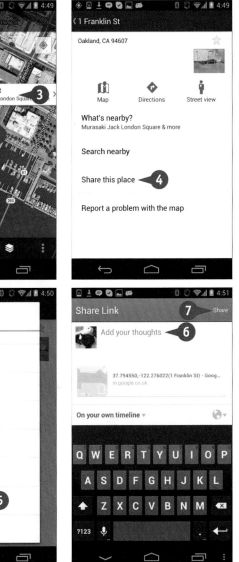

The Share this place dialog box appears.

5 Touch the means of sharing to use. This example uses Facebook.

The Share Link screen appears.

6 Type any text needed to accompany the place.

7 Touch **Share** to post the place to your account.

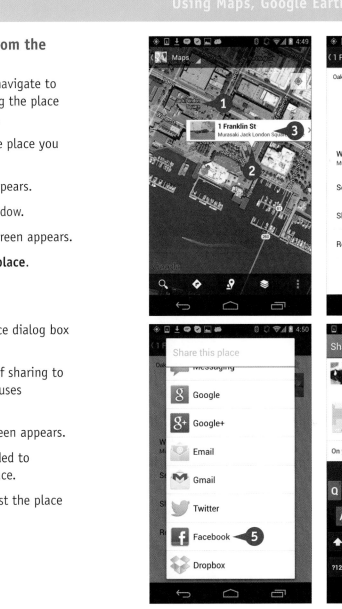

TIP

How can I mark a place so that I can go back to it later?

In the Maps app, navigate to the area that contains the place, then touch and hold the place until an info window appears. Touch the info window to display the info screen for the place, then touch the **Favorite** button, ☆ (☆ changes to ⭐) to mark the place as a favorite. To return to the place, touch the pop-up menu at the upper-left corner of the Maps screen, then touch **My Places**. Touch the **Starred** tab if it is not displayed, then touch the place.

Set Alarms

Android includes a Clock app that offers a wide range of features, such as displaying the time in several different locations at once, waking or reminding you with alarms, and measuring times with a stopwatch. You can use the Alarm feature of the Clock app to set as many alarms as you need, and create different schedules for the alarms. For example, you can set an alarm to wake you each weekday but not on the weekend.

Set Alarms

1 Touch the **Home** button ().

The Home screen appears.

(A) If the analog clock or digital clock appears on the Home screen, touch it to display the Clock app. Go to step **4**.

2 Touch the **All Apps** button (▦).

The Apps screen appears.

Note: If the Widgets tab is displayed on the Apps screen, touch the **Apps** tab.

3 Touch **Clock** (◉).

Note: If Clock is not on the Apps screen that appears first, scroll left or right until you find Clock.

The Clock app appears.

4 Touch the **Alarms** button (◉).

The Alarms screen appears.

5 Touch the **Add** button (➕).

A dialog box for setting the alarm appears.

6 Touch the buttons to set the alarm time. For example, touch 5 and 3 and 0 to set 5:30.

7 Touch **AM** or **PM**, as needed.

8 Touch **OK**.

The alarm appears on the Alarms screen.

9 Touch the alarm's switch to set it to On or Off, as needed.

10 Optionally, touch **Label**, type a name for the alarm, and then touch **OK**.

11 To repeat the alarm, touch **Repeat** (■ changes to ✔).

B The blue underline indicates the days of the week the alarm will repeat.

12 Touch a day to toggle the blue underline on or off.

13 Touch the **Collapse** button (◣◢).

The Clock app hides the alarm's details.

Note: You can now touch the **Add** button (■) to set another alarm if you want.

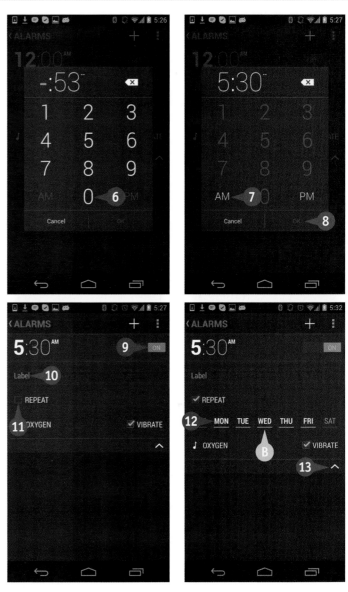

How do I remove an alarm?

When you no longer need an alarm, touch and hold it until the selection bar appears. Then touch the **Delete** button (🗑) to delete the alarm.

How do I change the sound for the alarm?

On the Alarms screen, touch the **Expand** button (▼) for the alarm. The alarm's entry expands. Touch the alarm's current sound — for example, Oxygen. The Ringtones screen appears. Touch the ringtone you want, and then touch **OK**. You can add your own alarm tones by copying music files to the Alarms folder using Windows Explorer or Android File Transfer.

Use the Stopwatch and Timer

The Clock app includes both a Stopwatch feature and a Timer feature. Using the Stopwatch feature, you can easily time events accurately down to hundredths of a second. You can also store lap times for each lap in an event that has intervals — for example, a track race. The Timer feature enables you to count down a set amount of time, which is useful for timed activities such as cooking. You can also easily add one or more minutes to the countdown time if you find you need to extend it without resetting the timer.

Use the Stopwatch and Timer

Open the Clock App

① Touch the **Home** button (■).

The Home screen appears.

Ⓐ If the analog clock or digital clock appears on the Home screen, touch it to display the Clock app.

② Touch the **All Apps** button (⊞).

The Apps screen appears.

Note: If the Widgets tab is displayed on the Apps screen, touch the **Apps** tab.

③ Touch **Clock** (◎).

Note: If Clock is not on the Apps screen that appears first, scroll left or right until you find Clock.

The Clock app appears.

Use the Stopwatch Feature

① Touch the **Stopwatch** button (◎).

The Stopwatch screen appears.

② Touch **Start**.

The stopwatch starts running.

③ Touch the **Lap** button (⟲).

Ⓐ The stopwatch records a lap time.

Ⓑ The progress circle shows red to indicate the current lap.

④ When you finish timing, touch **Stop**.

The stopwatch stops.

⑤ Touch the **Reset** button (Ⓞ).

The stopwatch resets to zero.

Use the Timer Feature

① Touch the **Timer** button (⊠).

The Timer screen appears.

② Touch the buttons to set the countdown time. For example, touch 4 and 3 and 0 to set 4 minutes, 30 seconds.

③ Touch **Start**.

The timer starts counting down.

④ If necessary, touch **+1**^{M} to add one minute. Touch again if needed.

⑤ Touch **Stop** if you need to stop the timer before it finishes.

⑥ Touch **Delete** (🗑) when you want to clear the timer.

TIPS

Can I run multiple timers at the same time?
No. At this writing, the Timer feature in the Clock app can run only a single timer at once.

How do I share times from the Stopwatch feature?
On the Stopwatch screen, touch the **Share** button (◁). The menu of sharing options opens. Either touch a displayed item, such as **Messaging**, or touch **See all** to see all the options for sharing, and then touch the option you want to use. Android starts a message or a post that you can then complete.

Set Up the Clock App with Multiple Cities

When you travel, or when you work with people in locations in different time zones, you may need to track the time in different time zones. You can set up the Clock app on your phone or tablet with the different locations you need so that you can instantly see the local time in each location you need to track. Seeing the local time can help you avoid contacting people at inappropriate times, such as in the middle of the night.

Set Up the Clock App with Multiple Cities

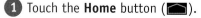

1 Touch the **Home** button (⬛).

The Home screen appears.

A If the analog clock or digital clock appears on the Home screen, touch it to display the Clock app. Go to step **4**.

2 Touch the **All Apps** button (▦).

The Apps screen appears.

Note: If the Widgets tab is displayed on the Apps screen, touch the **Apps** tab.

3 Touch **Clock** (🕐).

Note: If Clock is not on the Apps screen that appears first, scroll left or right until you find Clock.

The Clock app appears.

4 Touch the **Cities** button (📍).

The Cities screen appears.

5 Touch each city you want to add
(■ changes to ☑).

6 Touch **Cities**.

The cities appear on the Clock
screen.

7 Drag up to scroll down if
necessary to see the clock
you need.

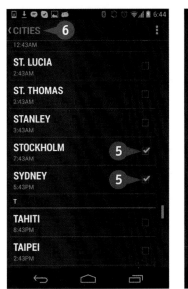

Your selected cities and their
time of day appear on-screen.

How do I remove a location from the Cities screen?
Touch the **Cities** button (🔲). The Cities screen
appears. Touch each city you want to remove
(☑ changes to ■).

What order does the Clock app use for the cities?
The Clock app presents the cities in time order, so
the city with the earliest time appears first and the
city with the latest time appears last.

CHAPTER 12

Playing Music and Videos

Your Android phone or tablet is great for carrying music and videos with you so that you can enjoy them wherever you are.

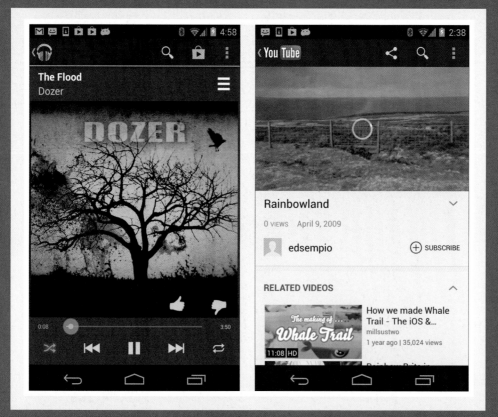

Copy Your Music and Videos to Your Device

Your Android device's Play Music app can play music stored in your Google Account across either a cellular or Wi-Fi Internet connection, but if you already have music files, you may prefer to store them directly on your device so they are always accessible and you do not use up your cellular data allowance. The easiest way to get your existing music files and videos onto your phone or tablet is to copy them from your computer. You can use either a Windows PC or a Mac.

Copy Your Music and Videos to Your Device

Copy Your Music and Videos to Your Device on Windows

1 Connect your phone or tablet to your PC via the USB cable.

Note: If the device's screen is protected with a PIN or password, unlock the device to allow your computer to access it.

The AutoPlay dialog box opens.

2 Click **Always do this for this device** (□ changes to ☑) if you want Windows to automatically open Windows Explorer when you connect your device in the future.

3 Click **Open device to view files**.

A Windows Explorer window opens showing your device's contents.

4 Double-click your device's name.

5 Double-click **Internal storage**.

6 Click **Music**.

Note: When transferring movies, click **Movies**.

The Windows Explorer window shows the contents of the device's Music folder.

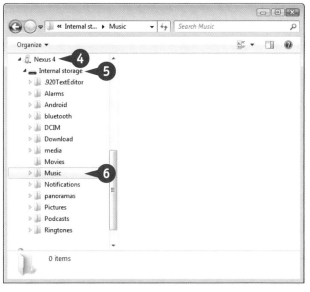

258

7 Click **Start**.

The Start menu opens.

8 Click **Music**.

Note: When transferring movies, click your username, and then double-click **Videos**. If you use another folder, open that folder.

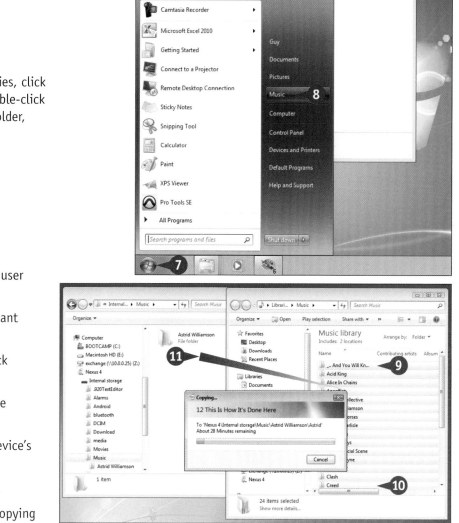

The Music library in your user account opens.

9 Click the first item you want to copy.

10 Hold down Shift and click the last item.

Windows selects the range of items.

11 Drag the items to your device's Music folder.

Windows copies the files.

12 When Windows finishes copying the files, disconnect your phone or tablet from your computer.

TIP

How do I copy music files to my phone or tablet on the Mac?

On the Mac, your phone or tablet does not appear in the Finder, so you must use a third-party app. If your device's manufacturer provides a custom app, such as Samsung Kies, use that app. If the manufacturer does not provide a custom app, download Android File Transfer from http://www.android.com/filetransfer/ and use it to transfer files from your Mac's file system to your phone or tablet. It is a good idea to follow the tutorial for Android File Transfer before using the app. To find the tutorial, click the **Help** link on the Android File Transfer web page.

Buy Music Online

When you want to buy music online, you can easily do so using Google's Play services, which offers millions of songs for sale. To access Google Play, you use the Play Store app, which comes built in to standard versions of Android. Songs you buy on Google Play become available both on your phone or tablet and on any other computers and devices you have linked to the same Google Account. You can also buy music from other online stores, such as Amazon's MP3 Store, or download music from sources such as a band's website.

Buy Music Online

1 Touch the **Home** button (▱).

The Home screen appears.

2 Touch the **All Apps** button (▦).

The Apps screen appears.

Note: If the Widgets tab is displayed on the Apps screen, touch the **Apps** tab.

3 Touch **Play Store** (▱).

Note: If Play Store is not on the Apps screen that appears first, scroll left or right until you find Play Store.

The Play Store app opens and displays the Google Play screen.

4 Touch **Music**.

Note: If the Listen to All Your Music screen appears, read the information it provides, and then touch **Start Shopping**.

The Music screen appears, showing the Featured list.

5 Touch **Genres**.

The Genres list appears.

6 Touch the genre you want to browse.

The Top Albums screen for the genre appears.

Note: From the Top Albums screen, swipe left once to display the Top Songs screen. Swipe left again to display the New Releases screen.

7 Touch an item you want to view.

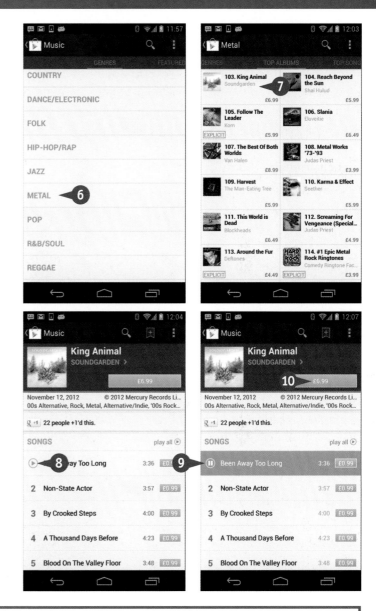

The screen for the item appears.

8 Touch **Play** (▶) to play a sample.

9 Touch **Pause** (⏸) to pause playback.

10 Touch the price button to buy an item.

TIP

Which music formats can the Play Music app play?

The Play Music app can play a wide range of music formats including MP3, AAC without digital-rights management protection, FLAC, Ogg Vorbis, and WAV files. The one widely used music format that the Play Music app cannot play is Apple Lossless Encoding, a format Apple provides in iTunes. If you have Apple Lossless Encoding files on your computer, use iTunes to convert them to AAC files and put those on your phone or tablet. You can also create MP3 files, but AAC gives slightly better audio quality than MP3 at the same file size and so is usually a better choice.

Play Music

After loading music onto your phone or tablet, you are equipped to enjoy the music wherever you go. To play music, you use the Play Music app, which enables you to browse your music collection by artists, albums, songs, and genres. You can also use the Recent screen to review and access music you have recently added to your phone or tablet and music you have recently played. You can also browse the Last added playlist and the Free and purchased playlist that Play Music creates for you, and you can create further playlists of your own.

Play Music

1 Touch the **Home** button (■).

The Home screen appears.

2 Touch the **All Apps** button (▦).

The Apps screen appears.

Note: If the Widgets tab is displayed on the Apps screen, touch the **Apps** tab.

3 Touch **Play Music** (🎧).

Note: If Play Music is not on the Apps screen that appears first, scroll left or right until you find Play Music.

The Play Music app opens.

The Recent screen appears, showing music you have recently added or played.

Ⓐ You can touch **Shuffle all** to shuffle all the songs.

4 Swipe left.

The Artists list appears.

5 Swipe left again.

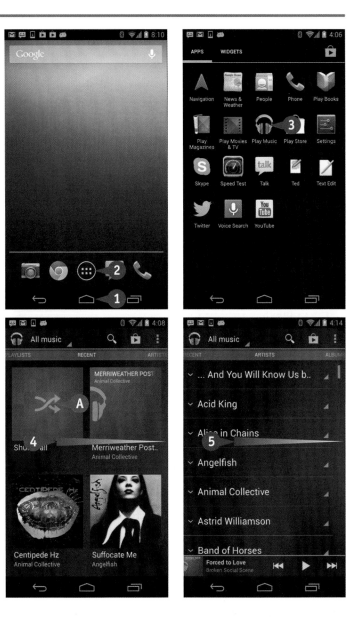

The Albums list appears.

6 Swipe left once more.

The Songs list appears.

7 Touch the song you want to play.

The song's screen appears, and the song starts playing.

8 Touch **Pause** (⏸) to pause playback.

9 Touch **Next** (⏭) to skip to the next song.

10 Touch **Previous** (⏮) once to go back to the beginning of the current song. Touch **Previous** (⏮) again to go back to the previous song.

11 Touch the screen to display additional controls.

12 Drag **Playhead** (⬤) to move forward or back through the song.

13 Touch **Like** (👍) if you want to rate the song positively.

14 Touch **Dislike** (👎) if you want to rate the song negatively.

TIP

What do the other controls do?
Touch **Shuffle** (⤫ changes to ⤫) to shuffle the current album, list, or set of songs into a random order. Touch **Shuffle On** (⤫ changes to ⤫) to turn off shuffling. Touch **Repeat** (🔁 changes to 🔁) to turn on repeating for all songs in the current album, list, or set of songs. Touch **Repeat All** (🔁 changes to 🔁) to turn on repeating only for the current song. Touch **Repeat One** (🔂 changes to 🔁) to turn off repeating. Touch **List** (☰) to hide the song's artwork and display the list of songs.

Adjust the Sound with the Equalizer

You can use the Equalizer feature in the Play Music app to adjust the sound to your liking. The Equalizer is especially useful when you use your phone or tablet with different output devices, such as portable speakers and headphones. The Equalizer includes a number of presets designed for different types of music, such as Folk, Heavy Metal, Jazz, and Rock, but you can use them freely for any type of music you listen to. You can also create your own custom preset called User to give exactly the balance of frequencies you prefer.

Adjust the Sound with the Equalizer

1 Touch the **Home** button (▬).

The Home screen appears.

2 Touch the **All Apps** button (▦).

The Apps screen appears.

Note: If the Widgets tab is displayed on the Apps screen, touch the **Apps** tab.

3 Touch **Play Music** (🎧).

Note: If Play Music is not on the Apps screen that appears first, scroll left or right until you find Play Music.

The Play Music app opens.

4 Navigate to the song you want to play, and then touch it.

The song starts playing, and its screen appears.

5 Touch the **Menu** button (▮).

The menu opens.

6 Touch **Equalizer**.

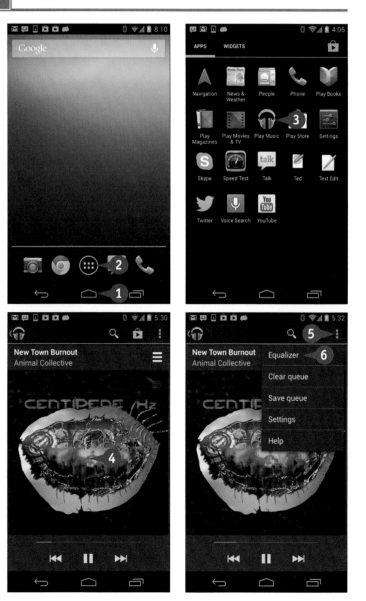

The Equalizer screen appears.

7 Touch the **Equalizer** switch to set it to On if you want to use the Equalizer.

8 Touch the name of the current equalization.

The pop-up menu opens.

9 Touch the equalization you want to apply.

The menu closes, and Play Music starts using the equalization on the song you are playing.

10 To adjust the sound further, drag an equalization slider (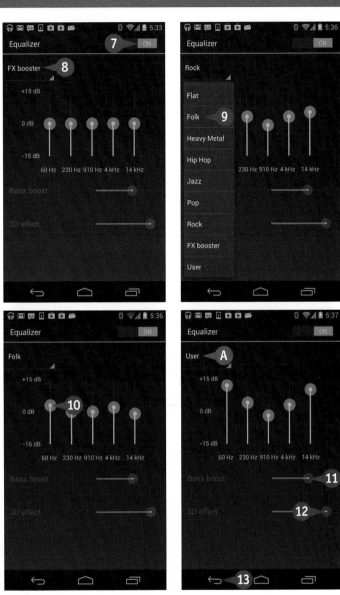) up or down.

A The Play Music app changes to the User equalization when you customize a preset equalization.

Note: You can reapply your latest custom equalization by opening the pop-up menu and touching **User**.

11 If Bass boost is available, drag its slider (⬤) to adjust the bass.

12 If 3D effect is available, drag its slider (⬤) to adjust the 3D effect.

13 When you finish choosing an equalization, touch the **Back** button (⬅).

The song screen appears again.

TIPS

Why does the Equalizer command not appear on the menu in the Play Music app?

Some Android devices do not support the Equalizer feature. If your device does not support Equalizer, the command does not appear on the menu. If your device provides another app for playing music, see if that app provides equalization.

How do I choose a suitable equalization?

Simply listen to the effect each equalization has on the music you play, and decide which you prefer. Pay little attention to the equalization names, because their effects vary depending on the speakers or headphones you are using. For example, you may find classical music sounds best using the Heavy Metal equalization.

Create a Playlist

Instead of playing individual songs or playing a CD's songs from start to finish, you can create a playlist that contains only the songs you want in your preferred order. Playlists are a great way to enjoy music on your phone or tablet. You can easily create a playlist in either of two ways. The first is by starting the playlist and then adding songs to it whenever it suits you. The second is by adding songs to the queue in the Play Music app and then saving the queue as a playlist.

Create a Playlist

1. Touch the **Home** button ().

   The Home screen appears.

2. Touch the **All Apps** button (⊞).

   The Apps screen appears.

   Note: If the Widgets tab is displayed on the Apps screen, touch the **Apps** tab.

3. Touch **Play Music** (🎧).

   Note: If Play Music is not on the Apps screen that appears first, scroll left or right until you find Play Music.

   The Play Music app opens.

4. Swipe left or right one or more times to reach the music screen you want to use. This example uses Songs.

   Note: You can also start a new playlist by going to the Playlists screen, touching the **Menu** button (⋮), and then touching **New playlist**.

5. Touch and hold an item.

   The pop-up menu appears.

6. Touch **Add to playlist**.

   The Add to playlist dialog box appears.

7. Touch **New playlist**.

The Playlist name dialog box appears.

8 Type the name.

9 Touch **OK**.

10 Touch and hold another song.

The pop-up menu appears.

11 Touch **Add to playlist**.

The Add to playlist dialog box opens.

12 Touch the playlist.

13 Swipe right one or more times until the Playlists screen appears.

14 Touch the playlist.

The playlist starts playing.

Note: You can rename a playlist from the Playlists screen. Touch and hold the playlist, and then touch **Rename** on the pop-up menu.

TIP

What is the queue and how can I use it to create a playlist?

The queue is the list of songs that is currently playing. You can add an item to the queue by touching and holding the item and then touching **Add to queue** on the pop-up menu. When you have the queue displayed on-screen, you can remove an item by touching and holding the item and then touching **Remove from queue** on the pop-up menu. You can clear the queue by touching **Menu** (▤) and **Clear queue**. To save the queue as a playlist, touch **Menu** (▤) and **Save queue**. In the Playlist name dialog box, type a name and touch **OK**.

Customize the Audio Settings

You can customize Play Music's settings to make the app work your way. You can connect Play Music to Google Play using your Google Account so you can stream audio you have stored in your account. This enables you to listen to your online music collection using your phone or tablet. You can choose whether to automatically cache music on your phone or tablet, limit streaming to Wi-Fi connections to reduce your cellular data usage, and decide whether to stream music at high quality. You can also prevent Play Music from downloading audio files over a cellular connection rather than Wi-Fi.

Customize the Audio Settings

1 Touch the **Home** button (⬭).

The Home screen appears.

2 Touch the **All Apps** button (▦).

The Apps screen appears.

Note: If the Widgets tab is displayed on the Apps screen, touch the **Apps** tab.

3 Touch **Play Music** (🎧).

Note: If Play Music is not on the Apps screen that appears first, scroll left or right until you find Play Music.

The Play Music app opens.

4 Touch the **Menu** button (▤).

The menu opens.

5 Touch **Settings**.

268

6 On the Music settings screen, touch **Google account** if the readout does not show the correct account. Otherwise, go to step **9**.

7 On the Google account screen, touch the correct account (◉ changes to ◎).

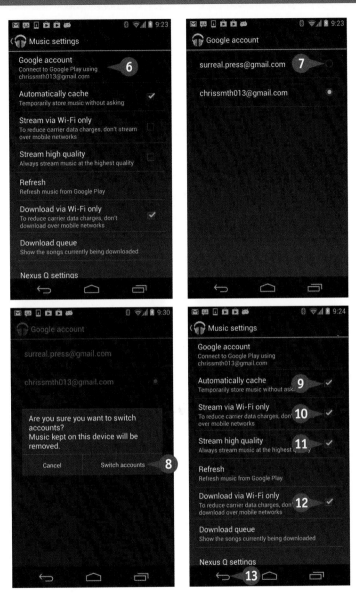

8 In the confirmation dialog box, touch **Switch accounts**.

9 Touch **Automatically cache** (■ changes to ☑) if you want to cache music.

10 Touch **Stream via Wi-Fi only** (■ changes to ☑) if you want to avoid streaming via cellular connections.

11 Touch **Stream high quality** (■ changes to ☑) if you want to use high quality always.

12 Touch **Download via Wi-Fi only** (■ changes to ☑) if you want to prevent cellular downloads.

13 Touch **Back** (⬅).

TIP

How do I store music in my Google Play account?

When you buy songs from the Play Store, using either your computer or an Android device, the Play Store places the songs in your Google Account so you can play them from any computer or device. To put songs from your computer into your Google Play account, use the Google Play Music Manager app to upload them. You can download Google Play Music Manager for free from https://play.google.com/music/listen?u=0 - manager_pl.

Watch Videos

To play videos — such as movies, TV shows, or music videos — you use the Play Movies & TV app. This app can play back both your own videos, such as those you shoot with your device's camera, and movies and TV shows you buy. You can play back a video either on the screen of your phone or tablet, which is handy when you are traveling, or on a TV to which you connect the device. Using a TV is great when you need to share a movie or other video with family, friends, or colleagues.

Watch Videos

1 Touch the **Home** button (⬛).

The Home screen appears.

2 Touch the **All Apps** button (⬛).

The Apps screen appears.

Note: If the Widgets tab is displayed on the Apps screen, touch the **Apps** tab.

3 Touch **Play Movies & TV** (⬛).

Note: If Play Movies & TV is not on the Apps screen that appears first, scroll left or right until you find Play Movies & TV.

The Play Movies & TV app opens.

4 Touch **Personal Videos**.

The Personal Videos tab appears.

5 Touch the video you want to view.

The video opens and starts playing.

6 Touch the screen to display the playback controls.

Ⓐ Touch the **Pause** button (▐▐) to pause playback.

Ⓑ Drag the **Playhead** (⬤) to move forward or backward through the video.

Ⓒ Touch **Play Movies & TV** (🎬) when you are ready to return to the list of videos.

7 If the video uses landscape orientation, rotate your phone or tablet into landscape mode.

The video appears in landscape orientation, and you can watch it full screen.

TIP

Which video formats can the Play Movies & TV app play?
The Play Movies & TV app can play videos in the formats H.263, H.264 AVC, MPEG-4 SP, and VP8. The video files themselves can use various different file types and file extensions, such as the MPEG-4 file format and .mp4 file extension, the Matroska file format and the .mkv file extension, and the 3GPP file format and the .3gp file extension. To determine whether the Play Movies & TV app can play a particular file, try to play that file. If the file will not play, you may be able to convert it using HandBrake, free from http://handbrake.fr.

Buy Videos Online

As well as apps and music, Google's Play Store also offers a wide range of movies. You can access the Play Store using the Play Store app built in to your phone or tablet and browse the Movies section to find movies that interest you. You can read the details and reviews of each movie, and for some movies you can watch a trailer. Movies you buy in the Play Store become available both on your phone or tablet and on any other computers and devices you have linked to the same Google Account.

Buy Videos Online

1 Touch the **Home** button (⬛).

The Home screen appears.

2 Touch the **All Apps** button (⬛).

The Apps screen appears.

Note: If the Widgets tab is displayed on the Apps screen, touch the **Apps** tab.

3 Touch **Play Store** (⬛).

Note: If Play Store is not on the Apps screen that appears first, scroll left or right until you find Play Store.

The Play Store app opens and displays its home screen.

4 Touch **Movies**.

Note: If the Watch HD Movies and More screen appears, read the information it provides, and then touch **Start Shopping**.

The Movies screen appears, showing the Featured list.

5 Touch **Categories**.

The Categories list appears.

6 Touch the category you want to browse.

The Top Selling screen for the category appears.

Note: From the Top Selling screen, swipe left once to display the New Releases screen.

7 Touch an item you want to view.

The screen for the item appears.

A Touch **Play** (⊙) to play the trailer in the YouTube app.

8 Scroll down to see the synopsis, cast and credits, reviews, and other information.

9 Touch the price button to buy an item.

B If a Rent button appears, touch to rent the movie.

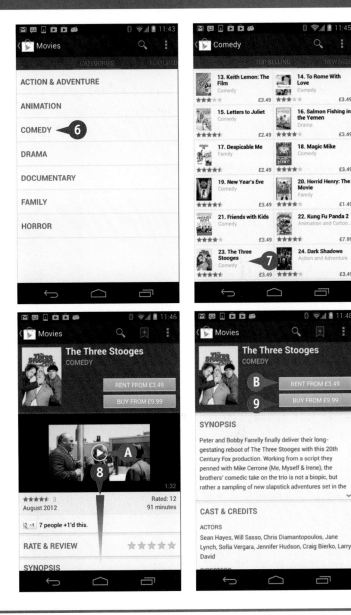

How can I play a video from my phone or tablet to my TV?

If your TV has an HDMI port, buy a Slimport-to-HDMI adapter and use it to connect your phone or tablet directly to your TV. This method is straightforward and works with older versions of Android as well as with Android Jelly Bean. If your Android device runs Jelly Bean, another option is to use Android Wireless Display to connect your device to your TV wirelessly. The TV must have either Android Wireless Display built in or an Android Wireless Display adapter connected to it. The Android device must also support Android wireless display.

Find Videos on YouTube

If you enjoy watching videos, you can find a wide variety of entertainment on YouTube, Google's video-sharing website. Your Android phone or tablet comes with a built-in YouTube app that enables you to access YouTube easily and find the videos you want to watch. You can browse YouTube and watch videos without logging in to your Google Account. But if you want to use all of YouTube's features, including rating videos and flagging them, you must log in.

Find Videos on YouTube

Open the YouTube App and Browse Videos

1 Touch the **Home** button (⬒).

The Home screen appears.

2 Touch the **All Apps** button (▦).

The Apps screen appears.

Note: If the Widgets tab is displayed on the Apps screen, touch the **Apps** tab.

3 Touch **YouTube** (▣).

Note: If YouTube is not on the Apps screen that appears first, scroll left or right until you find YouTube.

Note: If YouTube displays the Choose an account dialog box, touch the appropriate account (◉ changes to ◎) and then touch **OK**.

The YouTube app opens and displays its home screen with the Trending category selected.

4 Swipe left.

The list of trending videos appears.

5 Swipe up.

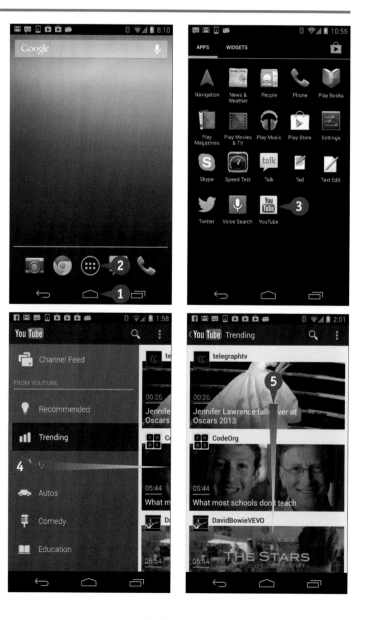

More videos appear.

6 Touch a video.

The video's information screen appears, and the video starts playing.

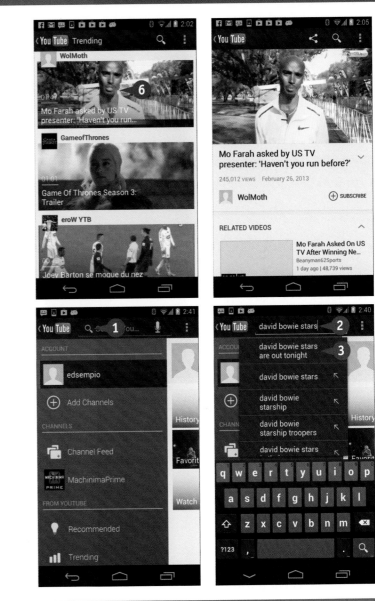

Search for Videos

1 Touch **Search** () at the top of the YouTube screen.

2 Type your search terms in the Search box.

A list of search results appears.

3 Touch a search result to view that video's page.

Watch, Rate, and Flag YouTube Videos

When you find a video that interests you on YouTube, you can watch the video on your phone or tablet. If you have signed in to YouTube using your Google Account, you can also give the video a rating. Your ratings can help other people decide whether to view the videos you have watched. If you find a video offensive, you can flag it to help YouTube identify problems with it. For example, if you discover dangerous acts in a video, or if it infringes your rights, you can flag it.

Watch, Rate, and Flag YouTube Videos

1 Touch the **Home** button (▱).

The Home screen appears.

2 Touch the **All Apps** button (▦).

The Apps screen appears.

Note: If the Widgets tab is displayed on the Apps screen, touch the **Apps** tab.

3 Touch **YouTube** (▤).

Note: If YouTube is not on the Apps screen that appears first, scroll left or right until you find YouTube.

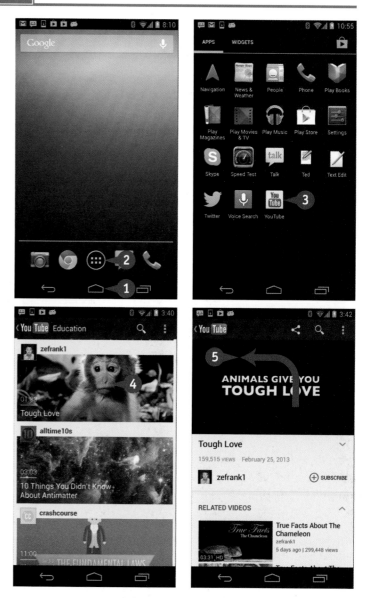

The YouTube app opens, and you can find a video by using the technique explained in the previous task.

4 Touch the video you want to view.

The video's screen appears, and the video starts playing.

5 Turn your device to landscape orientation.

The video appears in landscape orientation, filling the screen.

6 Touch the screen.

The controls appear.

7 Touch the **Menu** button (▤).

The menu opens.

8 Touch **Like** or **Dislike**, as appropriate, to rate the video.

TIP

How do I flag a video?

1 On the video's screen, touch the **Menu** button (▤).

2 On the menu, touch **Flag**.

3 In the Flag this video dialog box, touch the appropriate option button. For example, touch Hateful or Abusive Content (▣ changes to ◉).

4 Touch **Flag**.

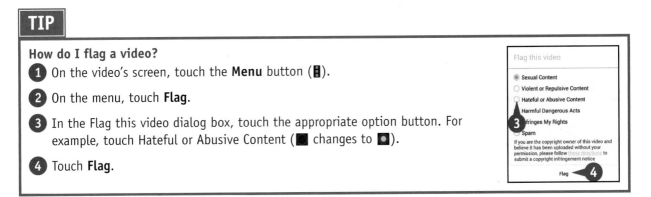

CHAPTER 13

Troubleshooting Your Device

To keep your phone or tablet running well, you should update its software, keep backups against disaster, and learn essential troubleshooting moves.

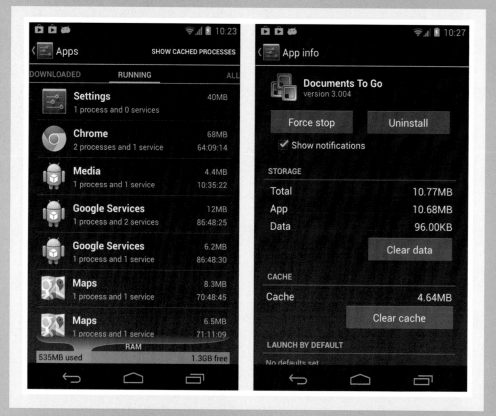

Close an App That Has Stopped Responding

Developers make their apps as reliable as possible, but sometimes an app stops responding to your input. When this happens, you need to close the app and then restart it so that you can continue using it. You can close an app either from the Recent Apps list or from the Apps screen in the Settings app. It is usually easiest to try the Recent Apps list first; if it does not work, you can then use the Apps screen.

Close an App That Has Stopped Responding

Close an App from the Recent Apps List

1. When the app stops responding, touch the **Recent Apps** button (▭).

    The Recent Apps screen appears.

2. Touch and hold the app that has stopped responding.

3. If the pop-up menu appears, touch **Remove from list**.

    Android stops the app. You can then touch the **Home** button (⬡) to display the Home screen, touch the **All Apps** button (⊞) to display the Apps screen, and then touch the app to restart it.

Note: If the pop-up menu does not appear on the Recent Apps screen, follow the next procedure to close the app.

Close an App from the Apps Screen

1. Touch the **Home** button (⬡).

    The Home screen appears.

2. Touch the **All Apps** button (⊞).

    The Apps screen appears.

3. Touch **Settings** (▦).

Note: If the Settings icon does not appear on the first Apps screen, swipe left until you can see it.

The Settings screen appears.

4 Touch **Apps**.

The Apps screen in Settings appears.

5 Touch the app that has stopped responding.

The App info screen for the app opens.

6 Touch **Force stop**.

The Force stop dialog box opens.

7 Touch **OK**.

Android forces the app to stop running.

8 Touch the **Settings** button (▦).

The Apps screen appears.

9 Touch the **Settings** button (▦).

The Settings screen appears.

TIP

What should I do if my Android device stops responding to the touch screen?

If your phone or tablet stops responding to the touch screen, restart it. Press and hold the Power button until the dialog box shown here appears, then touch **Power off** (Ⓐ). If the dialog box does not appear, continue to hold the Power button until the device turns off. Wait 10 seconds, then press and hold the Power button until the Google logo appears.

Update Your Device's Software

Google periodically releases new versions of the Android operating system to fix problems, improve performance, and add new features. To keep your phone or tablet running quickly and smoothly, and to add the latest features that Google provides, you should update the device's software when a new version becomes available. Your phone or tablet checks periodically for new versions of Android and notifies you when they are available. Similarly, any companion software you run on a computer may also check for new versions of Android. You can also check manually for new versions of the software.

Update Your Device's Software

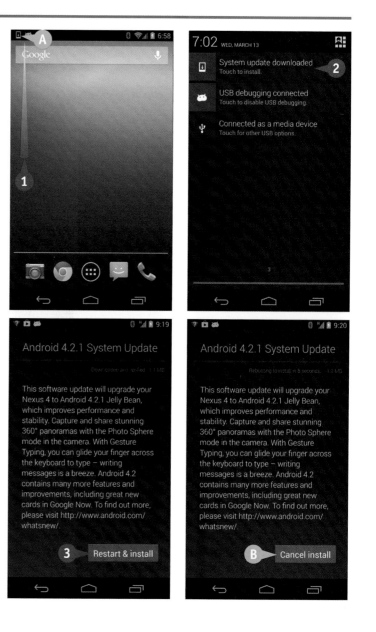

A When a system update is available the System Update button (▣) appears in the status bar.

Note: Android may also display a dialog box telling you that a system update is available.

1 Drag down the Notification shade.

Note: On a tablet, drag down the left part of the status bar to display the Notification shade.

2 Touch **System update downloaded**.

The Android System Update screen appears.

3 Touch **Restart & install**.

The update begins.

B You can touch **Cancel install** if you need to stop the update.

The Power off screen appears.

Your phone or tablet shuts down, and then restarts.

During the upgrade, Android optimizes the apps on your device, reorganizing their placement in the device's storage as efficiently as possible.

After optimizing the apps, Android starts those you were running.

The lock screen appears.

4 Drag the **Lock** button (🔒) in any direction to the edge of the circle that appears. Android unlocks the screen.

You can then start using your phone or tablet again.

TIP

How do I check manually for new versions of Android?
Touch the Home button (⬛) to display the Home screen, then touch the **All Apps** button (▦) to display the Apps screen. Touch **Settings** to display the Settings screen, then touch **About phone** or **About tablet** at the bottom. Touch **System updates** to display the System updates screen, then touch **Check now**.

Extend the Runtime on the Battery

To keep your phone or tablet running all day long, you need to charge the battery fully by plugging the device into an adequately powered USB socket, the charging unit, or another power source. You can extend your device's runtime by reducing the demands on the battery. You can turn off Wi-Fi and Bluetooth when you do not need them. You can dim the screen so that it consumes less power, and you can set the phone or tablet to go to sleep quickly.

Extend the Runtime on the Battery

1 Touch the **Home** button (⬠).

The Home screen appears.

2 Touch the **All Apps** button (▦).

The Apps screen appears.

3 Touch **Settings** (▦).

Note: If Settings is not on the Apps screen that appears first, scroll left or right until you find Settings.

The Settings screen appears.

4 Touch **Battery**.

The Battery screen appears.

5 Look at which items have been using the most power.

Note: To see further details, touch a button to display the Use details screen. You can touch **Wi-Fi** to see the Use details screen for Wi-Fi. Touch the **Settings** button (▦) to display the Battery screen again.

6 Touch **Settings** (▦).

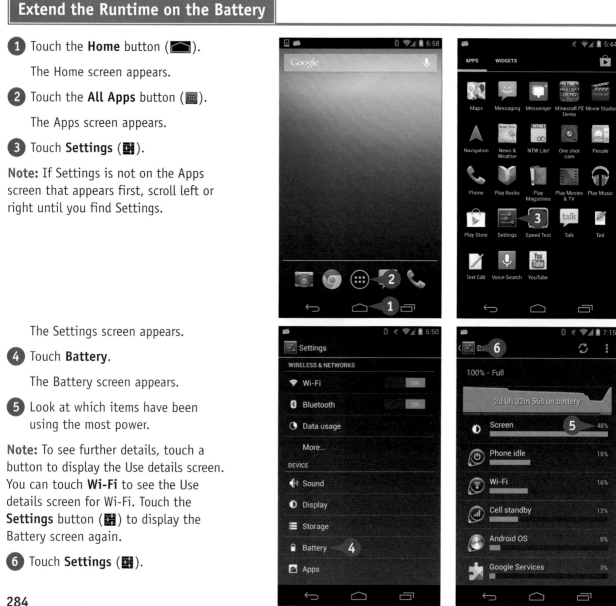

The Settings screen appears.

7 To turn Wi-Fi off, touch the **Wi-Fi switch** to set it to Off.

8 To turn Bluetooth off, touch the **Bluetooth switch** to set it to Off.

Note: Instead of turning off Wi-Fi and Bluetooth on a cellular-capable device, you can touch **More** on the Settings screen, then touch the **Airplane mode** check box (■ changes to ✔) to turn off all communications.

9 Touch **Display**.

The Display screen appears.

10 Touch **Brightness**.

The Brightness dialog box opens.

11 Touch and drag the slider to the left.

12 Touch **OK**.

13 Touch **Sleep**.

The Sleep dialog box opens.

14 Touch the option to set how long you want your your device to remain awake before sleeping (■ changes to ◉). To save power, choose a short time, such as 15 seconds.

15 Touch **Settings** (⊞).

The Display screen appears.

TIP

What else can I do to get more use of my phone or tablet between charges?
If your phone's or tablet's battery is easily removable, carry another fully charged battery with you, and swap batteries when the device runs low on power. Another possibility is to get a higher-capacity battery, but check that using it will not void your device's warranty. If you need more power on the move, buy a case with a built-in battery or a charger for charging the battery in a car.

Reset Your App Preferences

If your phone or tablet starts behaving oddly, you may be able to bring it back under control by resetting your app preferences. This move resets each app's preferences to their default settings. You can then set the preferences for any given app the way you want them. You may also find it useful to reset your app preferences when you have been experimenting with the settings for different apps but cannot find the settings needed to restore normality.

Reset Your App Preferences

1 Touch the **Home** button (▭).

The Home screen appears.

2 Touch the **All Apps** button (▦).

The Apps screen appears.

3 Touch **Settings** (▦).

Note: If Settings is not on the Apps screen that appears first, swipe left until you find Settings.

The Settings screen appears.

4 Touch **Apps**.

The Apps screen appears.

5 Touch the **Menu** button (▐).

The menu opens.

6 Touch **Reset app preferences**.

The Reset app preferences dialog box opens.

7 Touch **Reset apps**.

The Apps screen appears again.

8 Touch the **Settings** button (⊞).

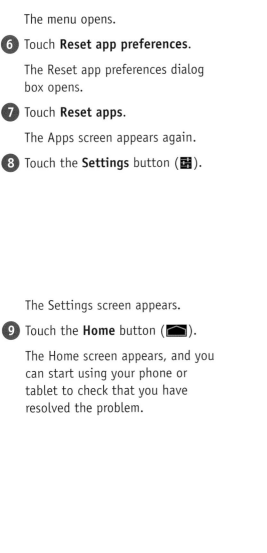

The Settings screen appears.

9 Touch the **Home** button (⌂).

The Home screen appears, and you can start using your phone or tablet to check that you have resolved the problem.

TIP

What other effects does resetting app preferences have?

Resetting app preferences also removes the associations you have made between particular file types and apps. For example, when you first try to open a movie file, Android displays the Complete action using dialog box showing a list of the available apps. You can then touch the app to use and touch the **Always** button or the **Just Once** button. If you touch the **Always** button, you make an association between the movie file type and the app you chose. The next time you open a movie file of this type, Android uses that app without asking. After you reset app preferences, Android prompts you again to choose which app to use when opening a file.

Check Free Space and Clear Extra Space

If you take your phone or tablet with you everywhere, you will probably want to put as many data and media files on it as possible. When you do this, your device may run low on free space. This can cause the device to run slowly or be unstable. To avoid problems, you can check how much free space your phone or tablet has. When free space runs low, you can clear extra space to keep your device running well.

Check Free Space and Clear Extra Space

1 Touch the **Home** button (⬟).

The Home screen appears.

2 Touch the **All Apps** button (▦).

The Apps screen appears.

3 Touch **Settings** (▤).

Note: If Settings is not on the Apps screen that appears first, scroll left or right until you find Settings.

The Settings screen appears.

4 Touch **Storage**.

The Storage screen appears.

Ⓐ The Internal Storage chart shows how much of the storage is in use.

Ⓑ The Total space readout shows your device's entire memory capacity.

Ⓒ The Available readout shows how much space is free.

Ⓓ The list breaks down the memory usage into categories: Apps; Pictures, video; Audio; Downloads; Cached data; and Misc.

5 To see which apps are installed, touch **Apps**.

The Apps screen appears.

6 To remove an app from your device, touch its name.

The App Info screen appears.

7 Touch **Uninstall**.

A confirmation dialog box opens.

8 Touch **OK**.

9 When you finish managing apps, touch the Back button (⬅).

The Storage screen appears.

10 Touch **Downloads**.

The Downloads screen appears.

11 Touch the check box of each file you want to delete (■ changes to ☑).

12 Touch the Delete button (🗑).

Android deletes the files.

13 Touch the **Back** button (⬅).

The Storage screen appears.

14 Touch **Cached data**.

The Clear cached data? dialog box appears.

15 Touch **OK**.

TIP

What other items can I get rid of to free up space on my phone or tablet?
You can remove miscellaneous files and media files. On the Storage screen, touch **Misc.** to display the Misc. files screen. You can then select the check box for each item you want to delete (■ changes to ☑) and then touch the **Delete** button (🗑). Although the Storage screen provides a Pictures button, a Video button, and an Audio button, it is easier to remove pictures, video, and audio files using Windows Explorer or Android File Transfer than directly using Android.

Back Up Your Phone or Tablet Online

To keep your valuable data and carefully chosen settings safe, you can back up your Android phone or tablet online to your Google Account. If your device has problems, you can restore it to factory settings and then restore your data and settings to it. Similarly, if your device gets broken, lost, or stolen, you can restore your data and settings from your Google Account to a new device. Restoring your data and settings enables you to implement your preferred setup on your new device without laborious customization.

Back Up Your Phone or Tablet Online

1 Touch the **Home** button (▟).

The Home screen appears.

2 Touch the **All Apps** button (▦).

The Apps screen appears.

3 Touch **Settings** (▦).

Note: If Settings is not on the Apps screen that appears first, scroll left or right until you find Settings.

The Settings screen appears.

4 Touch **Backup & reset**.

Note: On a phone, you may have to scroll down to display the Backup & reset button.

The Backup & reset screen appears.

5 Touch the **Back up my data** check box (▣ changes to ☑).

Note: When setting up your phone or tablet, you may already have set it to back up to your Google account. If **Back up my data** is already selected (☑) and **Backup account** shows the right e-mail account, you are all set.

6 Touch **Backup account**.

The Set backup account dialog box appears.

7 Touch the appropriate account.

Note: If the account does not appear, touch **Add account** and follow the instructions on the Add a Google Account screens.

The Set backup account dialog box closes.

8 Touch the **Automatic restore** option (■ changes to ☑) if you want to restore your settings and data when you reinstall an app.

9 Touch the **Settings** button (🔳).

The Settings screen appears.

10 Touch the **Home** button (🏠).

The Home screen appears.

Your Android device now backs itself up periodically to the account you designated.

TIPS

What settings does my Android device back up to Google?
Android backs up your personal data, such as your contacts, web bookmarks, Wi-Fi passwords, and custom dictionaries. Android also stores the list of apps you have bought or downloaded from the Play Store and your customized settings — for example, your Display settings and Sound settings.

Why does the Backup & reset button not appear on the Settings screen?
Most likely because you have a nonowner account on a tablet. On a tablet, only the owner — the first account set up — has access to the Backup & reset commands.

Back Up and Restore with a Computer

Your Android phone or tablet likely contains valuable data, so it is a good idea to back up the device. One backup option is to use your Google account, but if you have a computer, you can back up your device to the computer by using suitable companion software. Backing up to your computer is faster than backing up online, and you can restore your device without an Internet connection. For security, you may choose to back up your phone or tablet both to your computer and to your Google account to ensure you can restore your data after a disaster occurs.

Connect Your Phone or Tablet to Your Computer

To back-up your Android phone or tablet to your computer, or to restore the device from the computer, you must connect them. The best means of connection is a USB cable, but you may also be able to use Wi-Fi for backup. Normally, when you connect your phone or tablet to your computer, the computer's operating system launches your companion software automatically. The device then appears in the companion software window.

Run the Backup Operation

By backing up your Android phone or tablet to your computer, you ensure you can restore your data to the device, or to another Android device, if problems occur. To back up your phone or tablet, you use the companion software on your computer. In this program, you click the Back up/Restore tab, choose the items to back up, and then click the Backup button. The Backup dialog box shows the progress of the backup.

Prepare to Restore Your Phone or Tablet

After your phone or tablet becomes unstable or stops responding, you can restore it from a backup on your computer. To prepare to restore your device, connect it to your computer using a USB cable. If the companion software does not launch automatically, launch it from the Start menu or Start screen in Windows or from Launchpad or the Dock in OS X. You can then click the Back up/Restore tab and select the backup file from which to restore the device. Normally, you use the latest backup file.

Choose Which Data to Restore

You can choose which categories of data to restore to your device. Normally, you would restore all the data contained in the backup because this restores the data most completely. But sometimes you may choose to restore only some categories of data. For example, you may decide not to restore all video files because of the large amount of space they consume. After choosing which data to restore, you start the restore operation running.

Complete the Restore Operation

During the restore operation, the companion software copies data from the backup file on your computer to your Android device. The backup may contain many gigabytes of data, so the restore operation may take one or more hours to run. Be careful not to interrupt the restore operation. After the restore completes, your phone or tablet restarts, and then reestablishes its connection to your computer. You can then disconnect the phone or tablet and start using it normally again.

Restore Your Device to Factory Settings

Google makes Android as reliable as possible, but sometimes problems occur that need your intervention. If your computer has companion software for your phone or tablet, connect your device to your computer and try using the software offers to reset or restore the device. If those moves fail, or if you do not have companion software, you may need to restore the device to factory settings. Restoring to factory settings is an operation you perform on the phone or tablet itself to resolve severe problems. After restoring to factory settings, you can restore data to your device from your Google account.

Restore Your Device to Factory Settings

1 Touch the **Home** button (▬).

The Home screen appears.

2 Touch the **All Apps** button (▦).

The Apps screen appears.

3 Touch **Settings** (▦).

Note: If Settings is not on the Apps screen that appears first, scroll left or right until you find Settings.

The Settings screen appears.

4 Touch **Backup & reset**.

Note: On a phone, you may have to scroll down to locate the Backup & reset button.

The Backup & reset screen appears.

5 Touch **Factory data reset**.

The Factory data reset screen appears.

6 Touch **Reset phone** or **Reset tablet**.

Note: If the phone or tablet has a PIN or password, the Confirm your PIN screen or Confirm your password screen appears. Type your PIN or password and touch **Next**.

The Reset? screen appears.

7 Touch **Erase everything**.

Your phone or tablet restarts and restores its factory settings.

The Got Google? screen appears.

8 Touch **Yes**.

The Backup and restore screen appears.

9 Touch **Restore from my Google Account to this phone** (☐ changes to ☑) if you want to restore your data.

10 Touch **Keep this phone backed up with my Google Account** (☐ changes to ☑) if you want to keep your device backed up.

11 Touch the **Next** button (▶) and allow setup to finish.

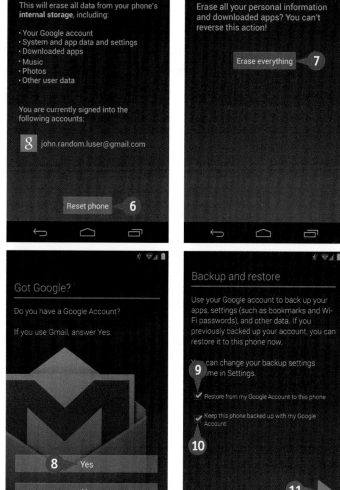

TIPS

What if I do not want to restore data from my Google account to my device?

If you do not want to restore data from your Google account, deselect the **Restore from my Google Account to this phone** check box on the Backup and restore screen. You can then set up your device manually.

Are there other reasons for restoring a device to factory settings?

Other than software problems, there are two other common reasons for restoring a device to factory settings. First, if you have encrypted the device, you can restore it to factory settings to remove the encryption. Second, if you plan to give or sell the device to someone else, you restore it to factory settings to remove all your data and settings.

Troubleshoot Charging Problems

If your computer is a few years old and you are having problems charging your phone or tablet, the USB ports on your computer may not supply enough power to meet the device's needs. In this case, you can use a USB charger to charge your phone or tablet from an AC outlet to see if that solves the problem. Another option is a powered USB hub. If you are having problems charging your device, you can try several moves to troubleshoot the issue. These moves can help you determine whether the problem is trivial or you need to get the device's battery replaced.

Check Your Cable Connections

If your phone or tablet does not charge, first check that the cables are actually connected and secure. Make sure that the micro USB connector is attached firmly to your device's SlimPort and that the USB end is firmly connected to your computer or charger. Verify that the connectors are free of any dirt or dust that could break the connection. If possible, try another charger or another wall socket in case the one you are using is faulty.

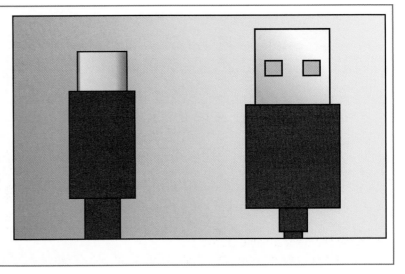

Switch USB Ports

If you are using your USB cable to connect your phone or tablet to your computer, you can also try connecting to a different USB port. Be aware that the USB ports on some keyboards do not provide enough power to charge a phone or tablet. If you are connecting to a keyboard USB port, try connecting to a USB port located on the computer instead. If you have a powered USB hub, you can try that, too.

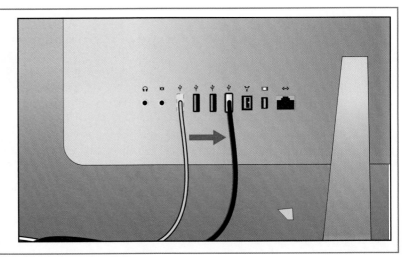

Update to a New Computer

If your Mac or PC is long out of date and you have tried using a powered USB hub but found it unsatisfactory, another solution is to update to a new computer. This is an expensive option, so normally you will want to exhaust all other charging options before pursuing it. The built-in USB ports on a computer more than a few years old may not supply

enough power to your phone or tablet. In this case, the USB ports may be good only for syncing your device with your computer, and you will need to use another power source to charge the device.

Wake Up Your Computer

Some computers do not charge connected USB devices such as phones and tablets when the computers are asleep; others do. If your computer does not charge your device when asleep, you can simply wake it up and configure your computer not to sleep while you are charging the device. Some laptop

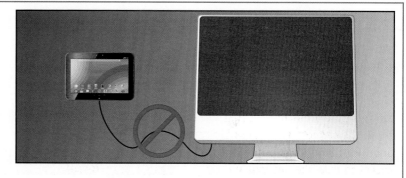

computers will charge connected USB devices only when plugged into a power source, not when running on the battery. In this case, you can plug in the laptop computer to make it charge your device.

Replace the Battery

If you still cannot charge your phone or tablet, you may need to replace the battery. How easy this is depends on the device. Some phones and tablets have easily removable backs that enable you to replace the battery in seconds. Others require surgery by a trained technician. If your device has no

obvious way of accessing the battery, consult its documentation before attempting to open it, because opening a device that is not designed to be user-serviceable may void the warranty.

Troubleshoot Wi-Fi Connections

To get the most out of your phone or tablet, use Wi-Fi networks whenever they are available. This is especially important for cellular-capable Android devices with meager data plans. Normally, your phone or tablet establishes and maintains Wi-Fi connections without problems. But you may sometimes need to tell your device to forget a network, and then rejoin the network manually, providing the password again. You may also need to find your device's IP address or its MAC address, the unique hardware address of its wireless network adapter.

Troubleshoot Wi-Fi Connections

Reestablish a Faulty Wi-Fi Connection

1 Touch the **Home** button ( ).

The Home screen appears.

2 Touch the **All Apps** button (▦).

The Apps screen appears.

3 Touch **Settings** (⊞).

Note: If Settings is not on the Apps screen that appears first, scroll left or right until you find Settings.

The Settings screen appears.

4 Touch the **Wi-Fi switch** to set it to Off.

Android turns Wi-Fi off.

5 Touch the **Wi-Fi switch** to set it to On.

Android turns Wi-Fi on and tries to reestablish the previous wireless network connection.

Note: If the Wi-Fi connection is now working satisfactorily, skip the rest of these steps.

6 Touch **Wi-Fi**.

The Wi-Fi screen appears.

7 Touch the network marked Connected.

298

A dialog box appears showing the connection details, including the IP address.

8 Touch **Forget**.

The dialog box closes, and Android forgets the network.

9 Touch the network's button again.

A dialog box opens prompting you for the password.

10 Type the password.

11 Touch **Connect**.

The dialog box closes, and your device connects to the network.

Find Out Your Device's MAC Address

1 From the Wi-Fi screen, touch the **Menu** button ().

The menu appears.

2 Touch **Advanced**.

The Advanced Wi-Fi screen appears.

3 Look at the MAC address readout.

Note: MAC is the acronym for Media Access Control. It has nothing to do with Apple's Mac computers.

4 Touch the **Settings** button (▥).

The Wi-Fi screen appears again.

Why may I need to know my device's MAC address?

Many Wi-Fi networks use a whitelist of MAC addresses to control which computers and devices can connect to the network: Any device with a MAC address on the list can connect, while devices with other MAC addresses cannot. A MAC address whitelist is a useful security measure, but it is not foolproof. This is because, although each network adapter has a unique MAC address burned into its hardware, software can *spoof*, or imitate, approved MAC addresses.

Index